THE LAST CRUSADE

To Deyna, a special daughter – I am very proud of you

THE LAST CRUSADE

THE SEVENTH CRUSADE & THE FINAL BATTLE FOR THE HOLY LAND

W.B. BARTLETT

TEMPUS

First published 2007

Tempus Publishing
Cirencester Road, Chalford
Stroud, Gloucestershire, GL6 8PE
www.tempus-publishing.com

Tempus Publishing is an imprint of NPI Media Group

British Library Cataloguing in Publication Data.
A catalogue record for this book is available from the British Library.

ISBN 978 0 7524 4389 8

Typesetting and origination by NPI Media Group
Printed and bound in Great Britain

Contents

Introduction   7

1   The Vow of King Louis   15
2   The Crusade in the Thirteenth Century   29
3   Preparations for Crusade   45
4   Rendezvous   65
5   Into Battle   77
6   The Serpent's Head   89
7   Massacre at Mansourah   107
8   Low-Water Mark   125
9   Prisoners of War   143
10   The End of the Beginning   159
11   Louis in Outremer   171
12   Louis the Diplomat   187
13   Consolidation and Disappointment   203
14   The End of the Dream   217
15   Homeward Bound   233
16   The Last Crusade   247
17   Postscript   261

Suggested Further Reading   265
Notes   269
List of Illustrations   275
Acknowledgments   277
Index   278

Introduction

On the Île de France, at the very heart of Paris, stands all that remains of the palace of King Louis IX. Nowadays, the Sainte-Chapelle is somewhat lost, surrounded by the roofs of the much larger buildings that now crowd it, mementoes of a later era, its spires here and there apologetically peering out and pointing upwards to the God that they commemorate. For this is a church like no other. And it is more than that. It is also a statement.

One enters the building through the lower chapel. This is the chapel used by the less important members of the palace staff in Louis's day. It is still impressive. Louis looks on in the corner in statue form, a pious, somewhat severe looking King, implicitly admonishing those using it to make sure that they look to the well-being of their souls. It is striking enough but does not prepare the viewer adequately for what is to come above it.

Make your way up a narrow flight of stairs and you enter the upper chapel, a building like no other in Christendom. It is a riot of colour. The windows are so large that the building seems as if it does not have walls. Every window is a kaleidoscope of blood-deep crimson, imposing royal blue or sun-blazed gold. All of them tell a biblical story. Anyone who sits in this building for any length of time cannot help but be led through the tales that they tell, following the trail from one small pane to the next.

The sanctity of this site was amplified by the objects that it once contained, for its purpose was to house two of the most prized relics in Christendom. A large platform was raised at the east end of the church, a focal point for the congregation. On it were placed the Crown of Thorns that had been placed on Christ's head and a piece of the Cross to which he had been nailed. Louis had spent a fortune in acquiring them for his collection. Around the walls, statues of the apostles looked on in approving admiration, mute witnesses to the glory of the scenes acted out. They are still there.

The Sainte-Chapelle is a testament to the ability of the Holy Land to inspire medieval man to attempt extraordinary things. For men like Louis and a host of others, it was a land like no other. It was not an immensely wealthy realm, though it brought with it trading advantages that could make men wealthy enough – the revenues of the port of Acre in the thirteenth century exceeded those of the whole of England. It was its sanctity that made it so significant. This was a vicarious situation, it was made holy through its associations with the life and death of Christ. But this was enough for men to attempt incredible things in its name.

What follows is the story of the last great Crusade to attempt to retake Jerusalem. To the Crusader, the Crusade was a penitential act that brought with it great spiritual rewards. He (or she) would benefit from the Papal Indulgences offered in return for their involvement. Put simply, by going on Crusade their sins could be pardoned and, as a result, their eternal wellbeing secured. For men with an intense personal faith such as Louis, that was no small attraction. And the greater the sacrifice, the richer the reward.

A succession of great Crusades were sent to the East between 1095 and the end of the thirteenth century but, in that entire span, few Crusaders were to suffer so many 'slings and arrows of outrageous fortune' as those involved in this one. At one stage seemingly on the verge of a great triumph, it would later plunge to the lowest depths.

Armies would be massacred, dreams shattered, thousands would endure years in captivity. If suffering truly earned spiritual rewards, then those earned by these Crusaders must have been great indeed.

What also makes this Crusade special is the presence on it of a great chronicler, whose quill brings these momentous events back to life. He was the Seneschal of Champagne, a region with a great Crusader tradition. His name was Jean de Joinville. He was still a young man when Louis's first Crusade took place, only twenty-four years old. He would witness more over the next five years than most men would see if they lived for a dozen lifetimes. Many years later he would reminisce and, as some older men do, would commit his memoirs to paper.

His account cannot be perfect. He was eighty-five years old when he wrote his account of the Seventh Crusade, but he did so with a freshness that suggests that the events he wrote of had only happened the day before. For the scale of those events was so great, their colour was so intense, that they seemed to sear themselves indissolubly into his memory so that he could bring them to life once more at will.

Through de Joinville's eyes, we can not only witness great events take place but we also get an extraordinary insight into everyday life. The history of Louis's first major Crusade, awarded the name of the Seventh Crusade by traditional historians, sub-divides into two distinct phases. The first is the invasion of Egypt, during which the great dramas of the Crusade took place. There are a number of surviving manuscripts that give us an insight into various Crusades, and the great actions that took place during their course.

But the less common feature found in de Joinville's chronicle relates to the second phase. This latter part of Louis's journey revolved around an extended stay that Louis made in Outremer (the name given to the territories held by Crusaders in the Middle East) before returning to France. De Joinville stayed with him, and gives us a rare insight into what it felt like to live on the frontiers of Christendom in the thirteenth century.

Here we find accounts of Louis's diplomatic contacts with a wide range of fascinating, and sometimes terrifying, peoples, whether it be the unbelievably ferocious Mongols or the mysterious Muslim group known as the Assassins. But there are also everyday touches that bring the period alive, such as a party of visiting Norwegian knights and their unusual tactics for hunting lions or the perils of a long sea voyage.

Backing de Joinville up, there is a range of other material available, from the formal, such as ecclesiastical documents, to the colourful. To this latter category particularly belongs the narrative of Matthew Paris, an English chronicler who is very anti-French but still finds it difficult to criticise Louis IX. Together, they weave a tapestry that is rich in colour and incident, bringing the thirteenth century back to life.

The story they collectively portray is of a world changing radically where traditional power bases are being replaced by new regimes. The very nature of the Crusading movement was going through a process of evolution and Louis's Crusade to Outremer would be the last great Crusade to the Holy Land. New forces were at work, which would dictate that the future battlegrounds of the Crusading movement would be on very different territory than had previously been the case. Therefore, the Seventh Crusade would in every sense be the end of an era.

At the outset, a note on numbers may be helpful. Economists are renowned for not being able to agree on anything but sometimes historians are not far behind. There has been a good deal of disagreement over whether or not the Crusade we are about to consider was the Sixth or Seventh. I am going for the Seventh, although the Sixth Crusade led by Emperor Frederick of Germany went without the blessing of the Pope.

But this is a slightly pointless argument. The truth is that both labels are wrong. There were a number of smaller expeditions, or Crusades, against groups elsewhere than the Holy Land that have not been granted the gift of a number by historians and this makes the numbering of Crusades somewhat suspect. But people like labels and I am sticking to that of the Seventh Crusade.

The title of this book needs to be explained. Crusades went on for centuries after King Louis's Crusades (he went on two, one in 1248, the other in 1270). Some commentators maintain that 'the Crusading movement ended with the fall of Malta on 13 June 1798'.[1] And, in accordance with the letter of the law, they are right.

But there is no doubt in my mind that the Seventh Crusade was the last of its type. Louis IX was the last King from the major Western European powers – that is, France, the German Empire and England – to set foot in the Holy Land, at the head of an army whose goal was to restore the Land of Christ, as they saw it, to its rightful Christian overlords. The Crusade of 1249 was also the last major expedition to set its heart on the re-conquest of the heartlands of Christendom (one cannot, in my view, equate the much smaller expedition of Prince Edward of England in 1270 with Louis's much larger venture).

Later Crusades would take place in very different geographical spheres, such as the lands surrounding the Baltic or deep within Europe itself, although a raid on Alexandria in 1365 briefly held the city for six days. In part this was due to changing external circumstances, as a resurgent Muslim world began to press hard on the outer borders of Christendom, forcing it in on itself. There were more pressing concerns for Europe than the far distant and increasingly remote regions of the Eastern Mediterranean coastline, as many areas increasingly felt the pressure of a Muslim revival.

But there were internal factors that resulted in a change of emphasis as well. The Papacy, in whose gift the spiritual rewards offered in return for Crusading lay, increasingly offered benefits for Crusades launched closer to home. The Albigensian, or Cathar, Crusade, as bitter an internal dispute as Europe had known for centuries, received Papal sanction for those who participated in the often vicious events of those wars, which were focused on the elimination of heretics rather than Muslims.

For a time, the threat posed by the Mongols also caused the Papacy to preach a Crusade against the threat from that direction too.

Pope Gregory IX preached such an expedition against them in 1241 (although he limited his appeal to the lands immediately adjacent to those subsumed in the Mongol deluge), to be followed by Pope Innocent IV in 1243. But these Crusades against 'external forces' happened alongside a number of campaigns that had as their object the assertion of supremacy by the Papacy over secular European powers, most noticeably the German Empire, particularly when Frederick II was its head. Such trends continued with the series of expeditions launched in the Baltic region.

In this respect, the year 1250 marked a watershed in European history, causing one historian to remark that the year 'may seem to be one of those pivotal dates which determine the destiny of peoples'. There were three major events that took place then that had a profound impact on Europe and the Mediterranean world. The first of them was the Seventh Crusade veering radically off course, the main subject of this particular book. The second event, which was intimately connected to the first, was the assumption of power by a new and assertive Mameluke dynasty in Egypt, the rise of which had a great effect on the course of Louis's Crusade. The third event was the death of Frederick II, a man who bestrode European affairs like a colossus, often leaving chaos in his wake.[2]

To these may be added a fourth factor that shaped the politics of both the Muslim world and Christian Europe for decades during the thirteenth century. The continuing incursions of the Mongols into both Asia and the fringes of Europe had a terrifying effect on the psyche of both Muslim and Christian powers which was an omnipresent factor on the evolution of world politics, and which shaped the atmosphere in which Louis, and others like him such as Christendom's great adversary, Sultan Baibars of Egypt, lived.

Palestine and the surrounding lands were on a fault-line where different worlds collided (a situation which the modern world can equate all too easily with). After the traumatic events of the thirteenth century, such as the terrifying raids of the Mongol hordes or the emergence of the powerful Mameluke dynasty the world would become a radically different place. It was as if a pack of cards, neatly sorted into a particular order, was thrown up into the air and fell to earth in a radically different sequence. Nothing would ever be quite the same again, especially the Crusading movement.

It was in this context that the Seventh Crusade became the last Crusade of a particular type, fought overseas beyond the boundaries of Europe, probing the torso of the Muslim world. The King was himself something of an anachronism, devoted to an idea that was changing radically, one suspects in ways that Louis found uncomfortable. He was not averse to supporting the Papacy in Crusades nearer to home (he reigned as France was still coming to terms with the effects of the Crusade against the Cathars) but his heart was always drawn to the Holy Land. The focus on Jerusalem, and the lands in which Christ walked, did not die with Louis but never again would a leading Western monarch set foot in the region and try to re-conquer its lands by force of arms.

One of the seminal works of Crusading history in the twentieth century recognised the importance of Louis's Crusade in the following terms:

> The Crusades of Louis IX mark both the culmination and the beginning of the end of the crusading movement. None of the earlier expeditions was as well organised or financed, none had a more inspiring leader, none had a better chance of success. The Crusade of 1249 was the last whole-hearted effort of Christendom against the infidel – it was watched with friendly interest even in regions which were jealous of the leadership of the French King and suspicious of the policy of the Pope. But the very magnitude of the undertaking brought disillusion when it failed.[3]

Not all of this analysis from Setton's monumental work has stood the test of time. Yet these expeditions, which were massive in the context of Crusading warfare, raised huge expectations that were subsequently unfulfilled. This in turn had an effect on perceptions of the Crusades, which consequently caused great damage to the morale of Christendom and its attitude towards future Crusades.

The character of the King of France dominated the Seventh Crusade. Many Crusaders displayed the quality of humility but none more so than Louis, whose spirituality was so marked that within a few decades of his death he would be canonised, partly (though not solely) because of his actions whilst he was involved in his Crusade. Whatever his faults as a tactician – and he was certainly not a military genius, although he was undoubtedly a brave leader – it is impossible to ignore the fact that in his own, or any, age he was a remarkable man.

Of all the men, great or small, rich or poor, who during the Crusader period ever left the safety of his home country for the uncertainties of the East few, if any, can show greater strength of personality than Louis IX, King, pilgrim and saint. The story of his last, great Crusade to Outremer is one in which the King's character and personality, warts and all, shaped events in a way that is rarely matched in the history of the Crusading movement.

The Vow of King Louis

In 1244, Louis IX, King of France, lay on his deathbed. His young body (he was only thirty years old) had been overwhelmed by a serious fever from which there seemed to be no hope of recovery. As time passed, his vital physical signs became weaker and his mind ever more contorted as the fever took over completely.

A hush descended on the room, broken only by the sound of sub-dued sobbing and laboured breathing. Around his bed, his family and his subjects gathered to pay their last respects. Many of them felt sincere affection for their King. No one could doubt his piety. In a religious age, the King had set an example that no other monarch of his time could match. Devout to the point of fanaticism, the King's short life would undoubtedly commend him to his maker, whom he seemed destined shortly to meet.

His struggles became ever more laboured, until they appeared to stop completely. In his dark chamber, fitfully lit by flickering candles, dutiful subjects paid their last respects to their dying King. His strug-gles for life diminished, and then appeared to end. To most of those gathered around his bed, it seemed that his saintly life was finally over. One of the ladies-in-waiting who stood next to the bed moved to cover his face with a cloth in a final act of service to her lord.

As she did so, however, another female servant on the opposite side of the bed restrained her. Weak as the King undoubtedly was, she insisted that he was still alive.

A lengthy debate began as the two servants argued with each other. As they did so, a miracle took place. The King had been dumb for days because of his illness, but God gave him the strength at last to speak. His health began to recover. From being at death's door, the King started to revive. When the power of speech was fully restored to him, he offered thanks to his Lord for the gift of life that he had seemed so shortly before destined to lose.

He would repay the debt he owed in the most practical way that he knew. That very year, Jerusalem had fallen to Khwarismian hordes, violent nomadic Muslim horsemen from Central Asia who had been ousted from their homelands by the teeming Mongol hordes that were sweeping across the Far and Middle East. The Khwarismians in turn descended on the Crusader kingdom of Outremer like a storm breaking over an unsuspecting land. The loss of the city signalled a dramatic and conclusive end to a short-lived Crusader revival in the region.

Propagandists had a field day with the loss of Jerusalem. A contemporary Spanish poem painted a bleak and desolate picture of life in Jerusalem following its loss:

> ... the tender maidens in chains and in torment. They weep greatly in their affliction and sorrow in Jerusalem. The Christians see their sons roasted, they see their wives' breasts sliced off whilst they are still living; they go along the streets with their hands and feet cut off in Jerusalem. They made blankets out of the vestments, they made a stable out of the Holy Sepulchre; with the holy crosses they made stakes in Jerusalem.[1]

Such dark tales are a feature of most major wars: in recent times references might include the bayoneting of babies in the Indian Mutiny or the alleged crucifixion of Canadian soldiers by the Germans in the First World War. But they touched a nerve, as those later accusations did. Indeed, they formed part of the classic sequence of events that generated Crusading euphoria: a major catastrophe, a Crusade in response (which normally failed to achieve its objectives), a loss of momentum and then apathy. Then, another major reverse would start the cycle off again.

For example, in 1187 Jerusalem — the most sacred city in the Christian World — had been lost by the Crusaders to Saladin. This led to an angst-riven outpouring of grief in the West and a major expedition. Although the subsequent Crusade of Philip Augustus of France and Richard I of England had failed to recover it, the city had more recently been restored to Christian ownership through the exertions of Frederick II, the extraordinary German emperor.

Now the transient nature of that revival had been brutally exposed for the deception that it was. If Jerusalem were to be won back again for the West, another Crusade would be needed. Louis, King of France, believed that he was the man destined to lead it, and that his illness and subsequent recovery were unmistakable signs from God that he must take the Cross.

Accordingly, with a strength in his voice that would have seemed unbelievable only a short time before, he announced to those assembled around his bedside his intentions. His mother, Blanche of Castille, was with him. She was overjoyed when she saw that her son had escaped from the jaws of death itself.

When she heard of his plans, however, her bearing re-assumed all the appearance of mourning. Crusading was a discredited ideal. It would mean the expenditure of huge amounts of money for no guaranteed return. It also meant the absence of Louis from his kingdom at a time when it was threatened by troublesome neighbours and dissentient elements within his own country. Nothing but harm would come from this expedition in her opinion.

Her exhortations, and those of many of Louis's councillors, fell on stony ground. To Louis, God had given an unmistakable sign and it would be a sin and a sacrilege to ignore the divine plan. Louis took his obligations as a King extremely seriously — indeed, they were only outweighed by his obligations to God. And, convinced as he was that God had spoken to him, there was a stubbornness in his character that would brook no opposition. He was a Christian monarch, who owed his position entirely to the will of God, and he would not abandon his stated intention to take up the cross of a pilgrim, a Crusader.

Louis was not the only pious member of this extraordinary family. He had a sister, Isabella, to whom he was very close and who may have encouraged him in his obstinacy. Just a couple of years previously, her mother had arranged a marriage for her to the heir of the German Emperor, Frederick II. Bringing together the two great mainland powers of Western Europe at the time as it did, it was a match that had much to commend it.

Isabella, however, refused to participate in this convenient arrangement. When shortly afterwards she had contracted a serious illness, she took a vow that she would dedicate herself to perpetual virginity which not unnaturally killed off any lingering thoughts about marriage arrangements. She did not enter a convent but led a very austere life, dressing in humble clothes and dedicating herself to the care of the poor. The influence of this powerful personality, capable of resisting the manipulation of a domineering matriarch, upon Louis must have been striking.[2]

Louis's life had so far been a difficult one. Born on St Mark's Day, 25 April 1214, he had ascended to the throne of France on 29 November 1226, when he was just twelve years old. His father, King Louis VIII of France, had died well before his time after an attack of dysentery (although some whispered that his demise had come about because he had been poisoned by one of his truculent barons).

It was a worrying time for the kingdom and a trying one for the child King. He was not even the eldest son – his elder brother, Philip, had died in 1218. However strict his upbringing may have been, it would have left him very unprepared for the challenge that lay ahead. The heir apparent was not even yet a knight. En route to his coronation in the ancient cathedral at Rheims, where coronations had taken place for a thousand years since the early days of the Merovingian dynasty, Louis was hastily dubbed a knight in the nearby cathedral city of Soissons.

Louis became King of a nation scarred with the flames of hatred and heresy. For twenty long years, his immediate predecessors Philip Augustus, his grandfather, and Louis VIII, had led a bitter and brutal Crusade against the Albigensian Cathars, a sect of heretics in the South of France.[3] The campaigns that had been fought had been characterised by atrocity and judicial execution as the heretics were systematically and ruthlessly expurgated by the armies of the King of France. It was in such a fundamentalist environment that Louis spent his early, largely unrecorded, years. Given such a background, it is little wonder that the King would develop such strong and unequivocal views with regard to Christianity.

His impressionable years were also spent under the influence of a person who was to become the dominant person in his life – his mother. Louis was far too young when he ascended the throne to rule in his own right and Blanche of Castille was declared Regent. She enjoyed the power that this offered her, even though her grip on it was by no means secure.

France was a country still in its formative years. The shape of the nation had changed dramatically in the preceding decades. During that period, a significant proportion of the territories owned by the English Plantagenet Kings had been conquered by the French. However, other territories were still owned by the English. Provinces such as Brittany were virtually autonomous, and the Burgundian territories in the east of the country were stubbornly independently minded. Allied to the fact that the South of France had to all intents and purposes recently been annexed in a campaign characterised by fire and blood, the ruling dynasty constantly had to be on its guard.

Blanche protected her position and that of her family so ferociously that, even when her son Louis became King in fact as well as name, she still exerted a suffocating influence over him. It was to her that the chronicler of Louis's subsequent Crusade, Jean de Joinville, attributed the King's piety:

[She] taught him to believe in God and to love Him, and to gather round himself all good people of religion. And, child as he was, she made him recite all the Hours, and listen to the sermons on festival days. He recorded that his mother had sometimes led him to understand that she would rather he were dead than have committed a mortal sin.[4]

The Queen developed a paranoia about the barons of France which was to an extent justified. She was a foreigner from Castille, and they had little love for her. She had few friends in the country. The actions of some of the leading barons in France during her Regency seemed tailored to countermand her influence. During her years of effective power, a strong baronial opposition party developed in France, centred on the Count of Boulogne.

Before considering Louis's part in the Crusading movement, it is important to understand something of the domestic challenges facing him, for these paint the backdrop against which his adventures overseas took place. In the early days of Louis's reign, opposition to the crown festered. It came to a head when the barons called an assembly at Corbeil. They demanded that they be given more lands, a demand that was predictably enough refused.

Louis was then at Montlheri. He would not return to Paris until a strong armed escort was despatched from the city to accompany him. Open rebellion broke out, led by Peter, Count of Brittany. It soon fizzled out. When it came to the crunch, Louis still retained the support of certain key members of the nobility, particularly the powerful Count of Champagne,[5] Tibald IV, and the rebel barons were forced to back down.

Little good did the rebellion do the Count of Brittany; he was forced to make sizeable concessions to earn the King's forgiveness, in the form of the counties of Anjou and Perche. This was not the end of the revolt though. Seeing that they would not be able to force the King into acceding to their requests without first of all besting the Count of Champagne, the barons turned their attentions towards Tibald.

Tibald's claim to Champagne was disputed. His father, the previous count, had been the second son in the family. He had an elder brother, Henry of Champagne, who had left a daughter, who was the Queen of Cyprus. Many of the barons sought to press the claim that Champagne was her land at the expense of the current count.

Not all were convinced that attacking Tibald's rights to the lands was the best way forward. By attacking his legitimacy, they were making a rod for their own backs. By challenging the legality of his position, they were challenging the status quo. By encouraging resistance to the Count, they were creating precedents that might be used against them and their own legitimacy in the future. Further, the Count was a very powerful man, and he would not meekly back down when faced with this attempt to deprive him of his power. So some of the barons sought accommodation.

This was to be brought about by the proposed marriage of Tibald to the daughter of the Count of Brittany. Louis however was enraged when he heard of the match, as it would radically shift the balance of power in France in a way that threatened the monarchy. He sent an unequivocal message to Tibald that the marriage must not go ahead. Despite the advantages that the marriage would offer him personally, Tibald decided to comply with his King's peremptory demand.

All this did was to provoke an angry response from Peter of Brittany's supporters. This was more than a slur on family honour, it was an act that foiled the count's dynastic and territorial ambitions. He resolved to take it out on Tibald. He would lead an army against him whilst his ally, the Duke of Burgundy, would attack him from another direction in a pincer movement. They also approached the Queen of Cyprus, implying that they were prepared to fight for her cause. They clearly felt that she would be a useful political ally.

The actions against Tibald were also implicitly directed at Louis himself as it had been on his orders that the marriage plans had been cancelled. Louis therefore assembled an army of his own with which to fight the rebels. The troublesome barons marched on the city of Troyes whose citizens appealed to Simon, Lord of Joinville, for help.[6]

Reinforcements were rushed in, enough to dissuade the rebels from attacking. They instead joined up with the nearby army of their ally, the Duke of Burgundy.

Louis then came up with his forces. He immediately made it clear that he planned to attack the rebels. It was a defining moment for his kingship. The barons were on the verge of outright rebellion. Faced with the King in person, many of them felt distinctly ill at ease at the prospect of making war on their lord. They had taken an oath of loyalty to him, a sacred act that in medieval eyes amounted to a divine contract which could not be broken without compromising the offender's soul.

The barons sent a message to the King, begging him to withdraw. Louis disdainfully refused. A counter-proposal was made; the barons offered to prevail on the Queen of Cyprus to make peace (an ironic suggestion as they had largely been responsible for drawing her into the dispute in the first instance). Once again, Louis responded in the negative – he would agree to no peace, nor would he allow the Count of Champagne to do so, until the barons had taken their armies away from the field.

Faced with Louis's continued refusal to negotiate, the barons' campaign stuttered and then fizzled out. They had effectively been faced down by the King. A peace was negotiated between the Count of Champagne and the Queen of Cyprus. Under its terms, some land was given up by the Count to the Queen – the Count also sold other lands to the King.

De Joinville discusses this incident in some depth in his chronicle, and it is worth pondering why he does so in a narrative that concentrates so heavily on Louis's involvement in the Crusades. Partly, there is a personal interest on the part of de Joinville, as his father had played a part in the campaign. It also illustrates several other points however, all of which are pertinent to our story. Firstly, it tells us much of the character of the King. He was a loyal man who did not hesitate to come to the aid of one of his subjects who was threatened because of his support of the monarchy.

He was also brave; his decision to personally involve himself in battle was very much in character with many of his other actions, and had in this instance proved decisive in resolving the dispute. And he was stubborn; faced with attempts at compromise on the part of the rebel barons, he refused to budge from his position.

In this instance, his stance had been successful. But this bravery and stubbornness were two sides of the same coin. Stubbornness can be a desirable quality in some situations, in others it leads to inflexibility. Louis's actions also show the pride that he had in the dignity of his kingship, and his anger at any who threatened it. He was humble as a man, proud as a King. These characteristics were to shape his reign and his career as a Crusader.

The incident also illustrates something else. It demonstrates that France was far from united. Although in the decade following this incident Louis established himself more securely, leaving France for any length of time could seriously threaten the position of the King. This also tells us something more of Louis. For him, matters of personal conscience would take precedence over affairs of state and politics.

This might serve well as the criteria by which suitability for canonisation is judged; they are less appropriate qualities for any man who would be a successful King. It has been argued[7] that the situation in France settled down significantly after the early days of Louis's reign. It has also been said that he and his mother had managed to introduce a degree of stability into France which created an environment in which Louis could afford to be away from the country for an extended period. This is only true up to a point.

Just two years before Louis took his vow to go on Crusade there was another outbreak of opposition that served to emphasise that France was still volatile. There was one other great player in the politics of France to consider, an old and future enemy. At the beginning of the thirteenth century vast swathes of the country had been owned by the King of England. France and England had been in a state of war or quasi-war for many years. Richard I for example had fought far longer in France than he had on Crusade.

Richard was a fine warrior whose reputation is well known. However, when he died his brother, John, succeeded. John was an unfortunate ruler. The biographies of his life that survive were largely written by enemies and consequently show him little favour. He has become stereotyped as one of the worst Kings ever to sit on the throne of England. This certainly overstates the case against him.

But what cannot be denied is that militarily and territorially his reign was a disaster for the Plantagenet dynasty in France. In a well co-ordinated and ferocious campaign, a large proportion of the dynasty's lands in France were lost, including Normandy. The territories belonging to the King of France were, in contrast, much enhanced. John spent much of the latter part of his reign distracted with serious problems in England. This prevented him from leading an effective counter-attack for some time.

This only delayed a fightback. John died in 1216, to be succeeded by his son who, at the tender age of nine, became King Henry III. It was a few years before France came under threat from the English. King Henry would not be a successful monarch, although he would reign for many years. In 1230, he launched a bid to recover the lost French territories. The campaign proceeded in a desultory fashion for a while but without any lasting success.

But further campaigns were always likely. In 1242 Isabelle of Angouleme, widow of King John and mother of Henry III, had remarried, to the Count of la Marche, Count of Lusignan and vassal of King Louis. The Count developed a close understanding with King Henry of England. He and Henry raised an army and led it through Gascony towards the territories of the French crown.

Louis marched to meet them. The two forces met outside a castle at Taillebourg. Here, there was a very narrow bridge across the River Charente certainly not wide enough for a great army to cross quickly. When the French saw their enemy approaching, they made their way across the river to face them, using a flotilla of small boats and pontoons that they had available.

There then began a battle described by de Joinville as 'grim and fierce'. The two armies hacked ferociously at each other. The French were heavily outnumbered but fought valiantly. Louis himself was in the thick of the battle. According to de Joinville, his presence proved decisive. When the enemy saw that Louis was fighting in person, they broke and fled.

It is conceivable that when the men of the Count of la Marche saw that they were fighting against Louis personally, their enthusiasm for the battle abated considerably. What is not in doubt was that the armies of King Henry and the Count of la Marche abandoned the field. Henry made his way back to Gascony, his tail between his legs. The campaign was over. The threat posed by the English King had, for the time being at least, been averted. Shortly after his triumph, Louis, possibly exhausted at his exertions, fell ill with a malady that presaged the more serious attack on his constitution that he was to face two years later.

Faced with the certainty of retribution from Louis, the Count of la Marche decided to sue for peace. He would pay a heavy personal price. He had to beg for mercy on his knees, his wife and children kneeling next to him before the King. He was forced to hand over large amounts of land to Louis. It was a great triumph for the King. It cemented his position as sovereign, clearly demonstrating that he was a force to be reckoned with. It was a great confidence-booster for him, and it meant that he could consider leaving France to take part in a great Crusade with a firmer sense of security.

It was still a very bold move to decide to take part in a Crusade so soon after these events. Henry of England would certainly not participate, although he did from time to time express an interest in making a pilgrimage to the East. With Louis away on Crusade, and a large part of his nobility likely to accompany him, France would be very exposed to a renewed assault from England, and this lay behind the concerns of people such as Blanche of Castille.

But Blanche's strategic arguments meant little to the King. If he was convinced that he had received a call from God, nothing would move him from what he perceived as his vocation. Sometimes, to be truthful, it seems to modern eyes that there is something of the fanatic about Louis. De Joinville describes his daily routine: a tiring succession of masses, private prayers in his chamber as soon as he awoke in the morning, even daily prayers for the dead. He would, according to the chronicler, delight in engaging in theological debates with his advisors after returning from church.

From early on, the prospect of leading a Crusade made a strong impression on Louis. He had already contributed significant sums of money to previous expeditions. And he was quick to encourage his countrymen to participate. He had previously insisted that some members of the nobility who had been involved in rebellion against him should serve their penance by Crusading in the Holy Land, and in 1237 he had demanded that the citizens of Narbonne should undertake a similar mission.[8]

There was another factor that also affected Louis's thoughts on the Crusading movement. Family history played a strong part in encouraging men to commit themselves to a Crusade. Louis's great-grandfather, Louis VII, was one important ancestor who had played a prominent part in the Crusading movement. Through such traditions and family pride Louis himself was encouraged to participate.

Neither were such traditions unique to the male line of his family tree. His mother, Blanche of Castille, came from a long line of Spanish warrior-kings who had taken an active role in the frequent clashes with the Moors in Iberia which took on the status of Crusades. Tales of their exploits would have resonated around the great halls of fire-lit castles during Louis's formative years, and must have had a great effect on him.

There would be many manifestations of his religious zeal and his burning faith during the course of the Crusade that was to follow. De Joinville's account is partly hagiographic. He would in later years be a witness to the Papal commission who, less than three decades after Louis's death, would approve the King's canonisation. Understandably, he may exaggerate features of the Louis's fanaticism.

For all that, there can be little doubt that Louis was an intensely devout man – few men, let alone monarchs, are canonised so soon after their death as Louis. On one occasion he declared that he would undoubtedly rather be a leper than commit a mortal sin. His reasoning was simple. As a leper, he would be freed of his bodily sufferings when he died, whereas a mortal sin imperilled the well being of his soul for eternity. In another instance, he rebuked his advisors for their view that washing the feet of the poor was demeaning, telling them that they should 'never disdain what God did for our teaching'.[9] Being a member of this King's court must have been an interesting and, one suspects, on occasion a very trying experience.

The King was also a generous benefactor of the Church, providing the funds by which many new religious buildings were erected, the greatest of which was the abbey of Royaumont. He paid for the maintenance of many groups of monks and nuns. Some of his advisors believed that he was being overly munificent with his gifts, but he refused absolutely to consider scaling down the size of his contributions towards the Church.

Later in his reign he would generously help create religious houses for monks around Paris. It would be wrong to assume that Louis would meekly acquiesce to every request of the church though. He could be stubbornly independent. He was once berated by a group of clerics whilst holding court in Paris. They criticised the King for being too lenient in his treatment of excommunicates in his realm. Their particular concern was that excommunicates were taking their religious punishment too casually, and many of them were consequently dying un-absolved of their sins.

The clerics asked that Louis should force excommunicates to seek absolution by depriving them of their possessions until they did so. Louis responded in a logical but completely unhelpful way. Many years before, the Count of Brittany had been excommunicated by the local church. For seven long years he had protested against his sentence and eventually it was lifted by none other than the Pope himself. Louis contested that, if he had acted as the delegation was now suggesting he should, he himself would have committed a great sin. Faced with such opposition, the pleas of the clerics were unsuccessful.

Such was the character then of Louis IX. Devout with streaks of stubbornness and fanaticism, once he had set his heart on achieving a particular objective, he would not be easily swayed from it, and so it proved with his Crusade. Those who opposed his decision to leave France for the East argued with passion that he could not be held accountable for his vow, as he had taken it when in a state of near-delirium. No one would think the less of the King if he were to withdraw from the Crusade: he had only promised to participate when he was in no position to think logically about his actions.

Louis tired of their protests. Eventually he appeared to accept their arguments. It was true that he was not in full possession of his senses when he had made his vow, being gripped with fever at the time. He ostentatiously took off his cross and put it down. Then in front of his entourage he picked it very deliberately again. Surely none of his subjects would have the temerity to aver that he was not of sound mind now?

Fully in possession of his faculties, Louis fervently gripped the cross. Effectively, he was re-taking his vow so that all could see. Faced with such determination, those who opposed his intentions reluctantly held their peace. The King was obviously set on a course from which he would not retreat. Indeed, if they understood him well, they knew that he could not retreat. A man of his piety could not contemplate turning his back on God, who had restored him to health when all hope seemed lost.

So France steeled itself for war. Recent Crusades had been blessed with intermittent success at best. But she was a confident country (if the loose alliance of counties and dukedoms that France then was could be granted such a grandiose title). Louis was a pious King who was totally committed to his religion. It was inconceivable that God would bless the expedition with anything other than resounding success.

The Crusade in the Thirteenth Century

The Crusading movement developed over time. It was based on an evolving, mutating concept which constantly reshaped itself as a result of events and experiences. By the time that Louis IX decided to set out on Crusade, the Crusading movement was unrecognisable from the early days of its evolution.

It all started in 1095, inspired by the preaching of Pope Urban II. His timing was propitious. The euphoria that greeted the call to arms for the First Crusade is one of the most powerful and amazing reactions in recorded history. His summons came at a time that fitted the contemporary mood of society perfectly. The reaction was a veritable tidal wave of support from all levels: rich, poor, male, female, young, old, peasant, warrior. In itself, this was problematic. What was clearly needed was a military force, well-armed under a unified leadership, which could retain some form of discipline under a loosely centralised control. The force that responded was, however, very different, far from what Urban expected or desired.

There were responses from the great warlords of Western Europe, it is true. But there was also an incredible groundswell of support from other strata of society; for example from the poor and idealistic who were patently unsuitable for involvement in a military exercise. What is most crucial to understand is not how this reaction manifested itself but why it occurred in the first instance.

The reaction pointed clearly to a great sense of spiritual longing that was present in society which expressed itself by involvement in the Crusade, effectively an armed pilgrimage. In return for involvement in this enterprise, which was plainly dangerous and would cost thousands of the participants their lives, the Pope offered great spiritual rewards in the form of Indulgences, offering remission of sins and, consequently, a more assured progression to the joys of paradise in the hereafter.

The Crusades were therefore religiously motivated. This may appear to be a statement of the blindingly obvious, but over the centuries many other motives have been ascribed to the Crusaders; the desire for new territories, the need for younger sons to search overseas for lands they could claim as their own, the thirst for plunder, glory and wealth. All these factors played their part, though the man who sought for wealth as a result of the Crusades was nearly always disappointed – involvement was inevitably an expensive option, and the great majority of Crusaders ended up vastly out of pocket. But they were, in many cases, secondary to the primary motivation: the desire to improve one's spiritual standing as a result of his or her pilgrimage.

The First Crusade (which was in fact a series of different 'invasions') achieved a miracle after a dreadfully inauspicious start. At the time, Palestine and Syria were under Muslim rule, in addition to large tracts of Asia Minor. The attack of the Crusaders was launched at a moment when their Muslim enemies were fatally divided. Unwilling or incapable of offering unified resistance, the Muslim rulers of the Levant let the forces of Christendom strike deep into their heartlands. After dreadful suffering, deprivation and attrition, the Crusade succeeded in taking Jerusalem from the Muslims.

The result was so unlikely that most people attributed it to nothing less than divine intervention. It was a crowning glory to the enterprise that appeared to give the lustre of heavenly approval to the whole concept of the Crusade. In the aftermath of the capture of Jerusalem, a small Kingdom was carved out in the surrounding territories. It was not large and it was certainly not secure, but it was nevertheless a Christian Kingdom established in the country of Christianity's birth. The territories formed there – Jerusalem, Tripoli, Antioch and Edessa – were given the collective name of 'Outremer' – 'the land beyond the sea'.

Despite a few decades of consolidation after the capture of Jerusalem in 1099, the outcome of the First Crusade, which was achieved just four years after Pope Urban had called the West to arms, would prove to be its greatest triumph. Although the fall of the Holy City was a tremendous success, retaining the city was always likely to prove a difficult challenge. For one thing, its capture was only possible because of the disunity of the Muslim world. If the Muslims were to act as a united force, they would have a vast numerical and logistical advantage that the Crusaders would find difficult to resist.

These disparities in the manpower available to either side were compounded by the inability of the West to provide suitable numbers of settlers in the region to compensate. As a result, whenever battle joined the Christians and the Muslims the former were almost invariably at a numerical disadvantage, often a significant one. This left the Christian armies with little margin for error. Sometimes a significant proportion of the fighting strength of the Christian kingdom was committed to battle in a major engagement, meaning that reserves were in short supply and consequently that a serious defeat with large numbers of casualties was potentially disastrous.

The twelfth century saw an increased unity in the Muslim world. A succession of outstanding and aggressive Muslim leaders eroded the gains made by the West. The first of these was Zengi, emir of Mosul. One of the first significant gains made by the First Crusade had been the capture of the ancient Christian city of Edessa. It lay in the outlying borderlands of the Crusader territories and as such was always strategically at risk.

Nevertheless, the fall of Edessa to Zengi in 1144 generated palpable shockwaves in the West. The triumph of the First Crusade created a sense of complacency. The fall of Edessa however shook Christendom from its apathy. A Second Crusade was launched. It was led by the two greatest magnates of Western Europe, the Emperor Conrad, ruler of the Holy Roman Empire, and King Louis VII of France.

It rapidly degenerated to the realms of farce. Poorly led, the respective armies were badly cut up making the crossing of Asia Minor. Then, when those who survived arrived in the Holy Land, they could not decide where to attack, so they besieged the strongly-fortified city of Damascus which, to cap it all, was currently held by an ally of the Christians of Outremer.

The Crusade achieved nothing, save to emphasise the paucity of strategic insight possessed by its leaders. But at about this time the Western settlers in Outremer began to perceive an Achilles Heel in the Muslim world. To the west of Outremer lay the state of Egypt. It was rich, and yet its wealth seemed to be in stark contradiction to the relative weakness of the country. The fiercest opposition by far to the Crusaders had come from the Turks in and around Asia Minor. In contrast, although the Egyptians had on occasion bested the Christian armies, they had suffered a number of defeats against the Franks. Further, the country appeared to be politically volatile. Egypt appeared to be ripe for the taking.

An invasion of the country was launched in 1162. It quickly lost its momentum when the Egyptians summoned help from the Turks around Damascus. This was despite the fact that there were fundamental differences between the Egyptians and the Turks. The Egyptians were Shi'ites, followers of a branch of Islam that was inimical to the beliefs of the Sunni Muslims, amongst whose number were the Turks. As such, there was a great deal of suspicion between the two groups, which had in the past led to open warfare between them.

In the long term, this was fatal for Egypt. The most powerful leader in Sunni Syria at the time was Nur-ed-Din, a man of extraordinary vision and decisive action. Further, he had a fiercesome lieutenant, a great warrior known as Shirkuh. Close to Shirkuh was a young ambitious individual called Saladin. It was a lethal triumvirate. In contrast, the weakly led Egyptian state was no match. The Syrian Muslims helped to fight off the Christian invasion with relative ease. Then, before long, they took Egypt for themselves.

Following the death of Nur-ed-Din, Saladin became the leader of the Islamic Empire. He launched a series of attacks on Outremer that threatened to drive the Crusaders back into the sea. These culminated on a battlefield outside of the town of Tiberias. Here, the largest Crusader army ever assembled, comprising nearly all the regular troops of Outremer, faced a huge Muslim force. Saladin had completely out-manoeuvred the Crusaders' leaders and had led them full square into a trap. Once in that trap, there would be no escape.

The Crusaders had been enticed from a position of defensive strength towards a strongly positioned Muslim army. Furthermore, they were forced to march across a region largely devoid of water in the midst of summer. The resultant battle at Hattin proved to be the blackest day in Crusader history. The Christian army was completely destroyed and the kingdom was laid bare before the triumphant Muslims. In the aftermath, city after city capitulated, incapable of resistance as most of them had been stripped of their garrisons to provide manpower for the now-defeated army. The greatest blow of all was the loss of Jerusalem itself.

Only Tyre held out in the territories immediately adjacent to Palestine. It did not seem that this could survive for long but against insuperable odds it did. The news of the loss of Jerusalem provoked a huge outpouring of grief in the West. Immediately, a recruiting campaign for a new Crusade was initiated. In response, a mighty army was assembled. To be more accurate, three were assembled; one led by Frederick Barbarossa, the German Emperor, another by King Philip Augustus of France and the last by King Richard I of England.

The Third Crusade emphasised once again the commitment of France to the Crusading movement, following on from the efforts already made during the First and Second Crusades. A Crusading tradition was developing that would help to shape the paradigms of future French monarchs. Indeed, the events of the Third Crusade were to resonate down through the years far after it had ended; de Joinville refers to them with a sense of almost reverential awe.

The Third Crusade was a partial success. Acre, the most important harbour in Outremer, was recovered along with some other territory. The greatest symbolic prize of all, however, remained in Muslim hands: Jerusalem was not re-taken. Philip returned to France early on and Barbarossa had died before he even reached Outremer. Although Richard of England fought on for several years, he never launched an assault on Jerusalem, which consequently remained a Muslim city.

However, Richard was no longer sure that Jerusalem was the main target. It was widely believed that he had identified the surest way of defeating Saladin. He had seen the inherent weakness of Egypt and there, he felt, lay the potential for destabilising the Muslim Empire. But before he could test his theories, he was forced to return home to England.

But there was sound logic behind this line of thinking. Saladin soon died, worn out by a lifetime of warfare, travelling and intense political activity. Internecine dynastic disputes followed in the wake of his death. The Empire fell apart, and Egypt reverted to a form of independence under one of his sons. The years immediately following Saladin's demise were characterised by incessant infighting within his family.

It was a time of great opportunity for those minded to launch another Crusade. But the potential offered by this internecine warfare was not exploited. Immediately following Saladin's death, Philip of Augustus and Richard of England were involved in a bitter war across a vast tract of disputed territories in France. Following Richard's death, the fighting continued between Richard's successor, John, and Philip.

A Crusade was finally launched just after the turn of the century. Although its ultimate objective was shrouded in mystery, there were strong rumours that it was headed for Egypt. It never arrived. In a bizarre turn of events, it diverted completely from its original destination, and arrived before Constantinople. In 1204, it attacked and pillaged the city, and set up a Latin Empire in what was formerly Byzantine territory. The Egyptians were no doubt greatly relieved at this turn of events, as it freed the Muslim world to carry on fighting amongst itself once more. Cynics also suggested that the Venetians, who had strong trading relationships with the Egyptians, were delighted as it meant that their commercial dealings could continue unhindered.

In many quarters in the West, the conquest of Constantinople was hailed as a spectacular triumph (which militarily it undoubtedly was, whatever the morality of the diversion against a Christian city). Further Crusading action was directed elsewhere, particularly against the heretic Cathars in the South of France, for the next few years. The Crusading movement began to look northwards and westwards.

But Jerusalem was still a powerful totem. Projects to retake it were regularly discussed though not often with much tangible end-result. But eventually another expedition was assembled to make just such an effort. In line with the thinking of the times, Egypt was definitively the target, the first step in a planned re-conquest of the East that was meant to culminate in the glorious recapture of Jerusalem.

It is worth dwelling in more detail on the course of this next Crusade, as there are certain precedents that could tactically have provided very useful lessons to Louis's crusade. The Fifth Crusade would be led by a Cardinal, Pelagius, a haughty and obstinate man with little tact and less vision. The secular leader of the army was John of Brienne, King of Jerusalem, a knight of French origin.

From the very beginning the two men were at loggerheads in an attempt to prove their right to overall leadership of the expedition.[1] However, at the beginning of the Crusade the cracks in the unified leadership were smoothed over. The first assault of the army was on the city of Damietta, a port at the mouth of one of the Nile

Delta's outlets to the Mediterranean. The city was strongly fortified, and held out for months before it fell due to an outbreak of disease inside its walls.

Once it had fallen, the army was unclear about its next move (a situation that would find an uncanny echo during Louis's expedition). For months, the army stayed in the vicinity of Damietta, encircled by a Muslim force. Here it was badly depleted by an outbreak of plague in the camp. Relations between John of Brienne and Pelagius sunk to unprecedentedly low levels.

It became clear that the enforced inactivity was doing enormous damage to the morale of the army. Accordingly, a breakout attempt was launched by the army. It succeeded in its attempts to move forward, and all appeared to be going exceedingly well. There was however one problematic, and as it turned out fatal, flaw in the Crusade's tactics. The timing of their breakout was hopelessly out of kilter.

Every year, with predictable regularity, the Nile inundation arrived. One of its effects was to transform dried-up riverbeds into fast-flowing streams, many of which consequently became navigable waterways. Oblivious to this fact – which could surely have been predicted from examining local knowledge, if any had thought to ask for it[2] – the army pushed on. After a time, the retreating Muslim forces made a stand, curtailing the Crusade's advance.

Shortly after, the floods came. The dried riverbeds filled up with water, turning them into a comprehensive network of canals. The Crusade ground to a halt, and it was eventually decided that a prudent retreat should be made. But the Christian army was still blissfully unaware of what was happening to their rear.

As they retreated, the full horror of their situation dawned on them. Behind them, large numbers of Muslim ships had used the network of newly formed, seasonal canals to both block their retreat and interfere with the progress of supplies that had been sent to re-provision them. It was a hopeless situation. A few Christian ships broke the blockade in a desperate attempt to escape, but the vast majority of the army was captured. It was a debacle of immense proportions.

The major tactical lesson of the fiasco was that great care should be taken when advancing along the Nile. The intricate nature of the canals meant that an enemy with local knowledge and a good supply of manoeuvrable, shallow-draft ships could threaten the lines of communication of any invading army. As the Muslims in Egypt were in possession of both of these, any invader should be on his guard at all times, otherwise the result would be disaster. Any future commander would be well advised to take good notice of this if he wished to avoid a repetition of this disaster.

The initial high hopes of this attack on Egypt were completely dashed by this fiasco. Rather than any reconquest of the Holy Land, the lasting legacy of the reverse was a further damaging blow to the fragile morale of the Crusading movement, and the creation of another strong counter-argument against those who wished to attempt to recover the lost territories of Outremer.

But the next expedition to set out would actually achieve a far greater degree of success than any other had since the First Crusade. Ironically, it would achieve its aims not by force of arms but rather by the power of diplomacy. In an even more unlikely turn of events, its leader would be a man that was so much at odds with the Papacy that, at the time he achieved his greatest triumph – nothing less than the recovery of Jerusalem itself – he would actually be an excommunicate.

Frederick II, Emperor of Germany, was no ordinary monarch. He dominated the political landscape of Western Europe in the first half of the thirteenth century, but this influence was not always positive. If there was ever a plot being hatched anywhere in Western Europe, it was highly likely that he was at the heart of it.

During the course of his reign, he certainly had diplomatic relationships with some strange bedfellows. For example, he was heavily involved in a series of diplomatic manoeuvrings with the Sultan of Egypt, al-Kamil, prior to his departure for the East. This is important to an understanding of relations between the Muslim Orient and the West at this time.

Certainly not everybody in the West believed that a violent assault on Egypt was the only option. Trade between Egypt and the West was at this time particularly brisk, with the Venetians having a strong presence in the country and other Italian maritime states also having interests there. A Crusade could cause great harm to these trading relations and could result in significant financial losses to a number of merchants in the West.

Similarly, others – especially Frederick II – saw that, if they acted astutely, they could advance their cause in the region without resorting to violence. This was not a view guided by moralities of warfare and Christianity. Crusading glorified war provided that it was fought in the name of God and by the sanction of His church. It was more the fact that political manoeuvrings could lead to more substantial results rather than trusting to the vagaries and uncertainties of warfare. And it also avoided much of the excessively high costs of war.

The time was ripe for a political approach to affairs in and around Outremer. An extended bout of uncertainty still pertained in the region following the death of Saladin. Even though by the time that Frederick set out for Outremer Saladin had already been dead for thirty years, political stability had still not returned to the Muslim world.

The Emperor played his hand for all it was worth. He negotiated with al-Kamil before he even left the West, offering his help in the Sultan's prolonged struggle to add Damascus to his territories. Ironically, by the time that he arrived, his help was no longer really needed. Even more bizarrely, he hesitated for so long before leaving for the region that Pope Gregory IX excommunicated him because of his prevarication.

Frederick however merely ignored the pontiff's injunctions that he was on no account to set out on the Crusade without first of all seeking the Pope's forgiveness. If he really believed that the Emperor would meekly acquiesce, Gregory badly misjudged his man. After sending out a missive to the leaders of Western Europe explaining his actions and appealing for pressure to be applied on Gregory in protest against his blatantly unfair actions, Frederick set sail anyway.

The plot predictably thickened on Frederick's arrival in Outremer. Within days of his landing there, he was scheming to overthrow a number of the leading local barons in the Christian kingdom and replace them with his own appointees. Something not far off a state of civil war followed closely in the wake of these actions.

In the midst of this chaos, the most unlikely scenario unfolded. When Frederick arrived in the Holy Land, al-Kamil no longer believed that he needed his help. However, the Sultan misjudged the situation and his attempts to gain Damascus without the help of the German Emperor foundered. Chastened, he re-opened negotiations with Frederick. In return for the help of the Emperor, al-Kamil offered the city of Jerusalem, which he presently owned. The deal was struck. In March 1229, Frederick entered the city of Jerusalem. On the 18th of that month, he was crowned King of Jerusalem.

It might be expected that this result would bring about an unprecedented outbreak of rejoicing throughout Christendom. However, the reaction proved to be the exact antithesis of euphoria. Firstly, the Emperor was an excommunicate. No other Christian dared openly support Frederick without risking incurring the wrath of the Church. No cleric would contemplate crowning Frederick. The Master of the Teutonic Knights, a military order in Outremer formed after previous German expeditions to the region, eventually performed the task. Even as he did so, the Archbishop of Caesarea arrived at the gates of the city and hurled abuse at Frederick.

Frederick had also caused a great deal of trouble in the region since he arrived, unable to restrain his flair for scheming, and had alienated large sections of Outremer society as a result. In addition, Jerusalem was virtually indefensible. The city walls were incomplete and the territories around the city that had traditionally provided it with a buffer zone were not part of the deal with al-Kamil. Any well-armed and determined Muslim enemy could easily recover the city should they so wish.

Frederick lingered in Jerusalem for just three days. Then, disgusted at the tepid reaction to his coup, he left, never to return. Ostensibly, he had achieved the ultimate dream of Christians all over the world, but few outside of his entourage rejoiced in the deed. He left Outremer soon after, pelted with offal as he paraded through the streets of Acre on the way to the ship that would take him home. It was one of the strangest interludes in Crusader history.

Yet, in the context of Louis's crusade there were two items of particular note with regard to the German Emperor. When Louis decided to set out on Crusade, Frederick was still very much alive and active in Western European politics, and remained one of the major players in the affairs of Christendom. And Frederick regarded Outremer as belonging to him and his dynasty.

His argument rested on sound legal grounds. He had married Yolande, Queen of Jerusalem, and when their son, Conrad, was born, he became legal heir to the throne. Therefore, Louis would need to ensure that any Crusade to the region did not antagonise the emperor. In addition, the character of Frederick, particularly his ability to alienate powerful men and make bitter enemies of them, was still alarmingly apparent nearly twenty years after he made his foray to Outremer.

By the time that Louis considered his Crusade, Pope Gregory had died but Frederick had managed to incur the wrath of Pope Innocent IV by his attempts to conquer all of Italy and add it to his already large Empire. Frederick currently held the upper hand in that particular dispute, so much so that the Pope had been forced into a state of virtual exile in the city of Lyon.

The ongoing warfare between Frederick and the Papacy caused several difficulties for Louis. There was firstly a practical problem. The war tied up vast numbers of men who would otherwise have been available for use during the Crusade. There would be very little chance of any sizeable German contribution to the expedition.

Further, as King Henry III of England was at odds with Louis there was not likely to be any significant input from that country either, though the attraction of the Crusades as both a source of chivalric glory and spiritual benefit would prove so strong that a small, independent English force would attach itself to Louis when it arrived in the East. The emphasis of the forthcoming Crusade would therefore be unmistakably French and as such there would be no doubt that Louis was the secular leader of the force when it eventually set out.

There was also a political difficulty for Louis. As Outremer was regarded by Frederick as being within his sphere of influence, Louis had to take great care to ensure that he did not antagonise the Emperor. After all, many of the Emperor's territories were dangerously close to France and, in Louis's absence, a hostile Frederick could stir up a hornet's nest. But Louis had been extremely astute in his political positioning as regards the confrontation between Frederick and Pope Innocent. He had managed to walk a very narrow line between paying all due respect to the Papacy whilst at the same time managing to enjoy sound relations with the Emperor.

As it transpired, so skilled was his handling of the situation that Frederick would offer no obstacle to the Crusade when it finally set out. In fact, quite the reverse would be the case; Frederick would appear to go out of his way to help Louis. It was a great diplomatic success for the French King, and suggests that Louis was a very efficient political operator.

With this backdrop of strife and uncertainty in Western Europe, Louis decided to depart for the East. It was undoubtedly a bold decision, and to fully understand it one needs to consider both the spiritual and chivalric attractions of such an adventure to a thirteenth-century French King, particularly one of Louis's character for whom the spiritual rewards on offer were enormously significant.

However, much had changed in the nature of the Indulgence since Urban II had summoned the First Crusade. At the beginning, the direct involvement of the Crusader in the pilgrimage to Jerusalem was required if he or she were obtain the spiritual benefits offered to them by the Church. Over time this strict interpretation of what was necessary was significantly modified.

In recognition of the reality that many who wanted to set out on a Crusade were debarred by age or infirmity from making an effective contribution to the expedition, it became acceptable for certain groups to offer money instead of their active involvement in the Crusade. In many respects, this was to be encouraged. It meant that no longer would hordes of ineffective non-combatants set out on Crusade, depleting already scarce food supplies and dying in their thousands of disease, exhaustion or wounds.

This relaxation was progressively enhanced, until many people who were quite capable of accompanying the Crusade did not in fact do so, but effectively 'bought' the benefits of the Indulgence instead. The practice of issuing such Indulgences was, by this time, beginning to damage the credibility of the Papacy. So serious was the problem that a particular phrase has been coined to describe the effect of the increasingly common use of Indulgences: 'spiritual inflation'.

A contemporary chronicler, Matthew of Paris, was scathing in his criticism of Pope Innocent IV for his lavish offers of such Indulgences (for example, the Papacy was by this time offering limited Indulgences even for those who had merely listened to a Crusade sermon). For some individuals, the lure of the many Indulgences available meant that they began to collect them with rapacious piety: King Louis IX was one such individual.

The potential targets of the Crusade had also been widened. The First Crusade was unmistakably summoned with the journey to the East in mind. However, since those early days of the movement other potential enemies of the Church had been identified. Pagan tribes around the Baltic would be identified as possible Crusading targets. Spiritual rewards were also offered for fighting the Moors in Spain.

More controversially, heretic Christians were also made into legitimate targets. The Cathars in the south of France were one example already discussed, but Indulgences were also offered for fighting against secular enemies of the Papacy, most notably against the Emperor Frederick.[3] The net impact of all this was negative for the Crusade in the East, as it reduced the pool of manpower potentially available for any Crusader army as it was more attractive for potential participants to take place in expeditions that were closer to home when they received the same spiritual benefits for doing so. Given the relative lack of success of the Crusading movement since the triumph of the First Crusade, the attractiveness of an expedition to the East had become somewhat tarnished.

There were therefore a number of practical reasons why the spiritual attractions of the Crusade, although still very real to some, were less enticing than they had once been. To compensate partially for this, the prospect of chivalric glory was becoming more important to the West than was previously the case.

The thirteenth century saw a blossoming of the chivalric movement in Western Europe, continuing the trend of the previous century. Tournaments were common by this time. As they were often accompanied by violence when near-riots broke out spontaneously at a number of such events, they were not always welcomed. By this time, they were becoming a real problem. The threat that they posed to the order of society can best be gauged by the number of attempts made to ban them. Papal decrees of 1215 and 1245 forbade them, whilst in England King Henry III refused to allow them to be held on five separate occasions between 1243 and 1248.[4]

Nevertheless, in the very frequent references to tournaments in the literature of the time we can perceive the development of a chivalric code in the West that was forming an integral part of society. Particular perceptions of the World were being shaped, as far as the nobility at least was concerned, by this development. Where spiritual benefits had once been the primary driver of the urge to set out on Crusade, the promise of honour and worldly recognition was now becoming an equally powerful motivator.

This trend has been noted by a number of historians. One notes that 'the later Crusades ... begin to look like an extension of the search for gloire, renown'.[5] Chivalry, and the paradigms that it gave rise to, was therefore an important part of the psychology of Crusading at this period in history.

Motivations for Crusading were, in summary, very complex. Further, they had subtly changed since the First Crusade was launched. A complicated mix of ingredients was present in society, which combined, in some quarters (particularly in France, where the chivalric code was especially prominent) to still make the prospect of a Crusade an attractive proposition.

Such lofty idealism was only part of the picture. For the Crusade to become a reality, practical considerations were a more immediate issue. Before any expedition could set out, a great deal of work needed to be done to assemble an army and to arrange for its transportation to the East. The days ahead would fully test whether Louis had completely recovered from his illness. All his energy and enthusiasm would be required if a Christian army led by him was ever to set foot in the East. It was time to stop dreaming and start doing.

3

Preparations for Crusade

It was much more difficult to organise a Crusade than it was to call one. Massive preparations were involved. One of the major practical considerations was recruitment for Louis had no standing army to call upon. Men must be encouraged to join; they could not be forced. The Crusade was a voluntary undertaking, a religious act, participation in which was a matter between each man and his conscience (though his priest had a big part to play in the process too).

Such an army also needed to be equipped and adequately provided with supplies, a huge undertaking as the army was likely to be away for a long time. This was likely to prove a major headache. An army on the march required a huge amount of food and to try to live off the land that they passed through was to invite disaster.

Both men and supplies had to be transported to the East. A land crossing through Asia Minor, the route chosen by the first Crusaders, was now an impossibility as most of the region was in the hands of the Turks, or threatened by the Mongol hordes who had arrived like a hurricane from the far corners of the world. No King had a fleet of his own that was remotely big enough to transport the sizeable force that would be needed if the Crusade were to be credible. It would therefore be necessary to approach maritime states such as Genoa and Marseilles for shipping.

Louis would also need to consider the security of his kingdom whilst he was away. Given the hostility of Henry III of England, strong government was essential in Louis's absence. He also needed to ensure the help, or at least the neutrality, of the Emperor whilst he was away. Frederick needed to be treated with respect if Louis's interests were to be protected.

There were also spiritual considerations to take into account. Relations with the Church needed to be carefully nurtured. Not only would its help be crucial in a spiritual sense but there were enormous practical concerns too. The financing of the Crusade was a huge undertaking, beyond the reach of even a King's purse. The only organisation capable of funding a Crusade was the Church, which had the ability to raise funds through special levies in every part of Christendom.

Without this support, there was little possibility that the expedition would ever be more than a figment of Louis's imagination. Louis would also require the political support of the Pope, particularly to discourage King Henry III from attacking France whilst he was away. This was an extension of the customary stance of the Papacy, which undertook to protect the property of Crusaders whilst they were absent.

Crusades were summoned by the Church: indeed, this was one of the factors that set the movement apart from secular warfare. And it was far from certain that the Church would welcome the absence of Louis from the volatile political landscape in Europe at this time. Louis's neutrality in the dispute between Pope and Emperor was a counterbalance in the delicate political equilibrium of Western Europe. His absence could have a decisive effect on the balance of power.

Events elsewhere were to lend a hand. The grip of the Christian forces in Outremer on recently-recovered Jerusalem was always tenuous. Far away to the east, thousand of miles away from Western

Europe and even from Outremer, events were taking place that were to throw much of the known world into turmoil. For the tribes that inhabited the little-known lands of Mongolia had recently been transformed into a cohesive unit by Genghis Khan. He shaped an army the like of which had rarely been seen by the world before, a cavalry force that swept across the lands of Asia like a tidal wave. None could stand in the way of these ferocious warriors. Their success was based on two weapons above all others; mobility and terror.

Their mobility meant that they travelled quickly and were capable of outmanoeuvring any who stood in their way. But, above all else, in an age of violence the Mongols exhibited a ferocity that far exceeded anything yet seen. Any city that had the temerity to stand in the way of the Mongol horde was ruthlessly exterminated, expunged from the face of the earth. Such tactics were barbaric but they were mightily effective. The fate of the decimated cities served as a warning to others.

Like a plague of locusts consuming everything in its path the Mongol army swept across Asia. Some had made their way to the very edges of Europe, to the plains of Poland and Hungary. Here they were faced with Christian armies who resisted gallantly but with painful futility. There was real concern that they might choose to sweep on into Western Europe itself. That did not happen but their impact on the psyche of the West was profound.

Other elements of the horde swept into Persia. Here they clashed with the Khwarismians. They were themselves a warlike people but they were no match for the Mongols. Totally defeated, large numbers of Khwarismians escaped westwards towards Outremer. Robbed of their territories, the Khwarismians looked for allies and gainful employment. The Sultan of Egypt was involved in a war against the Sultan of Damascus; one of many such conflicts at the beginning of the thirteenth century in the vacuum left after Saladin's death.

The Sultan of Egypt was delighted to employ the Khwarismians. The Sultan of Damascus for his part was allied to the Christian forces in Outremer; consequently, the country was a potential target for the Khwarismians. Despite their defeat by the Mongols, no one else in the region was able to stand up to them. City after city fell as they advanced through Syria towards Outremer. Only Damascus, surrounded by strong, high walls, seemed impervious to their assaults.

As the Khwarismians moved towards Outremer, it became apparent that the Christian kingdom was their objective. Jerusalem's defences had fallen into disrepair earlier in the century but work had been undertaken to restore them. But, this was not completed. Further, to properly man the walls would require a large number of men – far more than were present in the Christian garrison in the city.

Jerusalem was defended by various military orders, such as the Knights Templar, the Knights Hospitaller and the Teutonic Knights. These Orders had developed during the course of the previous century, effectively providing the regular defence force of Outremer. Organised along quasi-monastic lines, they exhibited a unique combination of religious discipline and military prowess, causing them to be described as 'warrior monks'. They formed the backbone of the regular army of Outremer. The leaders of these Orders decided that they would be unable to defend Jerusalem adequately against the Khwarismians, and abandoned it to its fate.

The Khwarismians moved on the city in July 1244, and 'began to make frequent incursions into Jerusalem, which was practically unfortified'.[1] The Christians left in the city were terrified by the Khwarismians' reputation for brutality. Six thousand opted to leave rather than take their chances. To escape they had to pass through Muslim territory and the Christians made a pact with the people there giving them safe conduct. However, it proved meaningless as large numbers of them were killed or enslaved en route. Others were trapped by the Khwarismians and slaughtered. Barely three hundred made it to safety.

Those that remained in Jerusalem were no more fortunate than these pitiful wretches. On 11 July 1244 the city fell to the

Khwarismians, never again to be in Crusader hands. Dreadful scenes of destruction and slaughter followed:

> They brutally disembowelled, before the Sepulchre itself [the Church of the Holy Sepulchre, the holiest shrine in Christendom], all the Christians who had stayed behind and withdrawn to the Church of the Holy Sepulchre. And, decapitating the priests who were celebrating Mass at the altars, they proclaimed together: 'Here we pour out the blood of the Christian people, where they poured out wine in honour of their God, who they say was hanged here.'[2]

They desecrated this great church, the holiest sanctuary in Christendom, which housed both the site of the Crucifixion and also Christ's tomb, carrying off the ornate columns within the church and violating the tombs of the Kings of Jerusalem for whom the Holy Sepulchre was a last resting-place. The chronicler of these terrible events, Robert, Patriarch of Jerusalem, in anguish compared the actions of the Khwarismians with the Muslims of old who had conquered the city – the latter had at least respected the sanctity of the Christian shrines.

This was a tremendous blow to Christian morale. Such losses were not unprecedented as the city had been lost in the past. But the deliberate destruction of so many sacred shrines in the city was a gross insult. Devastating as these tidings were, it was outweighed by news of a military defeat so disastrous that it called into doubt the very existence of Outremer.

After the fall of Jerusalem, the Khwarismians moved on to link up with the Egyptian army. Included in the Egyptians' forces were a group of fighting men that would become known as some of the foremost warriors in the world. The Egyptians had taken to recruiting troops from abroad, seeking out strong young boys who might be nurtured into great warriors. Once they arrived back in Egypt, they were taught all the arts of war and developed to form part of a formidable fighting force.

These foreign troops were known as Mamelukes. They were recruited from many areas, but the Caucasus region was a particularly rich source of supply. It was regarded as a great honour to be recruited as a Mameluke. These men were not like other slaves, being treated with respect and honour in Egypt. Their families sold them with enthusiasm, hoping to share in the reflected glory arising from the fact that their sons had been chosen for this special role.

In time, the Mamelukes would achieve great power in the politics of the East. Despite counter-measures to discourage them from becoming too powerful (for example, the sons of Mamelukes could not follow in their fathers' footsteps, in an attempt to prevent dynastic loyalties threatening the state) they would eventually form a dynasty of their own that would dominate Egyptian politics.

In the ranks of the Mamelukes was a blue-eyed, intelligent and powerfully-built bull of a man, Rukn ad-Din Baibars. Baibars would become the greatest enemy that the Frankish states in the East ever had. Far more ruthless than the great Saladin, he would strike terror into the hearts of Christians in a way that no other Muslim leader did. Cruel and merciless, he would wash the fragile state of Outremer away in a tsunami of blood.

The Crusaders assembled a large force to meet the threat of the Egyptians and the Khwarismians. The defence of Outremer relied heavily on the military orders. Although they had originally been formed to protect pilgrims travelling to Jerusalem and the other Christian shrines in the Holy Land, they quickly found a role as a key part of the standing army of Outremer.

Three orders in particular had risen to prominence. The Hospitallers had been present in the Holy Land for longer than any other order, although their original role had been a non-militaristic one. The Templars, on the other hand, had been formed with a military purpose in mind from the start. Their fame owed much to the sponsorship of their cause by Bernard of Clairvaux, one of the greatest figures of the medieval period.

The last group, the Teutonic Knights, had been formed much more recently and was heavily influenced by its German connections (they supported the claims of the Emperor Frederick during his sojourn in the Holy Land almost single-handedly). Although not as influential as the other two groups, and with their greatest days yet to come (they would eventually become much more famous for their exploits against the barbarian tribes of Eastern Europe than they would for their role in the Holy Land) they still provided valuable resources for the defence of Outremer.

The importance of the Orders as a source of military manpower to the kingdom gave them a pre-eminently powerful position. They answered direct to the Pope rather than any secular monarch due to their status as religious organisations. For they were effectively monks, living by a rule, practising chastity, with no possessions of their own (though their Orders were very wealthy) and required to obey instructions without question. This put them beyond the reach of secular law. But, unlike most other monks who lived a life devoted to passive spirituality, these men killed with the blessing of God – or, at least, of His Church.

But they were to some extent remote from ecclesiastical law, as they were not even answerable to local bishops. Their authority came direct from the Pope who was the only one who could hope to keep any semblance of control over their actions – and it was difficult even for him given the distance he was from Outremer. Even the King of Jerusalem could not control them

Unfortunately, the Orders had not always used this power wisely. They were often at odds with each other and their military tactics were sometimes rash. Their instincts encouraged them to commit everything to all-out attack when caution would have been the better option. Such had been the case in the campaign that had led to the catastrophic Battle of Hattin and the loss of Jerusalem to Saladin. Their tactics in the forthcoming campaign suggests that they had learnt little.

The Templars provided three hundred horsemen to the expedition, with the Hospitallers providing a similar number and the

Teutonic Knights somewhat less. Collectively, this represented a substantial proportion of the forces available to the Orders. Although the numbers might appear small when judged by the size of modern armies, the armoured troops of the West had an effect in battle out of all proportion to their size.

A charge by these armoured warriors could, in the right environment, smash through the defences of an enemy with unstoppable force. Man for man few warriors could match them. If co-ordinated, the charge of the Western knights would sweep aside all opposition as if it were a tempest whipping up the leaves. But if the charge were resisted then the Western knights quickly lost their cohesion. Although they lacked little in courage or bravery, sometimes their self-belief in both the righteousness of their cause and their invincibility led them to embark on missions which were, at best, unnecessarily risky and, on occasion, downright suicidal.

The Christian forces marched out, with an array of Muslim allies from the Sultan of Damascus to face the foe. The two armies met near the town of La Forbie, not far from Gaza, in October 1244. The Egyptian army was a large one, with five thousand Egyptian troops and ten thousand Khwarismian mercenaries. The Muslim allies of the Crusaders cautioned prudence.

The Khwarismian style of warfare was not well suited to assaulting a well-defended position and it was suggested that the Crusaders should adopt a defensive pose. Such cautious tactics were spurned by the Orders. Instead, it was decided that the Crusaders and their allies would attack at once, an aggressive reaction mirroring that adopted in the Hattin Campaign sixty years earlier.

The Christian army took up position on the right wing, with Muslim troops in the centre and on the left. Baibars positioned his best troops, his Mamelukes, directly opposite the Christian knights. The Khwarismians were detailed to take care of the other allied forces. They were also issued with orders that, should they drive their Muslim opponents from the field, they were not to pursue them but instead sweep behind the Crusaders and cut them off.

Battle was joined with the Christian knights crashing into the Mamelukes. Well organised and strongly armoured, the Mameluke line shook but did not break. Elsewhere, the Khwarismians more than held their own and the Muslim allies of the Crusaders began to waver. Panic spread, like a cancer eating into their resolve. Here and there a man started to edge away from the front-line. One or two became ten, twenty, and then hundreds. Soon, large groups of them started streaming from the field.

This was the crisis point. If the Khwarismians chased after the flee-ing Muslims, the Christian right might still extricate itself. However, the Khwarismians remembered their instructions, kept their disci-pline and began to sweep behind the Crusader knights who suddenly found that they were being hacked at from the rear and the side, as well as from the front. The battle degenerated rapidly into a brutal hand-to-hand fight, with hard steel crashing into armour and creat-ing a fearful din in the melee.

Heavily outnumbered, the strong armament of the Orders counted for little when faced with overwhelming odds. Inexorably, the Christian knights were overpowered and resistance petered out. They fought bravely enough but in a hopeless cause. Their losses were immense. Nearly ninety percent of the Templars' forces were killed or captured. The casualties of the other Orders were equally disastrous. In addition, the Grand Master of the Templars had been killed in the battle, and his equivalent from the Hospitallers captured. This was one of the blackest days in Crusader history.

Louis would not have known of the disaster when he decided to take the Cross but it meant that his timing was appropriate: an opportune turn of events for Louis for whom the news presented a valuable propaganda bonus to encourage recruitment. The disaster at La Forbie (also known as the Battle of Harbiyah) provided focus for his recruitment drive.

Pope Innocent IV called on the leaders of the West to prepare an expedition soon after he received tidings of this catastrophic reverse. In 1245, he commissioned his legate, Eudes of Chateauroux, to begin preaching the Crusade. The presence of the King of France in the East, although it might be unwelcome to the Pope given Louis's usefulness as a potential ally in his dispute with the Emperor Frederick, would certainly provide a welcome fillip to the kingdom of Outremer.

Many in the West were well aware that dramatic upheavals were taking place in the Middle East but it appeared to many that they had a more imminent danger to concern them, far more threatening than the 'Saracens' of the Levant. The annihilation of Polish and Hungarian armies by the Mongols in 1241 shook many a court in Europe to the core. It was said that Blanche of Castille, Louis's mother, had been driven to the verge of hysteria by the Mongol threat, convincing herself that even the French court was not safe. But before the Mongols could consolidate their gains in Europe, their Khan died and the hordes returned eastwards.

This was certainly not the end of the Mongol threat though. Domination of the Middle East was very much part of their agenda. They destroyed the Turkish forces that opposed them in Asia Minor, and forged an alliance with the Armenians in the area. Neither were the Christians of Outremer safe. A peremptory summons was despatched from the Mongols to Prince Bohemond V, ruler of Antioch. Dismissively, the Mongol Khan demanded that Bohemond should recognise the Mongol leader as his overlord. In 1244 the Patriarch of Antioch was despatched to the Pope to beg him for help. In response, Innocent had started to prepare the West for a Crusade against the Mongols.

But the Mongol threat was not prominent in Louis's mind as he prepared his army to sail towards Outremer. The King had other matters to distract him amongst the more traditional enemies of Christendom in the shape of the Muslims occupying the land of Christ. But it would be some time before Louis could lead his Crusade. Much preparation was needed.

He first sought to secure his political position. In 1245, Louis held talks with Pope Innocent IV, attempting to broker a compromise between the pontiff and the Emperor Frederick. The Emperor appeared to be willing to adopt a conciliatory stance but his friendly overtures towards Innocent were rebuffed.

Louis had to concede defeat, though he was annoyed at the intransigence of Innocent. The Pope's situation was now perilous and Innocent was forced to flee. He sought permission from Louis to set up his headquarters in Rheims but his request was refused. Instead, he took himself off to Lyon.

So bad were affairs between the Pope and the Emperor that at one stage it was strongly rumoured that Frederick planned to attack Innocent in Lyon but nothing came of this. Yet the failure of Louis's efforts was not total. Frederick appreciated the efforts at intercession made on his behalf by Louis. During the forthcoming Crusade, he would provide goods freely to the French troops and allow them safe conduct through his lands.

Even then though, his goodwill operated within strict limits. For years, Frederick had nurtured good relationships with the Sultan of Egypt and, according to Muslim chroniclers, he would provide an abundance of information to him about the projected movements of the forthcoming Crusade. Such Machiavellian dealings would have been fully in accord with his track record.

Louis next addressed the problem of Henry of England. After the war of 1243, a truce had been signed between England and France which was due to expire in 1248. All attempts on Louis's part to extend it foundered. So he sought and obtained assurances from the Pope that any chicanery on Henry's part would be severely punished by Innocent who agreed to raise an army to send against Henry if he broke the agreement.

Louis next looked to domestic affairs. He planned to take many of his family with him. His wife, Margaret, would accompany him and so would his brothers, Robert of Artois, Charles of Anjou and Alphonse of Poitiers. Louis trusted his mother implicitly. She had already served him well as Regent at a time when he was too young to rule, and it would have seemed to him the natural thing to install her in the position once more which he duly did. His attempts to achieve stability largely met with success and internal politics were not to prove problematic until the latter stages of the Crusade.

Louis then began to make meticulous material preparations. It would be several years before he left but he used the intervening period wisely. This would be the best-planned Crusade of all. Large stocks of provisions needed to be bought and stored. Not only were there human mouths to feed, there were also thousands of horses. And food was not the only problem: weapons must be transported and materials for siege engines were also necessary. Clothing for the army and tents for the nobility also needed to be packed.

All of these supplies would be moved by sea. Previous major expeditions had tended to rely on one major provider of ships for their transportation. For example, the Genoese were integral to the movements of French troops during the Third Crusade, whilst the Venetians had provided the transport for the Fourth with ultimately disastrous results.

Louis would however use a range of suppliers, which had the effect of limiting his risks. There would be Genoese, Pisan and Venetian vessels transporting the expedition. There would also be a large number of ships from Marseilles. Some of his barons looked further afield for transport, some hiring ships from England whilst one ship was built specifically for the Crusade in Inverness. Ships from as far north as Norway would participate.

Adequate provision of transport was critical, so much so that Pope Innocent granted an Indulgence just for those who provided ships. It was decided that the fleet would assemble at the port of Aigues Mortes in the south of France. It was not as large as Marseilles and it had some limitations as a result. Nevertheless, it would serve well enough as the major port of the forthcoming Crusade and also as its effective arsenal.

Well fortified and compact, Aigues Mortes offered a good illustration of the strength and vitality of the French kingdom at this stage of its history.[3] The port that Louis ordered to be constructed there was staggering in scale and proclaimed his ambitions to the world for all to see. It was more than a military asset that Louis had ordered to be built: it was a message to the world about his place in it.

Once he decided to build the port, nothing could distract him from his purpose, not even inconveniences such as the tendency of the port to silt up or the shortage of fresh water supplies. Recent additions included the construction of a canal and a new tower, magnificently proportioned, which would serve as Louis's residence whilst he was in the port.

Recruiting for the Crusade began in earnest in 1245. Eudes of Chateauroux was despatched by Pope Innocent to preach the Crusade and drum up support for Louis. The King was powerless to compel men to go with him. Although they were Louis's vassals, the barons were only required to serve him in a military capacity for a period of around forty days each year, by which time the Crusade would not even manage to cross the Mediterranean.

As compulsion was not an option, persuasion was necessary. The Church took the lead, appealing to the spirituality of the West and offering a range of spiritual inducements to encourage potential participants to declare their willingness to join the Crusade. Many of the leading barons would also be attracted to join the mission by its promise of chivalry and glory. In a ceremony in Paris on 9 October 1245, a number of Louis's barons as well as important churchmen such as the archbishops of Rheims and Bourges signified their formal commitment to the Crusade by taking the cross.

The recruitment drive would be relatively successful, although it would be several more years before it was completed. Louis adopted a variety of measures encouraging Frenchmen to take part, including giving some of his barons Christmas presents of robes with Crusaders' crosses already sewn on, implying that he believed they should commit themselves to the enterprise regardless of any personal qualms that they might have had.

Some French towns assembled bodies of men known as confraternities to serve on the expedition to the East. In one example, Eudes of Chateauroux gave his support to the townspeople of Chateaudun who adopted such a measure. Innocent IV himself approved the statutes adopted by this particular confraternity.

Ultimately, it is estimated that an army of around 25,000 men was raised.[4] This was composed of about 2,500 knights with perhaps twice as many squires and sergeants. There were probably around 10,000 infantrymen and 5,000 crossbow-men, the latter providing a potentially devastating array of firepower. But there was one distinguishing feature of the army that was eventually formed and that was its predominantly French composition.

There was an English contingent led by William Longspee ('Longsword'), although it was not large (perhaps containing 200 men in all).[5] William had been partly funded by elements in England who wanted to support the Crusade but were unwilling or unable to participate directly, the records of the time noting that funds were given by those who 'on account of the weakness of their bodies or other just causes are unable to go over the sea to that land in person'.[6]

Just a year before, Longspee had been stating that he did not have enough money to go. Now, only a large Papal grant made it possible. Henry of England had only been lukewarm in his support for Louis and it is quite possible that, as some have suggested[7], he only expressed an interest at all so that he could barter English support for the return of lost possessions in France.

Other groups – Scandinavian, German, Scottish and Italian – did not radically alter the national profile of the force. The result was that, although Louis could not compel his subjects to follow him on Crusade, the army nevertheless ultimately took on the appearance of a royal force. This at least meant that there would be few disputes over whom the leader of the Crusade should be (divided leadership had been an unsatisfactory feature of all previous major Crusades).[8]

All this cost a great deal of money. The King would be forced to pay for the maintenance of most of the army. To fund this from his own pocket would be impossible. It has been calculated that the Crusade would eventually cost in the region of 1.5 million *livres* – to put this figure in perspective this was six times the annual income of King Louis.[9]

However, even this apparently high figure underestimates the true cost of the Crusade. For it does not include the cost of subsidies that Louis paid to underwrite the Crusading expenses of Crusaders who were not wealthy enough to pay for themselves and their entourages. Neither does it take into account the costs of building Aigues Mortes. Including all these extra expenses it has been estimated that the final cost was more like 3 million *livres* – equating to twelve years' worth of income.[10] And this is only funding from royal revenues – in addition there was a huge amount of finance found from the pockets of individual Crusaders.

Louis took whatever measures he could to fill the gap. He put pressure on French merchants, then benefiting from a period of economic expansion, to contribute. But there was a limit to how much could be raised from his citizens in this way. Taxes levied by earlier Kings on the general populace had proved immensely unpopular. Louis was therefore forced to make recourse to the moneymaking powers of the well-organised machinery of the Church.

There was another way in which money was raised. Louis sent a team of inquisitors across his kingdom to hunt out abuses and levy appropriate fines. Louis took this operation very seriously. There were several reasons for his interest. As a King, he took a great deal of interest in the good government of his kingdom: generally his reign saw peace and stability in his kingdom if one excludes the problems in the early years of his kingship. Highlighting abuses in this manner was one way in which potential difficulties could be identified and avoided.

There is also a wider, more subtle point to consider. Before leaving on Crusade, it was necessary that the Crusader should be in a good state of grace and that any wrongs he had committed should be, as far as possible, righted. It is a relatively small step from understanding this at the personal level of an ordinary Crusader to seeing how it might be extended to the King.

For the King had a sacred, unwritten but publicly witnessed contract with God. During the course of his coronation he committed himself to governing with justice. His local officials were an extension of him. Wrongs that they had done were commensurate with wrongs that the King had vicariously committed against his country. They must be amended if the Crusade were to be blessed with the spiritual benefits that its participants wished for.

To achieve the benefits on offer from participation in the Crusade, the Papal Indulgences and the remission of sins, those involved must have a clear conscience. This involved making good any sins committed. There is an excellent example in the chronicles of de Joinville of this. De Joinville, the seneschal of Champagne, held a great feast in 1248 before he set out on Crusade. Those who owed him feudal allegiance were invited to his castle, where sumptuous dishes were laid before them for days on end. At the conclusion of the festivities, de Joinville called them all together, and addressed them:

> Lords, I am going overseas and I do not know if I shall ever return. Now come forward: if I have done you any wrong, I will make it good.[11]

De Joinville then withdrew from the chamber, leaving behind a panel to arbitrate on the complaints of those he had addressed and subsequently complying with any decisions regarding restitution that they might make. On a far greater scale, Louis was also aiming to ensure that everything was in order when he despatched his inquisitors throughout France.

There is no reason to doubt, given what we know of Louis's nature, that all the motives above were genuine concerns for the King. But a more cynical motive was that the money raised from fines levied would also prove very useful. This was a common way for Kings to raise money for their Crusades (King Richard I of England was a past master of the tactic). It was an invaluable method of increasing the income of the royal treasury. Whilst accepting that altruism was indeed a strong motivator, there is no real contradiction in accepting that more worldly motives played their part too.

Louis took measures to reduce the expenditure incurred on routine matters by the crown so that he could spend the money saved on the Crusade. He also confiscated money from heretics and adopted a common contemporary measure by extorting money from Jews. Louis also pressurised French towns and cities to make voluntary contributions, the accumulated result of which amounted to about 275,000 pounds tournois towards the cost of the Crusade.[12]

About two thirds of the Crusade's costs would be funded from Church resources. The clergy made a great deal of money from their benefices and a proportion of this income was taken by the Papacy to contribute towards the Crusade. Some, such as the Cistercians whose star was in the ascendancy, were exempted but these exceptions were few and far between.

The preparations made were thorough: it would not be through lack of organisation that this Crusade would fail. After three arduous years, it was time at last for the Crusade to depart. A great army started to wend its way towards Aigues Mortes and the rendezvous point at which they would all embark for the East and for glory. From points east, west, north and south slow-moving baggage trains lumbered along the uneven roads of France towards the shores of the Mediterranean, kicking up clouds of dust as they journeyed.

Before setting out on the journey Louis had to bid a formal farewell to his capital. He made his way first of all to the magnificent new church of Sainte-Chapelle, work on which had started in 1242. This amazing architectural marvel was a riot of opulent architecture, a paean of praise in stone and shimmering, vividly-coloured glass to the Almighty whose land Louis intended to recover for His people.

Here, almost in the shadow of the great cathedral church of Notre Dame, the new building was dedicated. Relics that had been brought back from Constantinople – at the time, the capital of the world trade in such icons – were paraded down the church in solemn ceremony and given places of honour.[13]

Louis then went to the great Cathedral church of Saint-Denis. Here, the protection of the Almighty was again invoked, and earnest prayers echoed around the sanctuary as the congregation begged that the tender mercies of God might be proffered both to them and their King during the dangerous days ahead. Eudes of Chateauroux then handed Louis a scrip and a staff. These were the traditional badges of the pilgrim. They symbolised that the Crusade was a sacred undertaking and that, when a man took part in it in whatever capacity, he was committing himself to an act of pilgrimage.

The pilgrim solemnly intoned his vows with a sincerity born from the depth of faith that he held. But this was no ordinary pilgrim as the King now demonstrated. The great war banner of France was brought to Louis and handed to him in solemn ceremony. In response to his investiture, Louis raised high the oriflamme, the banner of Saint-Denis traditionally handed to the King of France before he departed for war. Louis was summoning his nation to arms with him. The King and his army were now officially on Crusade.

This sacred ceremony now completed, Louis then processed to the church of Notre Dame. Finally, having surrendered his fine kingly raiment and adopted instead the simple attire of a pilgrim, this saintly man made his way barefoot to the Abbey of Saint Antoine. Here, he could make his own personal devotions, out of the eye of the crowd, before departing southwards with his army. Clearly, he was determined that his spiritual as well as his practical preparations were as complete as they could be before he set out on his perilous peregrination.

There is a neat symmetry around this series of events in Paris, which tells us much of the different aspects of the King's character. Sainte-Chapelle was in the King's palace and to an extent the service was therefore intimate, although held in surroundings of sumptuous magnificence. The ceremonies in Saint-Denis and Notre Dame were more public, in sanctuaries that were venerated in the consciousness of the King's people, the one dedicated to the patron saint of France, the other to the Virgin Mother of Christ.

It is fitting and quite deliberate that the final part of what can be read as one extended ceremony of dedication took place with the King alone, out of the public eye and dressed instead in the humble garb of a pilgrim, stripped of the trappings of royalty. The King had during the series of dedications done much to emphasise his kingship, to accentuate the importance of the Crusade to his country and to invest it with overtones of glory. But his final, private act was a recognition that, although he had a unique place in the expedition, he still had as many personal and spiritually inspired reasons for taking part as the most devout pilgrim of the army that marched behind him.

When he left Paris, his mother, Blanche of Castille, went with him for a short way. However, the experience proved to be too traumatic for her to endure and she was overcome with grief. She took her leave of Louis, turning back at the town of Corbeil, weeping hysterically and crying that she would never see her son again. The poignancy of this parting ceremony was made all the more moving by the fact that these predictions were all too accurate.

For those leaving, a variety of emotions were present, a heady mix of excitement, fear and perhaps even relief that at long last they were underway. For many though there was surely one emotion above all others that was present. The last word should go to de Joinville. After receiving his pilgrim's badge from the Cistercian abbot of Cheminon, the seneschal left his castle after many tender farewells to his wife and two young children. Then he left.

As he moved away 'never would I turn my eyes towards de Joinville for fear my heart would melt at the thought of the fair castle I was leaving behind, and my two children'.[14] Throughout France the scene would be repeated in a thousand villages and towns as families took their leave of one another. All over the country, families bade their tearful farewells to their menfolk. In far too many cases, they would never see each other again.

4

Rendezvous

Louis made his way down towards the coast and the rendezvous point at Aigues Mortes. En route, there were several incidents that highlighted that there were still potential for trouble whilst he was away. There had been an untoward incident even before the army left Paris. It demonstrated well the violent era in which Louis lived and although it was not in itself of major significance, it says much about the mores of the time.

De Joinville was on his way to meet the King in Paris when he came across a cart carrying three bloodied corpses. He was told that the three men had robbed a priest of his clothes. This man of God however showed a singular reluctance to turn the other cheek. He ran back to his lodging house and picked up his crossbow and a sword (the fact that he possessed these in the first place says much for the non-pacific nature of the times). Chasing after the brigands who had robbed him, he shot one through the heart with a bolt from his bow. He than ran another through with his sword. The third he caught as he was about to enter a house and 'struck him in the middle of the head with his sword so that he clove his head to the teeth'.[1]

Realising that he had overstepped the mark the priest then handed himself over to the authorities for suitable punishment. He was taken before Louis. The King ruled that he had surrendered his right to remain a priest by his violent actions. However, so impressed was the King by the priest's martial prowess that he took him instead into his service to travel on the Crusade with him so that 'my men fully understand that I will uphold them in none of their wickednesses'.

When the army left, they came to a castle at Roche-de-Glun, astride the River Rhone. The custodian, Roger of Clerieu, by tradition exacted tolls from travellers who passed. Louis refused to comply. He was King of France, and he was leading the army in the service of God. To Louis, the demands were both immoral and unreasonable. At a low level they also typified the contemporary struggle between King and barons for supremacy, not just in France.

Roger reacted angrily and seized hostages. But he badly misjudged Louis, who would not tolerate such an open affront to his authority. He laid siege to the castle, eventually storming the walls and subsequently raising them to the ground. Roger had made a grave error of judgement but it demonstrated that the barons of France were no weak pawns of the monarchy. But it was also good practice for the King and his army.

The Crusade then passed through Languedoc. The region had been decimated by the Albigensian Crusade, and there was a deep undercurrent of smouldering resentment against the monarchy still palpable. The local inhabitants thought of themselves as a nation apart as indeed in many senses they were. They had only been annexed by France after the recent Crusade which left many open wounds still unhealed. With a different attitude towards religion, their own traditions and even their own language, it was understandable if some saw the French King as the heir of a violent aggressor who had torn the region apart.

Simmering discontent turned to open violence at Avignon where, according to the English chronicler, Matthew Paris, the local inhabitants were insulted by French troops who called them heretics and poisoners.[2] Incensed, large numbers of the locals attacked stragglers from the French army as it travelled through a nearby pass robbing some and killing others. Louis's barons urged him to lay siege to the city and punish the miscreants severely, but the King refused to be diverted from his final destination, the East. The city therefore escaped what could have been an apocalyptic retribution. But the incident again served as a useful reminder to Louis: there were still many hostile elements in his country who might seek to take advantage of his forthcoming protracted absence.

Louis had already been thinking about this problem. His army had not moved rapidly. The pious monarch had stopped off at many of the hermitages and abbeys that he had passed in order to pray and to ask for the prayers of other holy men whilst he was in the East. On a more practical level he had also detoured to Lyons for an audience with Pope Innocent IV. This clearly had a significant religious element to it, as Louis sought the prayers and intercession of the holiest individual in Christendom. There was though a more pragmatic edge to the conversation too, as Louis confirmed that the pontiff would come to the King's aid should his kingdom be attacked by Henry III of England whilst he was away.

After his measured progress through his kingdom, Louis finally arrived at Aigues Mortes. Here, one of his leading barons, Raymond VII, Count of Toulouse, met him with a sizeable company as his contribution towards the expedition. The town itself was the subject of much interest as it had only recently been constructed and still had novelty value. It had been built as the result of the vision of the King who had wanted a new port on the Mediterranean coast.

Aigues Mortes was built on an island in a lagoon that was linked to the mainland by a specially-constructed causeway. A mole of large rocks offered shelter to any ships that took refuge in the harbour, and an aqueduct had been erected to supply clean water to the town. The whole was surrounded by strong fortifications. It had only just been completed, and as such was a very appropriate departure point for Louis, demonstrating as it did his confidence and power.

Not everyone joined the King on his journey all the way from Paris. De Joinville made his way independently to the port, transported by river with his baggage whilst his horses walked along the banks, a much more pleasant mode of transport than following the tortuous roads one would imagine. The rivers of France formed a vital part of the communications network in the country. It was common for barges and riverboats to be used to transport men as well as larger items of cargo such as siege engines.

The army, when it assembled, was a large one and the adventure was full of promise. Louis appeared to be taken by surprise when a large number of unexpected recruits arrived at Aigues Mortes seeking to join his army. Unable to transport them all, he had to refuse their offers of assistance. With a mixture of excitement and apprehension, the troops designated to depart for the East boarded the ships.

For many, the greatest ordeal was the sea crossing: it is a safe assumption that many of the Crusaders were more nervous of the journey to the East than they were of the prospect of being involved in hand-to-hand combat. The ships of the time were not particularly robust. Shipwrecks were common, and the lack of stability meant that, even though the lives of the Crusaders might not be forfeited on the voyage, they might nevertheless suffer dreadfully from seasickness.[3] In addition, conditions onboard were cramped and unhygienic. Even King Louis would live in much less comfort than he was accustomed to.[4]

Because of the fragility of the ships of the period, there were only two periods during which a crossing to the East would be made, one in the spring, the other towards the autumn. The Crusade, leaving as it was in August, was making the later crossing. With great care, the provisions of the Crusade (of which, thanks to Louis's organisation, there were a huge store) were placed onboard ship.

The horses of the expedition were loaded especially carefully. For them in particular, the voyage would be a great trial. Packed closely together, they could not exercise properly and many of them would become lame during the journey, which meant that it would be some time after they landed before they fully recovered their mobility. Most of the ships had doors in their sides through which the horses were loaded. Often, the doors were very close to the waterline and, as a result, they were sealed with pitch when the loading of the horses had been completed.

The loading of the horses was the last stage in the embarkation. When they had all been put onboard, the captains of the ships asked their men to confirm that they were ready to sail.[5] Receiving an affirmative answer, one final vital ceremony had to be performed. The priests onboard ship were asked to step forward, and bless the men. They then sang out the chant *Veni Creator Spiritus*, an old Crusader hymn. Their invocations travelled across the stilled waters as men, rich and poor, great and lowly, bowed their heads in earnest supplication. The blessing of God being duly invoked, the sails were now unfurled. Propelled on a wave of enthusiasm, on 25 August the ships sailed forth from France towards the shores of destiny.

They were quickly out of sight of land, alone in a vast expanse of water. Most of all, they worried about the wind. If it were too strong, the flimsy vessels could be tossed about like corks or, at the worst, dashed to oblivion against some rocky headland or overwhelmed by the seas and sunk in a watery grave. De Joinville was well aware of this fact, writing that 'when you lay down to sleep at night onboard ship, you lie down not knowing whether, in the morning, you may find yourself at the bottom of the sea'.[6]

However, a lack of wind was almost as worrying. After a few days sailing, de Joinville's ship was sailing close to the shore of Africa. As the countries of North Africa were in Muslim hands, the Christians would not want to tarry in this area any longer than they had to. The Crusaders sighted a mountain on an island near the coast. They sailed all night but, when day broke, the Christians were dismayed to see exactly the same mountain before them. They were becalmed in potentially dangerous waters.

It was a threatening position to be in but one of the priests onboard, the Dean of Maurupt, believed that he had the answer. He told the men that when his flock in France had been threatened by any danger of whatever nature he organised religious processions to be held for three Saturdays running. Invariably, God and the Holy Mother came to his aid when this simple scheme was adopted.

The Crusaders formed up to perform the ceremony, it then being a Saturday. They marched round the two masts of the ship (de Joinville was so ill because of his seasickness that he had to be carried in the procession). On cue, the wind picked up and they were quickly carried away from the coast and danger. On the third Saturday, the island of Cyprus – the appointed rendezvous for the fleet – hove into view. The first part of the journey had been successfully completed.

It would have been impossible for the fleet to stay together during the crossing. The winds and currents would have inexorably forced the fleet apart. Therefore, King Louis had decided that the fleet would re-assemble off the island of Cyprus. It was a sensible choice for a rendezvous point. The island had been part of the Latin territories in the East since Richard I had conquered it en route to the Third Crusade. It was consequently a friendly haven for King Louis. Further, during the winter months that were about to arrive, it had a mild and enticing climate, which would allow the Crusaders to gather their strength before the assault on Egypt, Louis's chosen target, commenced.

Most attractive of all, however, was its strategic position. It hugged the coast of Syria but it was also only a few days sailing from Egypt. It was therefore the ideal spot for Louis's fleet to regroup after its crossing of the Mediterranean and to husband its resources before the invasion of Egypt began. It was too late in the year for the Crusade to consider launching its attack on Egypt so Louis set up his headquarters on the island.

When de Joinville arrived on Cyprus he found that the King was already there. Louis had landed at Limassol on 17 September 1248. Most of the fleet had enjoyed an uneventful voyage. Only one ship foundered during the voyage, a small loss by the standards of the day, although many other ships had been scattered by a sudden, unexpected wind that had blown up en route.

The huge quantities of provisions that had already been unloaded on the island by the time that he landed particularly impressed de Joinville. Vast stores of wheat and barley lay in heaps, which looked to him like mountains because the rain that had fallen had caused the grain to sprout so that they looked for all the world as if they were covered in grass.[7] Stacked by the side of the sea were great piles of barrels containing wine. These had been bought for fully two years before the King's arrival on the island. They were stacked so high that they seemed like barns to the chronicler.

According to de Joinville, King Louis was all for pushing straight on to Egypt but his advisors argued successfully against this. Although they were undoubtedly right in that the army would run a great risk of being cut off from Cyprus if they had done so, the stopover on Cyprus nevertheless saw the first signs of difficulty for the expedition. Although Louis had been meticulous in accumulating supplies before the expedition set out, they were inevitably depleted during the four months of inactivity that the army was to spend on the island.

The situation became serious enough for Louis to send one of his barons, Tibald II, the Count of Bar, on a journey to ask for more provisions. He visited a few islands near Cyprus with some success. The Venetians were happy to help out, and sent six galleys loaded with corn, wine and other supplies to the French. The emperor Frederick was also fulsome in his assistance, so much so that Louis wrote to him to personally thank him. In addition, Louis again wrote to the Pope, telling him of Frederick's help and asking Innocent to seek an accommodation with him, although with little more success than the previous efforts he had made.[8]

There were some losses of men due to illness during the winter. Louis was forced to issue an order that no one should attempt to make their own way from the island before the expedition was ready, and he armed his galleys to enforce it. In addition, the great expense involved in the Crusade was already proving too much for some of the less wealthy barons with the expedition, and Louis was forced to buy them into his service so that they could remain with the army. Jean de Joinville was one such baron who had to rely on the generosity of the King. With the wonderful gift of hindsight, the problems of these delays could have been avoided if Louis had made the early summer passage across the Mediterranean. It meant effectively that the timing of the Crusade was already out of synchronisation.

The time spent on Cyprus was not entirely wasted though. Whilst he was there, Louis received embassies from several rulers seeking his help. The first embassy came from what was ostensibly a most unusual source. The Mongols had great designs in the Middle East. The major obstacle to their complete conquest of the area were the Muslim powers in the region, especially the Mamelukes. Obviously believing in the maxim that 'my enemy's enemy is my friend', the Mongols sent two representatives, the Westernised version of whose names were Mark and David, to Louis asking for an alliance. In return, the Khan of Khans was prepared to return Jerusalem to the Crusaders.

Louis received the embassy graciously, obviously seeing an opportunity for mutual advantage in the arrangement. Further, he had heard that some of the Mongols were Christians, though they were in a minority. Louis was not merely a passive Christian, he was an evangelist. The depth of the King's religious devotion can be judged by the fact that he seriously considered becoming a monk in later life (his wife, Margaret, managed to talk him out of it, possibly horrified by the fact that he also expected her to become a nun as part of the bargain). He wasted no opportunity that presented itself for converting the pagan to the ways of Christ. In the approach of the Mongols he saw just such an opening.

In response to the Mongols' approach for an alliance, he sent an exotic present to the Khan. Louis had with him a tent made of scarlet cloth, formed in the likeness of a chapel. It was a very expensive piece of work. Inside the tent, Louis had images of the Virgin Mary painted on the walls, along with other scriptural representations. He sent the tent, in the company of two friars who knew something of the languages of the East (though their knowledge must by definition have been imperfect), as a gift to the Khan. By the combination of the portable chapel and these two preachers (who, judging by the ferocious reputation of the Mongols, must have been exceedingly brave men) Louis hoped to convert the Mongols to Christianity, no doubt aiming to facilitate better relations between the Mongols and the West as a consequence.

Louis had many qualities as a man and a King, but he was sometimes errant in his judgement of men and events. There is no better example of this than in his interpretation of the approach of the Mongols for an alliance. In the proposed arrangement, Louis undoubtedly saw himself as at least an equal, and probably more, of the Mongol Khan. Nothing could have been further from the mind of the Mongols however.

The perception that the Khan held of himself is perhaps best described in the words of the most terrible Mongol lord of all, Genghis Khan. Some decades previously, following the capture of the ancient and beautiful city of Bokhara, Genghis had told the city's leaders that 'I am Heaven's scourge, sent to punish'. Genghis had died in 1227, but the current Khan was no different than his predecessors. The only way to truly enter into any form of alliance with the Mongols was to submit to them absolutely. The Mongol Khans believed that it was their destiny to rule the world and that it was, therefore, necessary for all other men to pay homage to them. In their eyes this was no alliance of equals but rather one in which they would expect and demand ultimate power.

There was certainly ample evidence around to alert Louis to this fact. The horrific excesses of the Mongols were well known in the West, particularly as Hungary and Poland had so recently suffered from them.[9] Further, Pope Innocent IV had only recently sent several embassies to the Mongols. He had sent a letter, demanding that the Mongols should accept Christianity. Although the Khan, Guyuk, was kind enough in his treatment of the ambassadors, he wrote a reply ordering the Pope to accept his sovereignty and to come with all the Kings of Christendom to do him homage.

The reply sent to the Pope was unequivocal in its import. Guyuk told Innocent plainly that 'now you must say with a sincere heart "We will be your subjects; we will give you our power." Come yourself, in person, at the head of all the Kings without exception, come to offer us service and homage. Then, we will recognise your submission. And if you contravene our orders, we will know you to be our enemies.' One imagines that Innocent was not used to this kind of forceful language being directed at him.

Surprisingly undismayed by this unequivocal rejection of his authority, Innocent subsequently sent another delegation, which had reached the Mongols in 1247. In response to this, the Mongols had sent envoys to Rome seeking an alliance. Innocent received them warmly, giving them presents of scarlet robes and squirrel-pelt furs, as well as precious ornaments made of gold and silver. It is quite probable, given the timing, that the embassy to Louis came about directly as a result of Innocent's initiatives. Nothing tangible, however, would ever come of this proposed alliance and within a few years Louis himself would realise that he had misinterpreted the Mongols' attitude totally.

He was equally wrong, as also was Pope Innocent, in his perception of the Mongols' attitude to Christianity. There were some Mongols who were Christians, although there were many that were not. These were Nestorian Christians though, an eastern form of Christianity that owed little to Western paradigms as far as its theology was concerned. Most of the Mongols were still pagan, followers of shamanism, and even those that were Nestorian Christians would regard acceptance of the Pope as the ultimate authority on Earth as a totally alien concept. The absolute authority of their Khan made the Papal vision of subservience by the Mongols to the Pope a totally naïve hope.

Just as Louis was to be disappointed by the proposed alliance as far as his political and military expectations were concerned, so he would be equally unsuccessful in his evangelical efforts. The idea of an alliance with a Christianised Mongol Empire was fatally flawed from the beginning, given the complete lack of similarity between the views that each side held of the other. Wrong-headed and based on completely erroneous assumptions, it was doomed to fail from the outset.

Louis also received the Empress of Constantinople, Mary, whilst he was on Cyprus. She had suffered a traumatic experience whilst anchored at the Cypriot port of Paphos when the cables securing her ship were broken and it was driven eastwards to Acre. As a result she had lost nearly all her baggage, with virtually nothing more remaining to her than the clothes she stood up in.

The Crusaders received her very graciously. They were very well disposed towards the Latin Empire of Byzantium, which had been in existence only since 1204 when the Fourth Crusade had captured the city of Constantinople. As most of the Westerners involved in that expedition were French, and the Latin Empire formed as a result of the conquest kept very close ties with France, it was little wonder that Louis's army was well-disposed towards the Empress. De Joinville was so moved by the lady's plight that he sent her cloth to make new dresses and an ermine fur. Many of the other barons were ashamed that one of their own had shown them up by his generosity, as they themselves had not taken similarly practical measures to help her.

But the Empress was after far more substantial help from the French expedition than new clothes or ermine furs. Since its heady early days, the Latin Empire centred on Constantinople had been increasingly threatened by a resurgent Greek Byzantine Empire. Little by little, the Latin territories in the Empire had been lost, whittled away in a succession of reverses. It did not take a military genius to hypothesise that the ultimate aim of the Byzantines would be the reconquest of Constantinople, a city that held an almost mystical place in the hearts of the Greeks.

Mary sought military help from the expedition to protect the Empire against such a threat. She pleaded her case so eloquently that she took away with her the promise of three hundred knights to journey to Constantinople and enlist in the Latin forces there after the Crusade was over. It was a heartening response; three hundred knights would be a very useful contribution towards the defence of an Empire that was, to be honest, already on its last legs (Constantinople would be lost by the Latins in 1261).

Sadly for Mary, she or her husband, Baldwin II, Emperor of the Latin territories, would see few of the army arrive. By the time that the Crusade in Egypt was over, few of the Western knights would have the appetite, or indeed the money, to make the journey to Constantinople. A good number of them would be dead.

Winter passed and spring came, and with it the promise of great adventures ahead. It appears that the Crusade became slightly too comfortable on Cyprus; certainly morale appears to have dropped over the winter months. Anxious to set out for Egypt and fulfil his Crusader vows, Louis was infuriated when an outbreak of hostilities between the crews of some Pisan and Genoese ships, which had anchored off the Syrian coast for the winter, delayed his departure still further. Commercial rivalry between the Italian maritime city-states was intense and such violence was far from unique, but it must nevertheless have caused Louis great angst to see yet another delay hold back the Crusade. This irritating interlude came to an end when the two sides managed to settle their differences, safe only in the knowledge that there was bound to be more trouble in the near future. The fleet was at last ready to sail.

As Louis prepared to board his ship, he heard the siren call of destiny calling him to Egypt. For Christian men, the Crusade was the ultimate adventure, and there was no more Christian man in Western Europe than Louis IX, King of France. The winter months on Cyprus seemed like an extended period of phoney war. It was agony for Louis to know that he had been only a few days sailing away from the fulfilment of his greatest objective in life. Now, at last, Louis need wait no longer. His meticulous preparations, the years of planning and organising, were almost at an end. The time for talking was over. It was time for the real action to begin.

5

Into Battle

As spring arrived, the King ordered his fleet to re-provision and make ready to sail. The grain was carefully stored onboard, along with large stocks of wine. By the end of May, preparations were complete. The King and queen embarked on their ship, the *Montjoie,* on 21 May 1249, the Friday before Pentecost. The next day, the ships weighed anchor. The Crusade was now really underway.

Before leaving, the King confirmed Egypt as the destination of the Crusade. This was a controversial decision. Jerusalem had only recently been lost to the enemies of Christendom, a factor that would have helped Louis considerably in appealing to the emotions of all devout Christians to recover it once more. Many of his followers would be disappointed that Jerusalem was not to be the target.

The city of Jerusalem held an almost divine status to most Christians. Many equated the earthly city of Jerusalem to God's heavenly Holy City. Robert the Monk, inspiring would-be Crusaders at the time of the First Crusade, had said of it that it was:

… the navel of the world, a land which is fruitful above all others, like another paradise of delights. The redeemer of the race illumined this land by his coming, graced it by his living there, made it holy by his suffering, redeemed it by his death, distinguished it by his burial. This royal city, set in the centre of the world [where it was depicted on Medieval European maps], is now held captive by its enemies and is enslaved in heathen rite by people who do not know God. Therefore, the city demands and desires to be set free, and calls upon you without ceasing to come to its assistance.

It was this mystical status of the city that had appealed to the hearts of those first Crusaders back in 1095 most strongly. It had continued to do so ever since. A Crusader was a pilgrim who was not relieved of his Crusading obligations until he reached his stated destination. In most cases, this was the Church of the Holy Sepulchre in Jerusalem.

Gregory X, installed as Pope after travelling to Acre in 1270, chose to preach on the following text before his journey East some twenty years after Louis's first Crusade, quoting from Psalm 136 that 'if I forget thee, O Jerusalem, let my right hand forget her cunning. If I do not remember thee, let my tongue cleave to the roof of my mouth, if I prefer not Jerusalem above my chief joy.' In such reverence was the city held in Christian eyes and many would have been disappointed and even angered concerning his choice of Egypt rather than Jerusalem as his destination.

Louis instructed his barons to rendezvous with him off Egypt. As they prepared to leave Cyprus, the priests with the expedition invoked the help of God in their efforts again. After all, the clash of arms was only days away now. They had not only the perils of a sea crossing to contend with, they were also faced with the prospect of going into battle with a fierce enemy defending his homeland. The fleet looked magnificent. De Joinville described it in awed tones, saying that 'it seemed as if all the sea, so far as the eye could reach, were covered with the canvas of the ships' sails', further adding that there were 1,800 ships, large and small, in this armada.[1]

There were several options open to Louis regarding a landing place. The sentiment of the expedition probably leaned towards Damietta from the start, given its close association with the previous Crusade to Egypt. There were however some disadvantages with this destination. Damietta was strongly defended and had held up the last expedition for many months before it fell. In preparation for what was expected to be a renewed attack from the West, the defences had been strengthened. Trenches had been dug and the river that acted as a moat by the walls had been widened.

On that previous occasion, the city had only succumbed to an outbreak of disease within the city. Force of arms alone could not take it then. From Damietta, the route to Cairo was not a straightforward one. There were a number of canals branching off the Nile that could be used to impede the Crusaders progress after they had captured Damietta. In addition, in response to the lessons of the previous Crusade, the Egyptians had constructed a new fortress town right on the road to Cairo at Mansourah.

The other obvious alternative for the Crusaders was Alexandria. Both Damietta and Alexandria were vital to the viability of Egypt. The loss of either to the Crusaders would be a very serious blow. But although the route to Cairo from Alexandria did not have the obstructions of the route from Damietta, much of it was across desert. It was eventually decided that Damietta should be the goal for Louis's crusade, and it was accordingly towards this city that the armada set its course.

The Muslim chronicler Maqrizi describes how Louis sent an imperious summons ashore to the Egyptians ahead of him, demanding their capitulation. Louis reminded the Egyptians of recent victories won by Christian armies in Spain and tells them of his determination to take their land by force, for 'even if you were to promise me anything on oath and to appear before the priests and monks and carry a candle before me as an act of obedience to the Cross, it would not deter me from attacking you and fighting you on the land that is dearest to you'. He goes on to tell them of his armies 'filling the mountains and the plains, numerous as the stones of the earth and poised against you like a stone of destiny'.[2]

The journey to Egypt only took a couple of days. The armada reassembled on its first night off a headland known as the Point of

Limassol. Their first act was to hold mass onboard ship. It did them little good. Shortly afterwards, a strong wind blew up from the shore. Many of the ships were driven away from the coast, and nearly three quarters of the knights with the Crusade were separated from the King as a result, a number of them not eventually touching land again until they reached Acre, the major port of the kingdom of Outremer. A good proportion of these would not return to Louis for some time.

The next day, the wind dropped, allowing the Crusader ships that remained to regroup. The residue of the fleet set sail for Egypt. These ships left on the Monday, and by the time that day broke on the Thursday following, the Crusade was adjacent to the shore of Egypt. The navigation of the mariners was excellent, and the Crusade arrived close to Damietta. There was a reception party arrayed to meet them, and it was not a friendly one.

Probably armed with intelligence from both the Venetians (trading partners of the Egyptians) and the emperor Frederick, who was a master of playing off two sides against each other, the Sultan of Egypt, an elderly and infirm individual named Ayub, knew that the arrival of the Crusade was imminent. However, Ayub did not personally take much of a role in preparing to rebuff the invasion. He had spent the winter in Damascus and was involved in warring against other Muslims in the region of Homs. The defence of Egypt was put in the hands of his trusted and capable vizier, Fakhr ad-Din, who was on excellent personal terms with the emperor Frederick.

Damietta was a tough nut to crack. It was garrisoned by a force of Bedouins, renowned for their ferocity in battle. They moved out in force to repulse the Crusaders' landing, judging rightly that this was the moment of greatest danger for any amphibious assault. The enemy troops made a great impression on the Crusaders, arrayed as they were in golden armour, from which the sun's rays reflected fiercely. The Egyptians attempted to strike further terror into the hearts of the Crusading host by making a fearful racket, a cacophony of horns and cymbals being used to create a deafening maelstrom of noise.

It was the first military moment of truth in the campaign. Many of his counsellors advised that Louis should wait until his numbers had increased. But Louis certainly did not lack for personal courage. He outlined his reasons for proceeding without delay. He told his counsellors that any sign of weakness would offer a psychological advantage to the enemy.

In addition, there were no ports close at hand where Louis could wait for the rest of his scattered fleet to rejoin him. And if he could not find a safe anchorage for what remained of his fleet then that, too, could be blown off station. Louis's decision to proceed with the attack was brave, but it was also undoubtedly the right one. He could not be sure if and when the others would ever rejoin him – in the event, a number of them would be desultory in doing so. After a winter of delay in Cyprus, the loss of momentum again at such an early stage would be a very bad beginning to the attack on Egypt. Louis, therefore, gave the order to begin the offensive.

It was decided that the attack would be launched on the Friday, the following morning. The Egyptians did not have a particularly strong recent naval tradition and, although they had some coastal defence vessels and some larger galleys, they would not hinder the Crusaders unduly even in the unlikely eventuality that they would be used in an attempt against the Christian fleet. But the great Crusader warships would not be able to get close enough to the shore to help in the landings because of their draft. The troops therefore transferred to smaller galleys for this purpose.

De Joinville understood that he had been assigned to a galley with Lord Everard of Brienne. But on the Friday morning a dispute broke out over who should go ashore. There were too many men to all be transported in the flotilla of smaller boats at once. When it appeared that some of the men would not be in the first wave, they were so dismayed that they climbed down into the small boats that were towed astern of the great ships so that they might make their own way ashore. Before long one of the boats began to sink because it was overloaded. Some of the men consequently decided that discretion was the better part of valour and climbed back onboard.

Seriously concerned for the welfare of the men onboard this boat, de Joinville enquired of the captain as to how far over capacity it currently was. The captain replied that he would be able to take the men ashore if twenty men were removed. This excess load was removed from the boat and arrangements were made to ship them back to the larger vessel that de Joinville had sailed over from Cyprus in.

The intense frustration that this unseemly incident created was too much for some. One of the knights onboard the larger ship, a man named Plonquet, was bitterly aggrieved that he had missed out on the chance of glory. Determined that he would not be debarred at this late stage from participating in the landing, he attempted to climb into the boat. On the way down, he lost his grip and was thrown into the water. Before any could assist him, he had disappeared from sight and drowned.

There was one more act to perform before the landing. There were two knights on the boat who loathed each other. De Joinville made both of the men swear on holy relics that they would forgive the grudges that each held against the other: otherwise they would get no spiritual benefit from their participation in the Crusade. It was, even on the eve of battle, a moment of great solemnity, and the oath was binding and not to be taken lightly. This was no mere empty gesture.

By now the spiritual and practical preparations were almost complete. It was time for each man to commit his soul to the protection of his Creator and, swallowing his fears, his apprehensions, to place his life on the line for the cause of Christendom. The boats moved towards the shore which teemed with thousands of Muslim warriors prepared to drive the Infidel back into the sea, for just as this was a holy war for Christians, it was equally so for Muslims.

Before long, de Joinville's humble landing craft was alongside a barge that, in its turn, was adjacent to a great warship. Even if the chronicler did not recognise this vessel instinctively, the banner of Saint-Denis flying proudly at the bow of the barge told everyone who was onboard. The banner was by tradition carried into battle by the King himself: none other than Louis IX was in the barge.

The crew in de Joinville's boat suggested that they should stay alongside, but the more senior men present decided otherwise. Further up the beach, they had noticed a large squadron of Muslim cavalry, estimated at six thousand strong. It was towards this heavily defended section of the landing ground that they aimed their boat. Riding the waves as they struck against the shore, the boat eventually grounded on sand. As it did so, those onboard climbed over the side and made their way up the beach.

There was no time for celebration. The squadron of cavalry had spotted their boat, along with others that had landed alongside. This large force aimed its weapons at the invaders and charged. They must have been slightly slow off the mark though. The Crusaders had time to take sharpened stakes out of the boats. They thrust them into the sand with their points bristling in the direction of the Muslims. As the enemy approached, they were discomfited by the strategically placed stakes. Unable to break through the wall of impromptu spears, the Muslim horsemen backed off.

All along the shoreline, the events witnessed at this small beachhead were replicated. To the left of de Joinville's party, the Count of Jaffa had landed. He made a particular impression on the chronicler, perhaps because they were distantly related. His galley had come ashore in some style. It was brilliantly decorated all over with his coat of arms, gold with a cross superimposed. It was propelled by three hundred rowers, each carrying their own shield (rowers were at this time not slaves but free men). Each shield also bore the coat of arms of the Count.

So keen were the rowers to get ashore that it seemed to de Joinville as if they flew across the water. They had musicians of their own onboard: trumpets, cymbals, drums and horns blasted forth in response to the Egyptians' attempts to intimidate them. In the midst of this deafening confusion, the galley rammed into the sand in the shallow waters by the shore. The men onboard leapt out, their metal carapaces affording them some protection against the arrows that any Muslim archer dared loose at them. The newly-arrived Crusaders took up position next to de Joinville's group. Another part of the front had been formed, although it was still early in the battle and the line was by no means secure.

The Count of Jaffa was collected enough to order that his tents should be erected close to the shoreline. It was a clear statement that the Crusaders were here to stay. Infuriated at his temerity, the Egyptian forces renewed their attack with fresh vigour. They dug their spurs into the side of their mounts and threw themselves head-long at the Crusaders again. The line once more held firm. Dispirited by the Crusaders' refusal to show any sign of giving an inch, the charges declined in ferocity and then ceased altogether.

To the right of de Joinville (about a crossbow shot away, according to him) the barge carrying the standard of Saint-Denis had also landed its men. One of the enemy in particular showed commendable spirit in attacking the Crusaders single-handed. Against such a well-armed enemy, his action was brave but suicidal. He was quickly overpowered and hacked to pieces by the Crusaders, who were by now driven on by blood lust.

When Louis (who had not gone in with the first wave of the attack) heard that his ensign had been carried ashore, he could delay no longer. Inspired by the news, he leapt into the water, which was deep enough to come up to his armpits. He was fully armoured, with his shield around his neck, his helmet on his head and his lance in his hand. It was an impetuous if courageous act; not only did the King risk drowning if he misjudged the depth of the water, he would also be a prime target for the attacks of the enemy.

Louis waded clumsily ashore, a giant crab ploughing through the waves. When he reached land and rejoined his men, he asked them who the people arrayed to his front were. When his men confirmed that they were indeed Louis's Muslim opponents, the excitement overcame him. He put his lance under his arm, levelled it in the direction of the Egyptians and ran towards them. With difficulty, the French soldiers round about him restrained him.

But the Muslim army's attempt to drive away the landing had ended in failure. Although they had received ample warning that the Crusade was about to invade their country, their efforts had been in vain. There were a large number of troops in the garrison, yet the attack had been called off when the Crusaders were still very vulnerable. They would not, as yet, have had sufficient time to offload all their men or horses, and as such they had not by this point attained full strength. That the Muslim resistance was abandoned in this way suggests that their morale was not all that it should be. Events soon afterwards would demonstrate even more clearly that this was undoubtedly the case.

The counter-attack having been resisted, the Crusaders were euphoric. They were seasoned enough veterans though to appreciate that this was only the opening gambit in the campaign. The enemy was still numerous and was even now making his way back behind those sturdy walls that only a few decades before had resisted the Crusaders for the best part of a year. They were on home ground, fighting in defence of their own country, and able to draw on Egypt's resources to sustain them through the coming campaign. The garrison on the other hand knew that they must let the authorities in Cairo know that the defensive line of the country had been breached. Accordingly, they sent word by carrier pigeon to the city.[3]

Louis erected his red tent outside of the city and prepared for a hard siege. With the Crusaders now firmly encamped in front of Damietta, the garrison's messages to Cairo started to become ever more frantic. They had been complacent in advance of the landings, over-confident in their ability to drive the enemy back on the shore-line. Now the strength of the forces arrayed against them was painfully obvious. The Crusaders were well-armed, well-supplied and driven on by a fierce belief in the righteousness of their cause. They had already demonstrated their tenacity, and there were more of them to come. To the defenders of Damietta it was already clear that the enemy was here to stay.

Well aware that the Sultan Ayub was far from healthy, rumours soon spread around Damietta that he had died. This was bad news and it flew around the city like a fire catching hold of dry grass. Recent experience suggested that, in the aftermath of his demise, there would be a bitter succession dispute, with the participants too pre-occupied and divided to effectively resist the Crusaders' invasion. If the rumour were true then the defence of Egypt might crumble.

In fact, tidings of Ayub's death were premature, but the falsehood of the rumours made little difference. For the garrison believed them, and this was enough to create an enormous psychological backlash. Unbelievably, they lost the will to fight. Without any further resistance, they crept away from the city and abandoned it to its fate. Damietta, surrounded by those massive and daunting walls, was given up before a siege had even started.

It was a treasonable act of desertion, lacking both courage and morality, but it suggested more strongly than ever that there were very divided loyalties in the Egyptian camp. If the actions of common soldiers tell us anything about the morale of a nation, then that of Egypt must have been at a very low ebb indeed. When news reached Cairo of the abandonment of Damietta with the city completely intact, the reaction was instant and brutal. The leaders of the Bedouins who had been so lack-lustre in their defence of Damietta were, when they reached Cairo, strung up to encourage the others. The rest of the garrison was collectively tarred with a reputation for cowardice and shame.

A contemporary Muslim historian, Ibn Wasil, recorded an outburst of 'great grief and amazement' when news of the capitulation at Damietta was received in Cairo, describing it as 'a disaster without precedent'. The rest of Egypt was dumbstruck when they heard what had happened as the defenders 'had provisions, munitions and arms in great quantity, and could have defended the city for at least two years'. But he was at least lenient in his judgement of the citizens of Damietta, stating that they 'are not to blame if when they see the troops in flight and heard of the Sultan's illness they were afraid to face a long siege and to die of hunger'.[4]

The garrison had left in such a hurry that they made it very easy for the Crusaders to walk in and take possession of Damietta. A narrow causeway of boats linked the city to the rest of Egypt. The garrison did not even attempt to destroy the bridge. Consequently, what could have proved an active hindrance to the Crusaders was avoided. The retreating Muslims did, however, at least manage to set fire to the bazaar in the city, destroying some of the provisions stored within its walls.

With the garrison gone, Damietta had lost all hope of fighting off the Crusaders and it was soon surrendered. As Damietta was one of the few entry points into the arterial network of the Nile and the Delta, its capture allowed the Crusaders to exert great commercial pressure on the Egyptians. It also gave them a wonderful base for a prolonged assault deeper into Egypt, towards Cairo itself.

The Christians were undisputed masters of the seas, through their links with states such as Pisa and Genoa as well as many other maritime powers (even allowing for their friendly links with the Egyptians, the Venetians would happily assist the Crusade if the price was right). The Crusaders could be regularly re-supplied from Cyprus and points further west. This would allow food stocks to be brought in to replenish provisions. Possession of the port and dominance of the Mediterranean also allowed the Crusade to regularly receive reinforcements to replace men who decided to leave or who were lost to the ravages of disease or the violence of battle.

It was by any measure a spectacular start to the Crusade. Within the space of days the Crusade had made almost as many material gains as the previous expedition to Egypt had done in a year. The capture of so great a prize for so little cost was wonderful indeed. Not only did it have a dramatic effect on the strategic position of the Crusade, this triumph was perhaps even more important to the morale of the expedition. As the Crusade was a Christian enterprise, was indeed a Christian act in its own right, then it followed that God had shown His satisfaction with the aims of the Crusade and the actions of the participants thus far.

Certainly, King Louis was not slow to give thanks to his Lord for the triumph, and would have seen the glory for the success as belonging to God rather than man. He entered the city to find that, as well as the garrison, much of the population had fled. Many of those that remained behind were Christians that had been captured in previous battles between Islam and Christendom. These were released, all of which no doubt helped to fuel the sense of euphoria and exhilaration amongst the Crusaders.

That first night in Damietta was sweet indeed for the victors. Few would have anticipated such a quick and relatively bloodless triumph. Yet for those who knew their history, there were lessons to be learnt very close to home. A few decades before, in 1219, a triumphant Christian army also held Damietta. However, the lesson of that previous Crusade was that the fall of the city was only a beginning, not an end. That earlier expedition had in the end failed miserably because the Crusaders had failed to exploit their success at Damietta. They had fallen victim to the geography of Egypt and the determination of their opponents.

One other factor also soon became clear. The Crusaders had probably reckoned that it would take months to achieve a breakthrough at Damietta. The immediate actions of King Louis suggest that he had not yet thought beyond the capture of the city. The capitulation of Damietta had become his end, and he appears to have given little attention to his longer-term strategic objectives.

The King was a man of thorough planning and attention to detail; acting instinctively was essentially alien to his character. His preparations for the Crusade had been a masterpiece of meticulous organisation, not an impromptu response to a given situation. In the current context, the sudden collapse of Damietta may have been more of a hindrance than a benefit as it forced Louis to act in a manner that took him into areas where he did not feel comfortable. The impetus of the Crusade needed to be maintained, otherwise the adventure could peter out. For those who cared to look, there were worrying signs that the ultimate defeat of the Egyptians was as yet still very far from being a formality.

6

The Serpent's Head

The fall of Damietta had happened so quickly that Louis felt unable to follow up on his success immediately. He was particularly concerned that his army was still far from complete. As well as the elements of his fleet that had been scattered by the winds before the landings near Damietta had taken place, there were other large contingents still expected from the West. Louis's brother, Alphonse of Poitiers, was due to bring such a body with him but he had not yet arrived. Perhaps the King was unaware that Alphonse was not making the early summer crossing of the Mediterranean and would not arrive until later on that year, eventually landing at Damietta at the end of October 1249.

The immediate concern after the Crusaders captured Damietta however was the division of the spoils from the city. Although those on Crusade were there primarily for the spiritual benefits they hoped to gain in return for their participation, it would be wrong to assume that they had no interest in material profit. True, few who took part in the Crusade were mainly motivated by the lure of booty. In fact, Crusading was an extremely expensive act and it was rarely the case that those who took part ended the Crusade enriched as a result. But this meant there was all the more reason to ensure that the spoils of war were allocated fairly.

Booty was an important part of medieval warfare. Particularly if a city resisted calls to surrender, its possessions were fair game for a successful opponent to loot. There were strict rules and conventions about how this should be done so that none were unfairly disadvantaged. Frequently however there were complaints that these rules were not equitably applied. A hundred years after Louis's crusade, special laws had to be written for English troops on campaign because, after battle was over, the troops often started fighting each other because they could not agree on how the booty should be divided.

Louis summoned a council of his barons and other advisors to rule on the allocation of booty. The Church was the first to offer an opinion. The patriarch of Jerusalem, who had accompanied the expedition, stated that the King should retain the food supplies found in the city so that he could feed his army and his entourage. What remained was to be brought to the legate Eudes of Chateauroux's quarters under pain of a sentence of excommunication for those that failed to comply. Despite the implicit threat, many failed to fulfil their part of the bargain and turn over the goods they had taken for themselves, de Joinville for one being surprised at the small value of that subsequently handed in.[1]

The value of that eventually collected amounted to some 6,000 *livres*. The King wished to hand this amount over to one of his barons, John of Valery, whilst retaining all the provisions seized in the capture of the city. John refused to accept this proposal, arguing that by tradition the spoils of war had been divided by the Kings of Jerusalem: one third to the King himself, two thirds to the remainder of the pilgrims who were with the expedition. Therefore, the King should hand over two thirds of the provisions taken in the capture of Damietta to be similarly divided.

As John of Valery himself argued, such a distribution had taken place the last time that Damietta had fallen, when John of Brienne, King of Jerusalem, had followed the custom. Louis however was not persuaded by the counter-arguments and refused to move on the issue, much to the shock of many of the barons who were, as de Joinville described, 'ill-pleased that the King should set aside old customs'.[2] Even at this early stage, it was apparent that the King's authoritarian style might be the cause of friction.

Neither was this the barons' only bone of contention. The King had a sizeable entourage of administrators with which he intended to ensure that his control was absolute. The presence of merchants in Damietta was a crucial part of the supply chain that the Crusade would be forced to rely upon. It was important to ensure that their willingness to re-provision the expedition was not compromised. Yet Louis insisted on levying from them large rents for the shops in the city from which they sold their goods.

Rumours of the heavy payments demanded by Louis and his advisors soon spread, with the result that foreign merchantmen were reluctant to sail to the port. Although in the short-term the higher rents may have increased Louis's revenues, in the longer-term it discouraged traders from making their way to Damietta. It was an inept move on the King's part, doing little to secure his long-term supply position.

Louis was concerned with other issues, too; in particular that some of his army appeared to have extremely lax morals. The barons held sumptuous feasts, the lavishness of which took on the appearance to de Joinville of 'outrageous excess'. As for the common people, the King was annoyed to discover that many of them were consorting with what were described as 'lewd women'. It was naïve of the King to believe that men would forego sinful pleasures during the Crusade, although theologians frequently warned those involved that the spiritual rewards offered in return for Crusading would be compromised or, at worst, lost altogether by such immorality.

However, prostitutes were a common sight amongst the camp followers of medieval armies. Richard I had banned them from following his army out of Acre during the Third Crusade, probably more worried about their effect on discipline than any concerns for the spiritual welfare of his army. So affected was King Louis by the sexual activities of many of his supporters that he dismissed many of them from his service when he eventually returned to France. As these events at Damietta took place several years earlier, the freshness of the King's memories with regard to these matters evidences the seriousness with which he regarded the sins of his troops.

There were though more pleasant matters to attend to. Damietta was a Muslim city and a pressing concern for Louis was to convert it to a Christian one. There were of course mosques in the city. The largest of them, the Great Mosque of Damietta, was commandeered by the Crusaders and became the Cathedral of Our Lady. A priest in the King's entourage, Giles of Saumur, became Archbishop. He was given generous grants of land in Damietta and the immediate vicinity.

Many of the Crusaders were still encamped outside of the city. This was a dangerous position for them to be in. Because the Crusade had been slow to follow up on its initial success, the Egyptians had regrouped and had assembled a force to harass the Crusaders. A large unit of cavalry launched an attack on the camp, as a result of which a number of men, including de Joinville, rushed to the headquarters of King Louis, inside the city itself. They found the King fully armed and surrounded by his advisors and urged the King to hurry to the aid of the camp.

However, Louis and his advisors refused. The guard that had been left in the camp should be more than capable of beating off the attack. It was also felt that the Muslims planned to entice the army to sally forth from Damietta in an undisciplined fashion and lead it into a trap. It was a classic ploy, and it had led to the defeat of many Crusading forces in the past. Therefore, the plea to rush to the aid of the camp was rejected out of hand with one of Louis's advisors, Lord John of Beaumont, ordering de Joinville not to leave his quarters until the King so commanded him.

The advice was sound. Based on past experience, a disjointed counter-attack from the Crusaders might well lead to self-induced disaster. Further, the camp was currently under the command of

Imbert of Beaujeu, who as Constable of France was one of the country's leading knights. Along with the master of the King's cross-bowmen, who was also in the camp, the force protecting it should certainly be capable of resisting the Egyptian counter-assault.

But some of the defenders charged onto the offensive. Fired up by the adrenaline rush of imminent battle, one knight, Walter of Autreche, quickly armed himself. He dressed himself in his armour in his tent, and then ordered that his great war-horse be brought to him. He took up his shield and put on his helmet. Then he dug his spurs into the side of his horse and charged headlong at the enemy.

It was a courageous act, but also a stupid one. The attack of one headstrong knight, acting on his own initiative, was doomed to fail. He charged onwards, shouting his battle cry, 'Chatillon', at the top of his voice. However, as he approached the Muslim forces his horse threw him. He fell to the ground, stunned and defenceless, whilst his horse charged after the enemy without its rider (the knight's steed was a stallion; the Muslim cavalry, as was usually the case, was largely composed of mares; for the stallion, the attraction was too much to resist).

As he lay prone, four Muslim soldiers approached him and bat-tered him, still in his armour, persistently with their maces. Back in the camp, others had seen the knight's foolhardy actions and rushed to his rescue. The Constable and a small group of other knights rushed to his aid. Their presence was enough to drive off the enemy and Walter was taken, senseless, back to the camp.

Medical aid was summoned. It was of a fairly basic nature. The medical support on offer to western armies at this time was renowned for its crudity, and was infinitely worse than that available to Muslim or Byzantine armies. Often, the main medical aid was provided by virtually untrained priests and only a handful of relatively skilled doctors would be available to the army.

Some basic remedies were available – for example, simple fractures were dealt with by packing the damaged limbs in a herbal poultice – but medical knowledge was not at an advanced level. When the doctors arrived, they considered that Walter was in no imminent danger of dying, although his situation was serious. They therefore directed that he should be bled in both arms.

Later that evening, de Joinville made his way to the camp to enquire after the health of Walter. The knight was famed for his bravery and de Joinville particularly wished to see him. Entering his tent, his servants asked them to approach his bed of fur skins quietly so that they did not wake him. As they approached his side, they saw to their sadness that he had in fact expired. Although the loss of a valiant and renowned knight presumably caused great distress to other Crusaders, King Louis for one was not sympathetic. In his view, the rashness of the knight's actions was solely responsible for his death.

This was only the beginning of the attacks on the Crusaders' camp. Regular night-time raids followed. Many Crusaders lost their lives as a result. In one attack, the sentinel of the Lord of Courtenay was killed at his table, and his decapitated corpse left behind in the tent as evidence of the deed (the decapitation was not just violent bravado: the Egyptian leadership paid a gold piece for each Christian head delivered to them). In an attempt to protect the camp, the Crusaders had deployed mounted patrols as sentries. However, this measure was not successful as the raiders merely waited until they had passed before launching a raid to their rear when they had gone.

Consequently, a large number of men were posted as sentries on foot. They were very close together, which helped to protect the camp. Louis took further measures, erecting a large earthwork round the camp to prevent a mounted raid by the Egyptians. On these earthen ramparts, he placed crossbowmen as a further deterrent to the enemy. Matthew Paris notes that the situation became very serious for Louis and the army 'surrounded with trenches, in need and destitute of all kind of provisions'.[3]

There were many Egyptians in the hills around the city who were a constant source of harassment to the Crusaders. A large force of 500 knights was delegated to guard Damietta itself protecting, amongst others, Queen Margaret and her ladies in waiting as well as Eudes of Chateauroux. The position of the Crusaders worsened when the Sultan sent galleys from Alexandria to harass the army's supply lines across the Eastern Mediterranean.[4]

The King was also in need of money. Maintaining the army was already proving costly. The despatch of more funds to Louis from the vast amount collected for the Crusade in the West was timely indeed. Eleven long wagons, each drawn by four powerful horses, had been loaded with gold and silver coins and taken by sea on Genoese vessels along with desperately needed provisions for the army. There were two great casks on each wagon each loaded with the coins, which Matthew Paris stuffily declared 'had been extorted over a three-year period from the goods of the Church'.

Such help would, however, have been much appreciated by the Crusade, who were according to Matthew now seriously short of food, so much so that they began to eat their horses. This was a serious matter for the French then, as now, were renowned as 'people who are clean and fastidious in food and drink', but they were now forced to eat 'dirty and detestable food'. Some of the Crusaders became so desperate that the English chronicler claimed that they crossed over to Muslim lines, in certain cases disowning their faith rather than starve to death. According to him, in return for their desertion and the intelligence about the Crusade's future plans that they willingly gave to the Egyptians, the deserters were provided with rations, and some of them were even generously endowed with wives and castles.

Louis was still unprepared to move until reinforcements had arrived from the West, in particular the force commanded by his brother, Alphonse, Count of Poitiers. The force from England did arrive in August 1249, led by William Longspee, son of the Countess of Salisbury. Although only a fraction of the French force in terms of size, it was nevertheless a welcome addition (Matthew Paris estimates that it numbered two hundred knights). Louis received them graciously, glad of any reinforcements. He placed them amongst his picked men, and asked that all parties might refrain from indulging in the traditional Anglo-Franco rivalry.

Sadly, his injunctions were ignored. The inherent distrust that both parties felt for each other would not be undone just by kind words – after all, the English and the French had been involved in bitter warfare not long before the Crusade had set out. There would soon be problems. Matthew Paris, hardly an objective judge, blamed the French for their jealousy at the superior prowess of the English. The truth of course was quite different. The English were unwilling to be ordered around by the French King (Henry III of England had taken steps before the English force left for the East to ensure that they retained an independent command) and would only co-operate if it were in their own interests to do so. With such strong-willed personalities involved, a fall-out was only a matter of time.

Inevitably a breach soon occurred. With undoubted patriotic jingoism, Matthew Paris places the blame for this fully with the French.[5] They were, according to him, incensed when William took possession of a tower close to Alexandria, an act that 'caught [the French] completely unawares … because of this, his renown, and fear of him, flew even to distant parts of the East'. The French enviously attempted to destroy his reputation, apparently even shocking King Louis, who attempted to dissuade his subjects from alienating such an invaluable ally in the process. Of course, a degree of caution should be exercised in relying on the information of Matthew too much as he undoubtedly brings a great deal of subjectivity to his relation of these events.

There is no reason to doubt though the broad outline of Matthew's account when he relates the incident that caused the complete breakdown of relationships between the French and the English contingent. William learnt through espionage of a caravan, fully laden with great riches, that was planning to make its way to Alexandria. He lay in wait for the merchants, marching on them at night and catching them completely unawares. In a lightning attack, he swooped on the caravan. Resistance was brief, although one knight and eight other men were lost in the attack. Within minutes, the caravan was overwhelmed, the merchants were despatched on the spot and the escorts killed, captured or driven away. The treasures carried by this caravan were rich indeed. As well as provisions (of immense practical importance to the Crusaders) there were gold, silver and spices.

William returned to the camp at Damietta in triumph. It was undoubtedly a singularly successful raid. However, the French were outraged by the coup. They berated William for launching a raid on his own initiative, against the dictates of King Louis who did not approve of such rash actions. They were presumably also far from impressed at missing out on a share of what was a very valuable haul.

In an attempt to pacify them, William offered to distribute the food amongst the whole army but, not satisfied with this compromise, they took all his booty. William appealed to Louis for restitution but, although the King was sympathetic, he was berated by his brother Robert of Artois for his soft words towards the Englishman. In sorrow, Louis turned to William and told him that he could not help him as, because the Crusade must be held together at all costs, he must not risk alienating the Frenchmen who formed the backbone of his army. Therefore, he could do nothing to improve his position.

Furious, William took himself and his troops back onboard ship and sailed across to Acre, where he was not slow to tell all the important men that he met of the perfidy of the French. William declared that he would on no account rejoin the Crusade but he would eventually return to it before it recommenced its advance on Cairo. He would have cause to regret this about-turn.

Matthew again gives a one-sided account of the events that led to William's departure but it is perhaps not too difficult to discern most of what really happened. That the raid took place, and that it was successful, is easy enough to believe. That it was contrary to Louis's general wishes is also very probable. The King was certainly against any rashness on the part of his army, as he wished to avoid the risk of unnecessary losses frittered away in actions that were of secondary importance to the aims of the expedition as a whole. Such an approach had been at the forefront of his strategy thus far. And he was also a practical man and any booty was needed to help fund the Crusade, a very expensive operation, and he would therefore have wanted to obtain a sizeable share of it.

It is therefore very believable that, once the raid had been success-fully completed, the French were especially keen to have an equal share of the spoils. Such an arrangement was not uncommon during the Crusading period; Richard I of England and Philip Augustus of France had, for example, agreed to split the spoils of war equally during the Third Crusade. And the sharing of booty of course had been a point of contention at Damietta recently.

However, the real issue was a much deeper one. William had acted independently because Henry III of England had specifically taken measures to ensure that this was an autonomous expedition, in no way under the control of the King of France. Indeed, it was unthink-able that the English force would be answerable to the French. On the other hand, Louis would certainly have wished them to become part of his army and to act in co-ordination with it, if not under his direct orders. The major reason for this fall-out then was in all prob-ability part of a wider power struggle over how the English force should act, and to whom they should be responsible.

This was a crucial point. Past Crusades had been dogged by the problems of a divided command. The first had been riven with dis-sension amongst the leaders of what were a number of different forces. The second had been marked by a lack of coordination between the Emperor of Germany, Conrad, and Louis VII of France. The Third had been problematic with Philip of France and Richard I of England fail-ing to see eye-to-eye: the lack of common purpose was later emphasised when Richard was held to ransom because of the actions of a former Crusading partner when making his way back home. Many other expe-ditions, not credited with a 'number' in the format traditionally applied by historians had also seen problems because of a lack of co-ordination.

Matthew's account also tells us something of a more personal nature. The villain of this particular piece is very clearly the King's brother, Robert of Artois. After the English sailed away in a huff, Robert was reported to have reacted with a laugh, saying that 'the army of fine Frenchmen is well rid of these people', though Matthew's version of events undoubtedly caricatures Robert as the anti-hero of the Crusade, and certainly exaggerates his actions and words as an example of the poetic license of a storyteller.

But Matthew is not alone in his views of the Count. De Joinville also tells us that he had great influence over his brother and suggests that he had a passionate and powerful nature. Robert is perhaps an all-too convenient scapegoat. Equally though there is some evidence that the Count was a powerful and sometimes disruptive influence who was capable, if he were given too free a rein, of leading the Crusade towards disaster. It is also clear that nationalist tensions were playing their part too. Nation states as we now understand them were still evolving at the time but it is interesting to note that the accounts suggest that patriotic tensions between Englishman and Frenchman was clearly in evidence. Some things, as they say, never change.

Autumn passed and still there was no sign of Alphonse of Poitiers. Louis became increasingly perturbed, fearing that if his brother did not arrive soon he might have to push on towards the heart of Egypt without him. Perhaps the lessons of the Crusade of 1218 were a source of concern to the King. That particular expedition had ended in fiasco partly because the army began to fall apart when it was inactive for too long. It was necessary to push on soon or the disruptive cocktail of boredom and apathy would inevitably start to cause stresses and strains within the army.

Seeing that Louis was anxious because of the late arrival of his brother, de Joinville reminded him that this might be an appropriate time to ask for divine intervention. He remembered the priest onboard ship who had told the pilgrims when they were becalmed off the coast of North Africa en route to the East that they should hold a procession for three successive Saturdays to win God's favour.

Knowing that his prayers had been answered on that previous occasion, de Joinville suggested that the King should try the same approach once more.

The King, being a deeply religious man, was very taken with the idea. Accordingly, on three successive Saturdays a great procession wound its way through the streets of Damietta, the ceremony culminating in the newly-founded Cathedral of Our Lady (previously the Great Mosque) with the legate, Eudes of Chateauroux, preaching an inspiring sermon. In the intervening weeks, a great storm blew up which caused significant damage to the fleet at anchor off Damietta. According to de Joinville, 240 ships were lost along with their crews.

This was a very serious blow to the Crusade, but it might well have become a disaster if Alphonse of Poitiers had been just about to reach Damietta when the gale struck. However, before the procession was held on the third Saturday, wonderful tidings reached Louis at his headquarters. Alphonse, his brother, had arrived at last. And, given the fact that he had managed to miss the terrible storm, his timing was just about perfect.

The arrival of this prominent man with a good number of reinforcements was a great fillip for the Crusade. Louis's spirits lifted as he was reunited with his brother. It was a double blessing: more troops to add to the cause and the arrival of a much-loved brother, too. Louis summoned a council of war, instructing all his leading advisors and major barons to attend and agree on a plan of action.

It comes as something of a shock to find that the next objectives of the Crusade were the subject of deep debate at this moment in time. Louis had been in Damietta for months, and had had ample time to decide on his next move. But at the council there were divided views about what this should be. Quite why they had not taken this opportunity of these months of inactivity to sort something out is not clear.

Many of the barons argued that the King should now move on Alexandria. However, this was a controversial strategic choice. If Alexandria was the target, it could well have been chosen ahead of

Damietta in the first place. To lay siege to the port now meant that the army would have to move along the coast and further away from Cairo, the capital of Egypt. It might well have to lay siege to the city for months before it fell, and it would also be exposed to being attacked from the rear by Muslim forces. It made the chances of success more difficult. Some argued that what was needed was a quick strike at the heart of Egypt before the Muslims could recover their balance after the loss of Damietta. Delay would give the enemy more time to prepare and strike back.

Although a number of the barons preferred Alexandria as the next target of the Crusade, others argued fiercely against it. Most prominent of the dissentients was Robert, Count of Artois, Louis's brother. He was a headstrong man, of passionate disposition with oratorical skills to match. His outspoken words obviously had a powerful impact on his listeners. For him, Babylon (the name by which Cairo was known to the Crusaders) was the capital of Egypt. As such, it was the focal point of the country. And if the Crusade 'wanted to kill the serpent, it must first crush its head'.[6] In other words, if Cairo were to fall, then Egypt would follow suit as surely as if the heart of the country were to stop beating.

On this occasion, logic was on Robert's side. Egypt was the Nile, and the army that controlled both Damietta and Cairo controlled much of the river, which acted as the arteries along which nearly all of the commerce of the country flowed. Further, as the political capital of the Egyptian regime, the loss of the city would be devastating to the morale of the ruling caste. Swayed by both the passion and the logic of his brother's arguments, Louis acceded to his advice. The time for debate was over. The army would move on Cairo.

It was a formidable challenge. Although the advance would be made during a time of year when the local weather was not at its most ferocious, the Eastern climate did pose real problems for Western soldiers with their heavy armour. Armour in the West was at a stage of transition from protection based around chain mail to full plate armour. The basic protection of the knight was a hauberk, a coat of chain mail, on top of which they would wear a surcoat. Plate armour was used to protect the legs (armour known as the *chauces de fer*) and the shoulders (*espaliéres*).

Underneath the hauberk a padded tunic known as the *gambisson* was worn. Helmets would be in several forms, such as the pot helmet, known as the *heaume à visière*, though other types were used. Horses, a hugely expensive commodity of which most knights would have several, would also be protected by armour. The knights' primary weapons were the sword, the dagger, the lance and a vicious spiked iron head on the end of a long handle, known as the *mace turquese*.

The combined weight of this equipment presented a considerable challenge to the knights. The heat of the East could quickly dehydrate them, on occasion causing collapse or even death. During the battle at Mansourah which would subsequently took place as part of Louis's campaign, a number of the soldiers would be desperate for water whilst the fighting was at its peak, and Louis himself would have to stop and take off his helmet to get some air.

Neither was the terrain conducive to their style of warfare. The knights would particularly struggle if they were required to fight on sand (probably an element in their disastrous performance at the earlier battle at La Forbie) as their cumbersome bulk was ill-suited to moving quickly and effectively on such a surface. Warfare in the East was certainly not without its problems for Louis's army.[7]

As the holy season of Advent began, the Christian host prepared itself to move south from Damietta towards Cairo. No doubt exultant at the prospect of going onto the offensive once more, the knights mounted their steeds of war and the foot soldiers marched with a spring in their step towards the heart of Egypt. The road to Cairo was not however a straightforward one. In this part of the Nile Delta, there were many small canals to cross. These formed difficult obstacles to the progress of the Crusade, and they might also act as focal points for an Egyptian force to obstruct the onward passage of the Christian army.

Further, in the season of the annual inundation, they were liable to fill up quickly. They might both be used as an obstacle to the retreat of the Crusade should it have to fall back, and also a means of moving enemy troops to their rear if the Egyptians used shallow draft shipping to transport them. The timing of the flood was well known to the Crusaders, and had influenced both the strategy of the current campaign and the previous Crusade in the country. Progress during the period of inundation would have been very difficult, and close to impossible. Such considerations played a part in Louis's decision not to push on immediately from Damietta after its early fall.

The army had not travelled far from Damietta before it was faced with its first obstacle. This was a small stream, branching off the main waterway of the Nile. To a great army, accompanied by its extensive baggage train, it was a barrier that could not simply be forded. The army therefore had to halt whilst the engineers with it built a dam across the stream. It was not a major operation and was completed in a day. However, the delay did allow the Egyptians time to prepare a hostile reception committee to impede further progress. When the stream was eventually traversed the army crossed to find itself faced by a force that included 500 of the Sultan's knights.

On 6 December 1249, Louis instructed the Crusade to recommence its advance. He issued strict instructions that, despite any attacks that might be launched by the Muslims, the army should keep its order at all times. No doubt aware that the indiscipline of Western knights had cost many a Christian soldier his life in the past, Louis was anxious that the army should maintain its formation. News of these orders reached the Egyptians, as they had managed to infiltrate spies into the Crusaders' camp. They saw that, as the Christian army advanced, it made no effort to drive away the enemy forces that were lurking in the vicinity. Emboldened by this, the enemy began to snipe at the edges of the force.

The Templars were in the vanguard of the army. These renowned, bearded warriors who had won the respect of their enemies in the region by their reputation for bravery in battle, were the shock troops of the Crusade. It was therefore logical that they should be at the head of the army and it was a position that they often held.

But they also had a reputation for arrogance and occasional bouts of recklessness.

One of the Egyptians charged into their ranks and brought down a Templar Knight, right at the feet of the Marshal of the Temple, Renaud de Vichiers. The Templars did not like passive resistance at the best of times. The psychology of the Western knight was ill suited to the philosophy of defence. Nurtured on a diet of tales of impetuous valour in battle, such meek passivity sat uncomfortably with the way that they thought and fought.

The unhorsing of his Templar brother was more than Renaud de Vichiers could bear. He had had quite enough of this passive approach. The clerics could turn the other cheek if they liked, but it was no way for a knight to carry himself in battle. The Marshal turned to his comrades, and shouted to them:

Out on them for God's sake! I cannot brook this.[8]

Then he levelled his lance at the enemy and charged. His comrades needed no further urging. Their horses were fresh, whilst those of the enemy, which had travelled some way to confront the Crusade, were tired. Further, it appears that the Muslims had become complacent and had placed themselves too close to the Christian army.

As one, the Templars rushed headlong at the Egyptians. The Egyptians may have tried to form a defensive line against them, but it would have been like trying to stop a tidal wave. A charge by heavily armoured Western knights, bristling with arms and protected by their virtually impenetrable outer shell, was, when launched in a confined space, irresistible.

As the Christian knights crashed into the Egyptian lines, the latter disintegrated. Swamped in the resulting melee, the Egyptians were struck down by the score. Some broke away from the murderous scrum and attempted to flee. However, when they tried to cross the river, the currents were too strong and, weighed down by their armour, they drowned. According to de Joinville, not one of the enemy force escaped.

Despite the fact that the counter-attack had been completely contrary to Louis's orders it had been devastatingly successful. The reputation of Western arms would certainly be enhanced by this overwhelming victory, although the fact that the Templars had so soon lost their discipline was a worry. On a different day, in a different battlefield environment, such rash courage might result in a very different outcome. Nevertheless, for most of the Crusading host this was a wonderful, a God-given, victory.

Ahead now lay the promise of adventure, plunder and glory. Babylon lay before them, the viper's nest, one of the great cities of the demonic Empire that they had come to overthrow. God was with them, and that was of great comfort to them as they contemplated the dangers yet to come. They were perhaps unaware of the fact that they were still faced with immense obstacles before they realised their dream. Several barriers lay before them, each of them presenting an individual challenge for the Crusade in the days to come.

One of them was Mansourah, the city built specifically with a view to defending the road to Cairo. Although they were wise enough to realise that some Christian blood must be shed before they feasted in the Egyptian capital, the Crusaders underestimated the scale of the challenge yet to be surmounted. The Crusade had started spectacularly well but it was a false dawn. Things were about to go badly wrong.

7

Massacre at Mansourah

The Crusaders advanced towards Mansourah. As the city had been built specifically as a major obstacle defending the approaches to Cairo, it was always likely that the attack there would be the defining moment of the campaign. If the city fell, the way to Cairo would be open. If on the other hand it were to be held, then the Crusader advance on Cairo would be halted and the Crusade must fail. In such an eventuality, the only option open to the Crusaders would be a race to escape back to Damietta. On the success or otherwise of the next stage of the campaign Louis's reputation would stand or fall.

Already, the defenders of Mansourah had taken time to strengthen the defences. Aware that they were on the most likely lines of advance for Louis's army, the Muslim army had been busy. Ibn Wasil tells us:

... the wall facing the Nile was rebuilt and faced with a curtain wall, galleys and fire-ships [were] brought up, loaded with ammunition and troops and anchored under the wall, and uncountable numbers of irregular infantry and volunteers for the faith flocked to Mansourah. A number of Bedouin Arabs also came and began to make raids and attacks on the Franks.

These raids had already taken effect in the period of months that elapsed between the fall of Damietta in June 1249 and the time that they left the city to move on Mansourah in November of that year. One raid on 13 July resulted in the capture of forty-six Franks, whilst several others each resulted in a similar number of captives being taken.[1]

On 24 November 1249 Ayub, Sultan of Egypt, died. Matthew Paris asserts that he was highly unpopular with his people, being 'proud and greedy and unjust to all'.[2] As a result, according to the chronicler, he was poisoned by one of his own citizens. He also relates that shortly before his death the Sultan had offered to strike a deal with the Crusaders if they would leave Egypt alone. In return for their withdrawal, he would give them Jerusalem and the surrounding region as well as all the Christian slaves he held. Louis was, in this narrative, prepared to accept what he regarded as generous terms but the intransigence of Robert of Artois, who demanded that Alexandria should be handed over as well, caused the deal to fall through.

The apparent generosity of the offer suggests a cautious interpretation of Matthew's account; if Ayub were to make such a suggestion, it would in turn lead to a serious counter-reaction from his own people who would consider the Sultan to have shown great weakness and cowardice in his dealings with the Crusaders. It is probable that the chronicler's information is, in this as in some other instances, more fanciful than factual.

The army advanced on Mansourah but it was soon faced with the most difficult obstacle yet. Barring further progress was a wide and deep stretch of water that the Crusaders had to cross if they were to advance further. The city stood on the eastern bank of the Nile and was separated from the stretch of land on which Damietta stood by a canal, the Ashmun Tannah. The only way that Louis could continue his progress was to somehow find a way across it.

He decided to construct a causeway. Aware that the engineers responsible for its construction would be subject to incessant attack from the Muslims on the opposite side of the river, he built two 'cats castles' to protect them. These were large roofed structures which could be moved on wheels. Their aim was to protect those involved in mining or engineering works.

The thirteenth century had seen some particularly large examples of these mobile shields. Simon de Montfort had used one during the Albigensian Crusade that was big enough to accommodate 400 knights and 150 archers. It was made of iron, steel and wood.[3] Louis also built two towers to act as further protection for his men on what would undoubtedly be a dangerous mission. As construction of these protective devices progressed, the artillery duel between the catapults of both sides intensified. Constant guard was kept on the castles and towers as they were being constructed to ensure that the enemy did not cause them irreparable damage.

As soon as the edifices intended to protect the engineers had been completed, the causeway proper could be built. The Muslim artillery aimed their missiles at the men bringing up earth for the causeway's construction. As this was not particularly successful, the Muslims opted for a simple alternative. As the causeway advanced into the river, the Muslims merely dug away the bank opposite so that the Crusaders never got any closer to crossing over to the other side. By this simple expedient, in a single day, they undid the Crusaders' three weeks' progress.

Even more worrying for the Crusaders was the fact that the Muslims had also managed to gather forces to attack their camp. One particularly ferocious assault took place on Christmas Day. Festivities were rudely interrupted by news that the Muslims were attacking and had killed several of the army already. A counter-attack was launched that succeeded in rescuing a prominent Crusader, Peter of Avallon, who had been struck to the ground in a fierce mêlée. The Crusaders then returned to camp in good order, the Templars covering their retreat in a disciplined fashion.

The attacks continued, and the assaults of the enemy became more urgent as further progress was made on the causeway. The bombardment of the Muslim artillery became increasingly ferocious, focusing particularly on the towers that protected the engineers. From the upper storeys of these, crossbow fire raked the enemy on the far shore. However, the damage caused by the Muslim's missiles was considerable. They brought up their petraries[4] so close to the shoreline that they created havoc with the Crusaders, both those on the towers and those on the causeway. So far, these machines had only been used at night to protect them from the counter-attacks of the Crusaders but the situation was now dangerous enough to merit risking them in the daylight.

These petraries now employed one of the most feared weapons in the medieval armoury. Greek fire was a concoction that, once alight, was very difficult to put out due to its chemical composition. It was a weapon that had been known for centuries, since the Byzantines had saved themselves from Muslim assaults on Constantinople during the eighth century. It made a huge impact on those who it was aimed at, one Russian commentator who had witnessed its use during the eleventh century describing it as 'lightning from Heaven'.

Its effectiveness meant that its actual composition was kept a very close secret, though descriptions of its effect suggest the inclusion of materials such as petroleum, resin and saltpetre. It was first used by a Western force in 1151. Various recipes were used to manufacture it, an Arab writer of the time suggesting that ingredients such as naphtha, olive oil and lime should be used (he also suggested that dolphin fat should be utilised).

The Muslims now hurled their own particular brand of Greek fire at the towers of the Crusaders. Flames quickly took hold of the highly combustible engines. In this hot, dry climate (even December is a relatively warm month in Egypt compared to Western Europe) the fire spread rapidly. Soon fire was licking the sky and the sound of crackling wood could be heard over the din of battle. When the Christian knights in the immediate vicinity saw this, they were beside themselves with rage but were powerless to do anything about it.[5]

Louis resorted to a desperate measure in response. In an attempt to ford the stream so that the Crusade could cross over more quickly and rid the bank of this troublesome enemy he searched around for more wood to build a replacement. The only immediately available source of building materials was the timber of the ships that had accompanied the expedition down river. A number were ripped apart so that a new tower could be built. This was kept well away from the enemy for the time being.

After a short respite Louis decided that he must risk this new tower. No doubt frustrated at what was now a worrying delay whilst he had attempted in vain to cross the river, Louis ordered it to be pushed onto the causeway. The Egyptians were however ready for this. They had no less than sixteen engines arrayed along the opposite shore with a view to repulsing the Crusaders and foiling them in their attempts to approach Mansourah.

A storm of missiles rained down on the Crusaders. The battle cries of those involved in the fierce fire-fight were regularly interrupted by the sound of boulders crashing into timber and the sickening thud of crossbow bolts driven into flesh and bone with brutal force. The missile shower was so intense that few Crusaders dared approach close to the tower, as this would require them to pass through what was now effectively a killing zone.

Within a very short time, those that manned the tower were faced once more with the terrifying vision of pots of Greek fire heading for them high in their lofty tower. Within minutes, this new tower was ablaze. Not long after, it was little more than a heap of smouldering timbers. All that was left to show for Louis's great efforts in building the tower, which had involved the sacrifice of a significant part of the fleet, was a blackened pile of charcoal.

But the Crusade's luck was about to change for the better. An old ally was about to come to their aid – treachery. A Bedouin had approached a knight, Imbert of Beaujeu. In return for monetary reward, he would show the Crusade where they might ford the river in relative safety. Wanting to ensure that the Crusaders kept to their part of the bargain, the Bedouin refused to tell them where this ford was until his blood money was safely deposited in his hands. Agreeing to comply with this request, the Crusaders duly assembled the money and handed it over.

The Bedouin kept his side of the bargain. Louis divided his army, leaving a strong guard under Count Peter of Brittany to watch over the camp. The attacking force would be led by the Templars and Count Robert of Artois in the vanguard. Their role would be to secure the crossing so that the rest of the army might cross over in some kind of safety. The honour of leading the troops was given to the Templars, with Robert of Artois following at the head of the second column.

It was a mark of great prestige to be given the vanguard to lead; on such apparently trivial details are wars won and lost, as would soon be discovered. Although we lack detailed battle orders for those at the head of the army, their role is clear enough. They were certainly there to fight off resistance near the crossing point. However, once they had done so they should hold the crossing for others to follow behind them. On no account should they abandon their position, whatever tempting targets they saw. Such a strategy required only a modicum of common sense and self-discipline to be put into effect.

The first part of the operation went well enough. As the first rays of the dawning sun tinted the Egyptian sky with its orange hues, the Crusader army moved towards the river, steeling itself for a decisive engagement. With the help of the Bedouin who had been bribed to assist them, the ford was found, and the vanguard crossed. There were even now a few alarms. By the time that the horses were in mid-stream, the water was shallow enough for them to stand. However, the banks on the far side of the river were slippery and fairly steep, and a few horses lost their footing and fell, throwing their riders, causing several of them to drown in the process.

But the opposition that the vanguard faced was brushed aside. The enemy saw that the Christian army was crossing in force, and broke and fled. The next move of the vanguard should have been to defend the crossing so that the King and the rest of his army could also traverse the river in safety. But seeing the Egyptians streaming away in blind terror and noting the panic-stricken retreat, Robert of Artois smelt the scent of glory. Its intoxicating aroma was far too strong for the headstrong prince to resist. Stopping only to encourage the Crusading army to follow him, Robert charged headlong after the fleeing Muslims. And so, on the morning of 8 February 1250, the Crusade began to plummet down the steep slope towards disaster.

Robert de Artois' actions placed the Templars in a quandary. They were led by their Master, William de Sonnac. He was an experienced warrior who had more than enough knowledge to know that he should stay and defend the crossing. However, he was the leader of a very proud organisation who prized honour above all other virtues. They had been given the vanguard to lead and now their place had been assumed by the reckless Count. It looked like cowardice rather than prudence to stand still whilst other knights were throwing themselves headlong into battle.

William was also fairly new to the role of Grand Master. He had been elected in 1247, following the death of Richard de Bures, the previous holder of his position. Bures had himself only been Master for three years, his predecessor having been killed at La Forbie. Aware of the potential slur on the honour of his Order, de Sonnac begged Robert to desist from his pursuit. If the Count decided to proceed with his plan to press on, then it was clear that de Sonnac would find himself under immense pressure to follow him.

According to Matthew Paris,[6] a furious row now broke out. The Count turned on the Master, berating him for his lack of courage. Others, more prudent than Robert, also attempted to calm his excitement. Prominent amongst them was the Englishman, William Longspee, who had returned from Acre in time to join the advancing Crusader army. But all efforts to persuade the Count to stay where he was failed. He turned once more on the Templars, angrier than ever, accusing them of all kinds of falsehood and treason.

To a man like William de Sonnac, inculcated with the code of honour that underwrote his Order, such gibes could not go unanswered. Infuriated by the insults of the Count, and against his better judgement, he turned to his standard bearer and told him to unfurl the battle-flag of the Templars. He turned his mount towards the fleeing Muslims. Then he led his men in a ferocious charge at the enemy. The sight must have been breathtaking but – to plagiarise a later military commentator – '*c'est magnifique mais ce n'est pas la guerre*'.

It was a fatal decision, although the seriousness of this incident did not immediately manifest itself. It was certainly clear that the army – or at least those in its vanguard – were rapidly spiralling out of control and that the battle-plan of King Louis was already seriously compromised. They had completely ignored their responsibility to guard the crossing so that others could follow in their wake. Unfortunately, few of them had enough wits about them in the heat of battle, with the next breath potentially their last, to coolly assess the situation. They were completely taken over by the events taking place around them.

The Crusaders chased the fleeing Muslims back towards their camp, outside the walls of Mansourah. Those in the camp included the vizier of Egypt, Fakhr ad-Din. He was in his bath, having his beard dyed with henna, when he heard a great commotion outside. Suspecting trouble, he ran out to see what was happening without putting on his armour. He found himself surrounded by a party of Templars who hacked him to pieces. He fell to the ground lifeless. It was a dramatic conclusion to an outstanding career, resulting in the elimination of an individual who, in the historian Ibn Wasil's opinion, had 'ambition that reached to the throne itself'.[7]

The camp was completely unsuspecting when the Crusaders attacked. Their charge hit like a thunderclap. Before many of the Muslims even had chance to understand the immediate danger, the Crusaders had rolled over the camp like an angry sea, flattening it in the process. Those of the Egyptians who were not cut down fled in terror towards the open gates of Mansourah.

In fairness to Robert of Artois, for all that his actions were rash they were so far stunningly successful. One of the leading men in Egypt now lay with the life flowing out of him in the ruins of a camp that had been completely overrun. Robert of Artois was on the verge of a spectacular victory, in fact he had already won one. The Crusaders, exultant and triumphant, were now approaching the decisive moment of the decisive battle of the entire Crusade. By their next decision they could either consolidate a wonderful triumph or turn overwhelming victory into catastrophic defeat.

The Crusaders watched as the enemy escaped in chaos through the open gates of Mansourah. Now more than ever their role was to stay where they were, consolidate their gains and enable the rest of the army to come up and join them. But still the gates of the city were ajar. Mansourah appeared to be there for the taking, with its defenders in a state of terror and abject confusion. Again there was a debate, with a number of voices once more advocating restraint. The end result was the same. Now completely convinced that he was destined to win the Crusade virtually single-handed, Robert bluntly told the other leaders that he would go on into Mansourah whether they joined him or not.

The recklessness of the Count again won the day. Matthew Paris is quick to point an accusatory finger solely at Robert of Artois, but in doing so oversteps the mark. There were a number of other leaders present of great experience who were more than capable of making their own decisions. Virtually without exception, despite their reservations, they all joined in the subsequent foray into the city. Motivated by thoughts of honour and glory, there was a collective culpability about this complete loss of discipline. Euphoric at the prospect of imminent, crushing, comprehensive victory, a wave of Christian steel swept towards the gates of the city.

The vanguard of Louis's army stormed through the gates of Mansourah. The Crusader knights were moving out of their natural environment, the wide-open spaces where their mobility could be used to overwhelming effect. Instead, the impetus of their charge was quickly lost in the narrow streets and restricted spaces of the city. The defenders of the city had been hurriedly reorganised following the death of Fakhr ad-Din.

Although in the current chaotic situation there would have been no time to formally adopt a new commander, one man above all others was prominent in the rapidly organised defence of Mansourah. He was a huge bear of a man, a Mameluke who had already caused much grief to the Crusaders' cause on a previous occasion. His name was Rukn ad-Din Baibars. Those who had not been present at the disastrous Battle of La Forbie were about to find out what a deadly adversary he was.

Even as the Crusaders charged without direction through the streets, men were placed on the rooftops overlooking the narrow roads that bisected the city. The Christian knights rushed on to the centre of Mansourah, where their progress was halted by a strong defensive force that had been thrown together. This force, composed especially of representatives of two Mameluke regiments known as the Bahrites and the Jamdarites, 'lions in war and mighty in battle, rode like one man upon the enemy in a charge that broke them and drove them back'.[8]

The Crusaders lost their momentum and, after some bitter hand-to-hand fighting, began to fall back. They started to retreat, but when they looked behind them the stark reality of their predicament suddenly dawned on them. Between the Crusaders and safety lay a warren of narrow streets, overlooked by the rooftops of houses that were now alive with defenders. What had seemed like a procession when the Crusaders teemed into the city now looked like a ride of death as they contemplated the journey back. The Crusaders had ridden headlong into a brilliantly organised impromptu trap.

As they fell back, a storm of missiles rained down on them. The defenders, seemingly beaten men shortly before, now reacted as they saw the plight of their foe, caught helplessly in a snare from which there was little possibility of escape. Blocks of wood and masonry were hurled into the struggling mass, along with more orthodox weapons of war. Organised resistance rapidly fell apart. Soon, all that was left were a myriad of individual battles for survival, most of which were lost.

Matthew Paris tells us that the Count of Artois tried to persuade William Longspee to flee with him in an attempt to save their lives but his implications of cowardice are hard to believe. If what we know of Robert suggests that he was a foolhardy man, his actions were generally those of a brave one. In the event, some knights managed to fight their way through to the river where most were lost as they tried in vain to cross to safety whilst still dressed in their heavy suits of armour. Robert paid for his recklessness with his life, one of those drowned.

William Longspee also fell, along with his standard bearer, Robert de Vere, and the vast majority of the English contingent which was decimated on the streets of Mansourah.[9] According to Matthew Paris, the news was not a complete shock to everyone; his mother Ela, Countess of Salisbury and abbess of Lacock, had been told of his death in a vision the night before. William de Sonnac fought heroically and escaped with his life, although he lost an eye in the process, hacked out in the ferocious infighting.

Unfortunately, most of his Templar brethren were even less fortunate. In all, 280 Templar knights died in the streets of Mansourah, in the slow-flowing waters of the river outside the walls or in the fighting leading up to the incursion into the city. It was a huge percentage of the Templars' fighting strength, one of the greatest losses in Crusader history. Coming only a few years after the disastrous losses at La Forbie, it decimated the orders' fighting strength.

They were the shock troops of the Kingdom of Outremer, the cutting edge of its army. Such defeats had a disastrous impact. Not only would they jeopardise the survival of the Crusade, it is debatable whether the Crusader states in the East ever recovered from the huge losses of this period in their history. Of all those present from the Orders, only three of the Templars survived. Five Hospitallers survived the massacre, one of whom later died of his wounds, and three Teutonic Knights. Matthew Paris says that in all 8,000 men of the Crusader army perished. Some of the other Crusader troops that survived the slaughter were terrified by these events and hid in ditches, waiting until night fell before attempting to return to their comrades on the other side of the river.

The Crusaders still crossing the river were not aware of the dramatic events affecting the vanguard. They had problems enough with their own local conflicts. On the riverbanks, a ferocious close-quarters battle was raging with swords and maces hammering away at the enemy. So intense was the fighting that some of the Crusaders attempted to return to the relative safety of the side of the river from which they had crossed but most drowned in the attempt.

De Joinville was in the thick of the action and described how he 'saw the river strewn with lances and shields, and full of men and horses drowning in the water'.[10] He saw that the King himself was right at the heart of the battle. He also noticed a small bridge over a stream near to Louis's position. If the Muslims were to take this bridge, they might well attack the King in flank creating a situation that was full of threat. The chronicler therefore took charge of this particular situation and led the defence of the bridge in person.

The situation was certainly a very dangerous one. After the battle, there were reports that Louis had at one point been close to capture and that several of the Muslim enemy attempted to grab the bridle of his horse and lead him from the field. It was apparently only the personal bravery of Louis that had fought off the immediate threat, striking down those who attempted to drag him away with his great sword. Inspired by his example, many of his men, who had been demoralised by the ferocity of the Muslim's attack on the King, found new heart and fought back all the harder. The immediate threat passed.

At this moment, a party of Crusaders was seen by de Joinville heading straight for the bridge that he was guarding. As they drew closer, their leader could be more clearly seen. Riding a powerful and imposing stallion, blood could be seen running profusely down his face and into his mouth. It was Count Peter of Brittany. He had been struck full in the face with a sword and continued to curse the enemy with dark threats, literally spitting blood in the process. He did not immediately pass on any news of the disaster inside Mansourah to de Joinville.

Close behind came more Muslim forces. They had not apparently noticed de Joinville and his small band of colleagues so far, but now they moved menacingly towards the bridge. De Joinville quickly assembled a small body of reinforcements. One of the men with de Joinville, a knight called Peter of Neuville, was struck senseless when one of the enemy approached him from behind (de Joinville was by this time in danger of being surrounded and cut off) and hit him forcibly with his mace, taking advantage of the confusion caused to gallop across the bridge to the other side of the stream whilst the Crusaders were distracted.

When the Muslims saw that the Crusaders would not be moved from the bridge, they instead attempted to bypass them. Aware of the threat, de Joinville and his comrades made ready to charge at the enemy and disperse them. They were however quickly disabused of this adventurous idea when the Muslims attacked in force. They had assembled a large number of infantrymen to drive the small group of Western knights from the bridge.

Some of them were armed with Greek fire. One of them threw a pot of the lethal substance into the midst of the Crusaders. It hit full on the face of the shield of a knight called William of Boon. The pot shattered on the shield to the great good fortune of the aforesaid William as he would surely have been incinerated, as de Joinville subsequently noted in his account of the battle.

Now Muslim archers were introduced to the battle for the bridge. Their arrows could cause serious wounds even to an armoured knight if fired at close quarters, and if they were lucky enough to find one of the weak-spots in the knight's armour, they were capable of causing mortal injury. At one stage, de Joinville and his comrades literally bristled with the arrows that were embedded in their armour. To help protect himself against this deadly downpour, de Joinville laid hold of the quilt jacket of a Saracen that lay close to hand, and used it as an improvised shield. It was apparently surprisingly effective, although some insight into the brutal nature of Medieval warfare can be gained from de Joinville's comment that he was fortunate to be only wounded by arrows in five different places.

De Joinville's vivid description of some of the scenes that he witnessed add further to the violent images of battle that resonate down the centuries from that fateful day, of a knight called Frederic de Loupey, who was struck by a lance that caused a wound so deep that 'the blood poured from his body as if from the bung-hole of a barrel' or of Erard de Sivery, whose nose was struck by a sword, so that 'it was left dangling over his lips'.[11] This was indeed a ferocious action.

As the afternoon wore on, the intensity of the Muslim counter-attack slackened. As darkness was about to fall, Louis deployed a screen of crossbowmen in front of his line. The crossbow was a terrible weapon, causing immense physical damage to anyone unfortunate enough to be hit by a bolt. So hideous were the injuries inflicted by the weapon that the Papacy had for a time tried to ban it from the field of battle. The Muslims attacking Louis's forces saw these harbingers of death arrive. It was, for them, enough. They took themselves away from the battlefield. The counter-attack had failed. But the news was still very patchy indeed for the Crusaders. Large numbers had been forced back over the river, some forced to attempt to swim back to safety, with many of them drowning in the attempt.

The camp of the Egyptians was in Crusader hands. The Bedouins had taken advantage of the confusion of battle to loot it. Although they were theoretically allies of the Egyptians, and had fought alongside them in the battle, no one was particularly surprised at their actions. De Joinville merely noted in a matter of fact manner that 'it was well known that the use and custom of the Bedouins is always to fall on the weaker side'.[12] Seeing that the Egyptians had lost the camp, the Bedouins were quick to improvise maximum profit from this particular opportunity.

Unaware of the catastrophe that had overtaken the vanguard, to the rest of the army it may at first have seemed like a wonderful victory for the Crusaders. The army had successfully crossed the river and now stood before Mansourah. Beyond lay the road to Cairo, not too far distant. At the beginning of the day, such an outcome would certainly have seemed like a victory. The primary objective of the day's operations had been to get the army across the river, and this objective had been achieved. The Pyrrhic nature of this victory was not yet clear.

Even on the Egyptian side, there was for a while confusion about the outcome of the battle. After the early dramatic successes of the Crusader vanguard's attack, a large number of Muslims had fled away from the city to Cairo. They arrived here at sunset and a gate of the city, the Bab an-Nasr, was left open to allow them to make their way to safety inside the walls on the assumption that a Crusader army would be following close behind, fired on by victory and hungry for more of the same.

But news of the ultimate triumph of the Mamelukes was received in Cairo during the following morning, a Wednesday, to be greeted ecstatically by the population, as 'the city prepared for a feast and the glad tidings were announced by a roll of drums. The victory over the Franks caused great joy and exaltation. This was the first battle in which the Turkish lions defeated the infidel dogs' (clearly, the writer is referring to the current campaign, and does not take account of the successes in earlier years against the Crusaders).[13]

For Louis as well, it took some time for the full import of what had taken place to sink in. Even in modern warfare it is difficult for the commander of an army to know what is going on in every part of the field of battle. It was far more difficult for the medieval commander, who had no technological help in evaluating battlefield progress. He relied on messengers to bring him news, and during the heat of battle it was often difficult for these to get through.

Even during the later stages of that day, the King had no idea about the final fate of his brother, although he had apparently been told earlier on that news had been received that the Count was trapped in a house in Mansourah and needed help. Everywhere the signs of the ferocity of battle were to be seen. The area around Mansourah was littered with corpses, while the eerie twilight, which is extremely short-lived in this part of the world, was rent by the sounds of the badly-injured and the dying, disfigured by hideous wounds for which there was little hope of succour.

Even cures for minor injuries were excruciating. For minor cuts, molten lead might be applied in an effort to stem the flow of blood. The injuries of those wounded were terrifying. Bones would be shattered under the impact of a lustily swung sword or axe whilst others, like the unfortunate William de Sonnac, might be blinded by full-blooded blows to the face.

Soon would come the night, the time for reflection and re-consideration of the day's events. For those that survived, there would be feelings of gratitude that God had let them see another sunset. But there would have been other more negative emotions; sorrow for friends lost, concern for those injured or captured, perhaps even guilt that they had survived whilst others had not. And, of course, fear and uncertainty about the immediate future.

There would be plenty of soul-searching to be done this night in the dust around Mansourah. The cream of the Crusader army lay trampled underfoot in the streets of the city. The Templars, the crack troops of the expedition, had been decimated, their Master in agonies both physical and mental as the pain from his shattered eyes seared through him and diverted him for a few seconds from the awful thoughts of brothers in arms who would never be seen again this side of Paradise. The English contingent, fine fighting men who would have been a great help to the expedition, were to all intents and purposes wiped out, their leader lying dead in the streets of Mansourah. As full details of the catastrophe inside the city became clearer, it became painfully obvious that the cost of this so-called victory was enormous.

Untold numbers of Louis's army lay dead and he was tortured by the lack of news. He waited desperately to find out what had happened to the Count of Artois. By this time, de Joinville had made his way back to his side. He was there when a dust-stained Hospitaller knight entered the King's pavilion. His name was Brother Henri de Ronnay, Provost of the Order. He kissed Louis's mailed hand and waited for the King to begin questioning him, as he had more news of the events inside Mansourah. Louis's first question was direct and to the point – did the messenger have any information about the Count of Artois?

Grimly, the Hospitaller replied to Louis that he knew for a fact that his brother, the Count of Artois, was even now in Paradise. Tears welled up in the King's eyes. His heart felt as if it would break: for all his faults, the Count was a much-loved brother. Seeing that Louis was much moved by this response, the knight bade him consider the wonderful triumph that he had won, by crossing a river under fire, taking on a fierce enemy in battle, driving them from the field, taking their tents and seizing their engines. It was a glorious outcome.

The King knew that all he said was true, but on this day the price of victory seemed far too high. Louis's real feelings were now all too clear for those in his presence to see. As he turned to the Hospitaller and said 'Let God be worshipped for all He has given me',[14] the tears streamed uncontrollably down his cheeks. Louis now knew exactly how extravagant the cost of honour and glory could be.

8

Low–Water Mark

The respite afforded the Crusaders after the battle at Mansourah was to be brief. The whole of Egypt was now very aware of the threat that the Crusade posed. The presence of the Crusaders so close to Mansourah, the gateway to Cairo, was a dagger pointed at the very heart of Egypt. They could not be allowed to stay where they were. A counter-attack was needed to push the Western army back across the river. It would not be long in coming.

After the battle outside of the city, the Crusaders – many of whom were wounded – were exhausted. A large number set up their tents in the camp that they had so recently taken from the Egyptians. De Joinville occupied one that had been given to him by the Templars and he put it close to the Saracen siege engines that had been captured when the camp had fallen.

He lay down and soon fell into a deep sleep, overcome with both tiredness and relief that he lived to fight another day. His slumber was disturbed well before morning. He awoke to find the camp in a state of chaos. The gloom of the pre-dawn hours was pierced by the cry of sentries shouting the alarm. Loud shouts of 'To arms! To arms!' rent the night. Few were in any doubt what this meant. The Muslims were assaulting the camp. The counter-attack had arrived.

De Joinville roused his servant and sent him out to discover what was happening. Terror-stricken, he returned soon after to de Joinville's pavilion. This was no minor raid. It was a major assault comprising both cavalry and infantry. The sentries that King Louis had placed to keep guard over the captured siege engines had already been killed or driven back. Even now, hand to hand fighting was taking place in the heart of the camp.

De Joinville sprang into action. However, he was severely hampered. The wounds that he had received in battle were so bad that he could not put his full armour on. He therefore had to throw on a thick quilted jacket and a steel cap. With other knights in the immediate vicinity, he charged headlong at the Saracens, driving them back past the siege engines, but beyond these was a large body of Muslim horsemen, menacingly facing down the Western knights.

Realising that he was in no position to defend his section of the camp adequately (many of his compatriots were also too badly wounded to put on full armour) he sent to the King for help. Louis responded by sending one of his knights, Gaucher of Chatillon, to assist. His presence was enough to dissuade the Muslim cavalry from attacking. It had been a close-run thing.

Seeing their initial attacks repulsed, the Muslims adopted other tactics. They hastily assembled a small entrenchment by throwing together a wall made of loose rocks and stones. This gave them some measure of protection against the lethal bolts of the crossbowmen. They then shot arrow after arrow into the camp, making a considerable nuisance of themselves, their effectiveness much enhanced because some of their targets were in no fit state to don armour.

Several of the defenders of the camp and some of their horses were injured. The Western knights decided that the troublesome archers could not be left where they were. They held a council and decided that, during the following night, they would advance on the entrenchment under the cover of darkness and remove the stones, thereby depriving the enemy of cover. One of the priests with de Joinville's entourage, John of Voisey, was present at the council. He said little but was soon to prove that actions speak far louder than words.

After the meeting, he walked straight out of the camp alone in the direction of the Muslim archers. He marched towards them with a steel cap on his head and a quilted tunic to protect him. Seeing him unaccompanied and seemingly unarmed, the Muslims believed that some lunatic was making his way out of the Crusader camp. They mocked him for his insanity. They were in for a rude awakening. The priest had hidden a spear and when he was close to the Muslim entrenchment he suddenly charged at them. Caught off guard by this unexpected turn of events, the Muslims panicked and fled.

This was the prelude to a full-scale skirmish. Seeing the successful one-man assault of the priest, a number of Crusaders were encouraged to sally out to his aid. Simultaneously, a group of Egyptian horsemen rushed to help their fleeing comrades. They wheeled around the Western soldiers, who were on foot, seeking for an opening but not closing with them.

After several of these probing manoeuvres, one of the Crusaders flung his spear powerfully at a Muslim horseman, striking him so hard that the weapon lodged in his ribs. The badly injured cavalrymen moved away, and discouraged by this incident his comrades followed him. This left the way clear for the Crusaders. The entrenchment of stones was then disassembled. The priest was henceforward renowned for his fighting prowess, an unusual accolade for a man of God.

These preliminary Muslim raids were merely a precursor to a far more serious attack. The Egyptian leadership paraded the arms of Robert of Artois around their army, telling them that they belonged to King Louis. Their aim was to encourage their troops to greater effort by convincing them that the Crusaders were leaderless. Without Louis at their head, the enemy would be demoralised and would be easily swept aside in battle.

Fortunately for the Crusaders, their spy network inside the Saracen camp was working efficiently. News of plans for a great assault on the camp of the Crusaders reached the ears of the King and his barons who took counter-measures. An enclosure of sharpened stakes had been hastily erected around the camp with the aim of keeping off the enemy cavalry. Orders were given that the Crusader army should assemble, fully armed, inside the camp at midnight to prepare for the attack that seemed imminent.

At dawn, the Muslims prepared to attack. A force of 4,000 mounted troops moved on the camp, supported by a large number of foot soldiers. The force arrayed was large enough to surround the Crusaders. The Muslims deployed their troops carefully, trying to ensure that they made maximum use of their numbers. A group of Bedouins was deployed towards the camp of Count Peter of Brittany, a separate encampment a short distance away. By this attack, they hoped to force Louis to send help to the Count, thereby dividing his force and weakening it.

These deployments took some time, and it was midday before the Muslims were ready to attack. The great kettledrums of the Egyptian army beat out their fierce rhythm, driving the troops on, and then the Muslims charged on the camp. The brunt of this first assault was taken by Charles of Anjou, King Louis's younger brother. The enemy attacked in tandem, interspersing infantry attacks with cavalry charges. The Western knights fought on foot. They were seriously discomfited by this first enthusiastic attack as the foot soldiers bombarded them with deadly jars of Greek fire.

Charles and his troops were rocked back by the ferocity of the assault. Frantic messages were sent to his brother, the King, begging him for help. According to de Joinville, Louis was so moved by his brother's plea that he himself spurred his horse straight into the heaving mass around Charles, personally leading the ferocious counter-assault that drove the Muslims back. He was at one stage in great danger – his horse was burnt by Greek fire during this skirmish – but he was successful in removing the immediate danger.

Along the line, the troops of Outremer – a number of whom had been sent to assist Louis in the expedition – also held firm, led by the brothers Guy and Baldwin of Ibelin.' Despite repeated attacks, the line here did not budge. Other Western troops were not so successful. William de Sonnac had arrayed the pitiful remnant of the Templar contingent that had survived the bloodbath inside Mansourah (a few had not been committed to the attack there) behind a wooden palisade. The timber was highly inflammable, bleached bone dry by the baking sun and the arid heat of the country. Greek fire was thrown at it and it was soon burning uncontrollably.

Even before the flames had died down, the Muslims poured through against the Templars. A vicious battle ensued. Days previously, Grand Master de Sonnac had lost an eye. Now, in this terrible struggle, he lost the other. He was removed from the field of battle to die not long after in agony. The area around the Templars was so heavily under attack that the ground could not be seen for the carpet of arrows that lay on it.

De Joinville had placed himself and his men close to another French knight, Guy of Mauvoisin, and Count William of Flanders – the chronicler was still suffering from the wounds he received in the great battle outside Mansourah and could not contribute much to the defence of the camp as a result. Guy's men were particularly worried by a heavy bombardment of Greek fire. It took them some time to control the resultant conflagration.

The Egyptians then turned their attentions to the Count of Flanders, charging at his troops fiercely. When de Joinville saw this, he directed his crossbowmen to enfilade the enemy in the flank. Once again, the Muslim army was much discomfited by the crossbow bolts and began to fall back. When the Crusaders saw this, they scrambled over the barriers they had erected around the camp and rushed at the enemy. A large number of the enemy were slain, and many prizes of war were taken.

Whilst these troops held firm, there was a scare close by. Alphonse, Count of Poitiers, commanded another part of the line. His men were all on foot, he himself being the only person there on horseback. The Egyptians attacked with much ferocity and for a short space of time they overran the defences. Alphonse was caught up in the melee, his horse was seized and the Muslims started to drag him away.

His capture would have been a great prize for the one side, and a great blow to the morale of the other. Behind the frontline there were a large number of camp followers, non-combatants who nevertheless were integral to the smooth functioning of a medieval army. When they saw that the Count had been captured, they threw themselves into the fray. This sudden and unexpected injection of new resources into the battle swung this particular skirmish the other way. The Egyptians were caught off-guard and the Count of Poitiers was rescued by a motley collection of butchers, smiths, cooks, even women. A catastrophe was narrowly averted.

All along the line, a series of vigorous Muslim assaults was launched. This was an intense and prolonged counter-attack. The only variation along the line was in the degree of ferocity. For example, at one place along the defensive perimeter there was a French knight, Joscelin of Brancion. He had twenty knights in his party (throughout the Crusade most men remained attached to their own individual lord, rather than officially being part of the King's army). Of these, twelve died in the bitter defence of the camp, as well as a large number of their men-at-arms.

Joscelin himself was so badly injured that, although he survived the battle, he never recovered from his wounds and died a short time after. His death fulfilled a personal wish. He had been so distraught whilst he was still in France at the constant wars between Christian neighbours in Western Europe that he knelt before the altar of a church and prayed fervently to God that he would 'take me out of these wars amongst Christians, and grant that I may die in thy service'.[2] God had honoured his plea.

This tremendous onslaught was resisted, although it must have stretched the resilience of the Crusaders to the limit. The ferocity of the Muslim attack was commendable given the political vacuum that existed within the country. Egypt had been rudderless since the demise of the late Sultan Ayub. His son and successor, Turanshah, was far to the East when he died, hundreds of miles away in Syria. An interim government of sorts was set up, but the stability of Egypt had been disturbed again with the death of the vizier, Fakhr ad-Din, in the recent battle.

The army was being led by the Mameluke Baibars, who had political as well as military ambitions. At the end of February 1250, just a couple of weeks after the events at Mansourah, Turanshah at last arrived in Egypt to claim his inheritance. He did not improve matters much, for he brought back his own favourites from the East with him. Traditional allies of the late Sultan were excluded from power. Worst of all, the Mamelukes saw their new ruler attempt to rein back their strength. Turanshah could not have made enemies of a more dangerous group of people.

The Crusaders were now under huge pressure, their forces badly depleted by the recent battles. The massacre in the streets of Mansourah was a dreadful blow to their military resources but the subsequent attempt on the camp by the Muslims was also a costly one for the Crusaders. The assaults had been beaten off but, as well as the loss of life, there were other serious strains on the army. The men were tired after their exertions. Many of them were wounded and with the primitive medical conditions available to the army that in itself could equate to a death sentence.

There was also the moral condition of the men to consider. So buoyed up by the capture of Damietta the previous year, they could have been forgiven for thinking that God was on their side and would grant them complete success in their endeavours. The failure to take Mansourah and move on Cairo – particularly given the fragile state of the Egyptian government during the interregnum following Ayub's death – must have shaken their confidence badly. Doubts began to creep into men's minds, fuelled by the tiredness and nervousness created by their constant need to be on their guard for a Muslim attack at any hour of day or night.

Of course, the problems were not one-sided. Despite the best efforts of the Muslims – and judging by the surviving evidence they were significant – the Crusader army was still stubbornly ensconced dangerously close to Cairo. This would have generated much anxiety amongst many of the Egyptians, particularly given the volatile politics of the region in this difficult period before the new Sultan could establish himself.

The Crusaders had demonstrated their fighting prowess. They were brave warriors, well armed and, in their own environment, fearsome. Not only had the heavy horse of the Crusader army been effective, judging by the frequent mentions in de Joinville's account the crossbow was also demonstrating itself to be a potent weapon. And in the defence of the camp, the cavalry had played a role but not the major one. The defence had been conducted largely by men fighting on foot. King Louis's foot soldiers had proved themselves doughty adversaries, brave, committed and resilient.

The resources available to either side were fairly well balanced. In such a situation, just one or two chance events could tilt the scales decisively in favour of one of the parties. Not long after the terrible battles fought at Mansourah, the river began to give up its dead, and there were many of them. It was soon a mass of putrefying corpses, its waters made rancid by its rotting burden. When the added ingredients of the searing climate and the intense heat of the remorseless sun were also taken into account, the conditions were ripe for a major epidemic.

The Crusaders were painfully aware of the decomposing corpses in the river and attempted to do something about them. It was a painstaking task, made worse by the nauseating state of the bodies. It was difficult to identify many of the badly rotted cadavers over a week after the battle. The Crusaders adopted a simple but effective form of identification. Any corpses of men who had been circumcised were assumed to be Egyptians; they were thrown beyond the pontoon bridge that the Crusaders had built across the river. They would float downstream and decompose well away from the camp. Those that were not circumcised were assumed to be Christians and they were buried in mass graves specially prepared for the purpose.

Matters were about to take a startling turn for the worse. Whether this human detritus was responsible or not is unclear but shortly afterwards disease hit the Christian camp with a vengeance. The symptoms of the illness were dreadfully apparent. The flesh of the legs dried up and ugly sores appeared. The gums of the sufferer receded. In the worst cases, blood was emitted from the nose; in such cases death was almost sure to follow.

It has been suggested[3] that the disease was scurvy and would not therefore have been directly connected with the large number of bodies decomposing in the vicinity of the camp. It is a very plausible diagnosis. The provisions of the army were poor: much of the food was heavily salted to preserve it and fresh food was hard to come by. During the period of Lent, for example, the only fish that the men had eaten were the eels that they had caught from the river.

De Joinville blamed the outbreak of disease in the camp on this, as he believed that the eels had feasted on the carcasses rotting in the river and thereby created an epidemic. But the problems of the army were compounded by another factor. Despite the fact that there were a large number of ships in Damietta that could easily sail down-river to re-supply the Crusaders outside Mansourah, none had arrived to so help the army for many days.

Then one day a wonderful sight was seen through the early morning haze rising above the river. It was a ship making its way towards the Christian army. As it drew close enough to hail, the men onboard shouted that the ship belonged to the Count of Flanders, who was with the army, and they were fresh from Damietta. When they landed, they delivered shattering news.

The reason that no ships had arrived for so long was simple. The Muslims had dragged a number of galleys across land on camelback to a part of the river to the north of the Crusaders and between them and Damietta. They had hidden their ships away in a back-water of the Nile known as the Bahr al-Mahalla, from which they had ambushed a number of Louis's ships attempting to make their way up-river. They had then created a blockade, which had been devastatingly effective. So far, eighty ships had been lost attempting to break through to the Crusaders at Mansourah. Without exception, their captured crews had been taken ashore and executed. Only this one galley had managed to force its way through.

The use of naval power by the Egyptians took them into an environment where they were not at their most comfortable. They were not unfamiliar with maritime matters, particularly given their situation adjacent to the Mediterranean. But militarily they tended to rely almost exclusively on land-based warfare to achieve their objectives. Naval warfare was held in comparatively low esteem, to the extent that many of those who manned the ships of war were convicts or prisoners of war.

During this very campaign, Turanshah himself would be rebuked by the chronicler Ibn Abd al-Zahir for taking a ship into battle, sailing on a boat 'like a spectator' rather than charging into the fray on horseback. The Mamelukes adopted a pejorative attitude towards naval warfare generally but it is noticeable that when Baibars later became Sultan he adopted a more pragmatic approach towards the navy and it is tempting to speculate that the crucial effect Egyptian ships had during this particular campaign had a decisive impact on his strategy in the future.[4]

This was dreadful news for the Crusaders. Without new provisions from Damietta, there was no chance of maintaining the siege of Mansourah for much longer. There was no prospect of living off the meagre resources of the land immediately around Mansourah indefinitely, and the Crusaders were now forced to rely heavily on the supplies that they had brought with them which could not last for much longer. As a result of the shortages that had already become apparent, there was rampant inflation in the camp and food was selling for extortionate prices.

The strategic priorities of the Crusade were in danger of being turned on their head. Not long before the army's objective was to take Cairo and drive out the Muslim enemy. Now, without yet appreciating the fact in full, it had already started down a road towards a new objective – that of survival. In this dreadful atmosphere, living in a camp hit by plague, famine, war and death, surely many a Christian mind turned inexorably towards the tribulations visited on this very country by the God of Moses in millennia before.

This bad news forced Louis to reconsider his options. When he discussed these with his Council, it was agreed that they should cross over to the north side of the river, into the camp of the Duke of Burgundy who had stayed there whilst the army had crossed over. Until they did so, they were in danger of becoming the besieged rather than the besiegers.

This action evidenced a change of thinking on the part of the leadership. They realised that the likelihood of a military triumph was now receding by the day. They were in no position for a protracted campaign against Mansourah, and each new dawn would see their fighting capabilities diminish. The emphasis was already turning irrevocably towards a negotiated settlement. This dramatic reversal in fortune had left the Crusaders with little option but to give up some of the gains that they had bought at such a great price.

To protect the retreat that now seemed inevitable, Louis ordered a fence to be built to act as a barbican for the troops. This was accordingly constructed, although it was not very high. It was the beginning of a new phase of the campaign. Louis's crusade had reached and passed its high-water mark. Before, there had only been thoughts of victory, now of nothing save withdrawal.

The first elements of the army to re-cross the river were the baggage train. Large numbers of armed men, including Louis himself, stayed behind on the south side of the river to protect them. The baggage train would make a tempting prize for the Egyptians and must be defended at all costs. When it had finally crossed safely, the King and his barons also crossed. Only Walter of Chatillon remained as his men formed the rearguard.

A force remained in the barbican. The Egyptians, who must have been able to see that large numbers of the Crusaders were heading back across the river, launched a strong attack on the hastily erected fortifications. Hordes of mounted archers circled the barbican, shooting clouds of arrows into its mist, whilst others even threw rocks into the camp. The defenders suffered much, their danger increased by the fact that the barbican was not high enough. During the actions of that day, Charles of Anjou particularly stood out for his valour and energy.

The crossing was nevertheless successfully negotiated. Safely installed in their new camp, the army hoped for a change in fortune. Unfortunately, things went on much as before. The health of the Crusaders did not improve as a result of the move. De Joinville was especially ill. Weakened as he was by his wounds at Mansourah, a fever took hold of him. He was forced to take to his bed, where one morning something happened that particularly moved the chronicler, an event that reminds us that his account is sometimes a very personal one.

De Joinville was lying in his bed listening to his priest saying mass, when he saw the cleric first sway and then start to fall. De Joinville moved from his bed and managed to arrest the priest's fall to the ground. The priest managed to recover himself and finish the ceremony but it was clear that he too was suffering from the illness that was sweeping the camp. With laconic simplicity, de Joinville noted that 'never did he sing mass again'.[5]

The continued deprivation of the Crusaders meant that negotiations must be started as a matter of urgency. Louis proposed that, in return for the restoration of Jerusalem to Christian ownership, Damietta would be handed back to the Egyptians. It was a proposition that closely matched that supposedly on offer from Ayub earlier in the campaign. As such, it intimated just how parlous the situation now was. Louis's confidence was very low, and this offer was in stark contrast to his peremptory rejection of any attempts to negotiate a settlement earlier in the Crusade.

His conciliatory stance came about as a result of his sudden position of weakness, a fact that his adversaries must have appreciated only too well and which would have encouraged them to force a harsh bargain. Under the terms of the offer, the Egyptian Sultan was to look after the sick in Damietta until they could be returned to the Crusaders; he was also to watch over their siege engines and stocks of salted meat until they could be handed back.

The Sultan asked for hostages. The Crusaders offered one of the King's brothers as surety, a sign of their increasing desperation. But even this was not enough for the Muslim leadership, who demanded nothing less than the custody of Louis himself. Such a move could not be contemplated, and the negotiations ground to a halt. Successful negotiation can only work if both sides have equal bargaining strength. In this particular situation, the Crusaders were arguing from a position of weakness and the Egyptians knew it. The latter could be as demanding as they liked in their terms and conditions, as in the warfare that must necessarily ensue if diplomatic contacts failed they would hold the upper hand.

In the absence of a peaceful solution, the condition of the Crusaders continued to deteriorate at an alarming rate. So bad did the sufferings of the Crusaders become that surgeons had to cut away the dead flesh from their gums so that they could chew on anything. De Joinville says that the camp was filled with the howls of men screaming like women in childbirth (his own descriptive phrase) as the surgeons performed their gruesome task.

Louis was now faced with an awful but unavoidable decision. If they stayed where they were, the army would just deteriorate further and they would become easy pickings for the Muslims in any subsequent assault. Attack was out of the question; the army was far too weak to have any realistic hope of success, whilst the Muslims, powerfully led by Baibars, were clearly a formidable foe. There was therefore only one option left.

A retreat to Damietta would be a bitter pill for the army to swallow. Much blood had been shed in the attempt on Mansourah, and the loss of life would have been in vain if the attempt on Cairo were abandoned now. But the Crusaders would still be in a strong position if what remained of the army could be brought back more or less intact to Damietta. They could be re-supplied from Cyprus and Outremer, although the coastal defence vessels of the Egyptians based at Alexandria were by now starting to make a real nuisance of themselves.

The army could lick its wounds at Damietta and build up its strength again. Reinforcements could make their way to the city, and a new attack could then be launched at some point in the future. Possession of the city also gave the Crusaders a strong bargaining chip. The Egyptians would certainly not want them to hold it in perpetuity. Once the army was safe behind its walls, there was a much better chance of successfully negotiating a trade-off, exchanging Damietta for Jerusalem. It was a much smaller gain from the Crusade than had been anticipated in the heady days of the previous year but it was, nevertheless, a gain of sorts.

It was time to think the unthinkable. Louis gave the order to retreat. It must have been one of the worst moments of his life. After all the suffering, the hope of great triumphs, the prospect of honour and glory, there was now only a race for safety to look forward to. And even that started badly. It was only just over a week's march back to Damietta. In the race that the army was now starting out on, hours would count. As soon as they were gone, the Muslims would be after them in hot pursuit. They must at all costs be obstructed at every opportunity to slow them down.

There was one particularly easy way of doing this from the start. The only way of crossing from the south side of the river (where the Muslims now were) to the north was over the pontoon bridge that the Crusaders had constructed. It would be a relatively easy task to destroy this, either by setting fire to it or cutting loose the ropes that held it together. A party was deputed to do this but for some reason failed to carry out its orders. The retreat therefore began with the Crusaders making a present of the bridge to their enemy. Nothing better typified the 'command and control' problems facing the Crusade.

Predictably enough, it was not long after the army began its demoralising journey that the Muslims started to harass them. The sick were placed onboard ship so that they might travel in relative comfort, although they still had the daunting prospect of breaking the Muslim's blockade of the river to negotiate before they reached Damietta. The Crusaders left their camp after dinner on 5 April 1250. The mariners onboard ship lit fires as a beacon for the sick to make their way towards.

Even before this initial manoeuvre was completed, the Muslims were in the camp, slaughtering the wounded. Louis himself was seriously ill by this stage. He was suffering from dysentery so badly that he had to have the lower part of his trousers cut away so that he could answer the calls of nature promptly. Despite this, he refused to be taken onboard ship, preferring to share the sufferings of his troops.

And so began a retreat that was akin to a journey through hell. Constantly attacked by a now exultant enemy, ravaged by disease and hunger, the morale of the men plummeted in diametric contrast to that of the Muslims. Despite his infirmity, Louis had placed himself in the rearguard where he would be in the thick of the action. He still rode proudly enough, seated on a horse draped in silk, but the predicament that he now found himself in was a humbling experience for the King.

Unable to defend himself as he was so ill, the King was forced to rely on the bravery of a loyal subject, Geoffrey of Sargines, for protection. Every time a pursuing Muslim got too close, Geoffrey would charge at him with lance levelled and either run him through or drive him away. The retreat was turning into a rout, a helter-skelter charge for safety.

The Mameluke regiment of the Bahrites again distinguished themselves 'by their courage and audacity: they caused the Franks terrible losses and played the major part in the victory. They fought furiously: it was they who flung themselves into pursuit of the enemy: they were Islam's Templars.'[6] They, and other Muslim troops, flung themselves incessantly at the backs of the Franks. The Crusaders were dogged every step of the way, unable to stop and rest, pursued relentlessly by a foe that scented blood.

As the retreat progressed, Louis's condition worsened. It eventually became obvious that he could go no further. They found a humble dwelling in a small village, where the King could stop and hopefully recuperate for a short while. Louis was asked if he wished one of his envoys to approach the enemy again with a view to re-opening negotiations. This can only mean that by now the army was in an parlous state, and that hopes for reaching Damietta in safety were already slim. Louis agreed to this request, and one of his ambassadors, Philip of Montfort, made his way to the Sultan to discuss terms.

Louis's personal situation was now critical. So ill was he that there were many that did not expect him to make it through the night. He had of course not been well for a while before leaving France and his exertions in this terrible war could not have helped. Philip was therefore embarking on a vital mission, on which might rest the fate of not only the expedition but also the life of his King. The Sultan expressed his willingness to discuss terms and negotiations commenced.

While they were still going on, the fate of the expedition was finally decided. There was a soldier in the camp by the name of Marcel. De Joinville says that he was a traitor but he may have just been a humble soldier in a state of blind panic. Whatever his motivations were, he started to cry throughout the camp of the Crusaders that Louis had given the order to surrender. It was not true but it was widely believed. Everywhere the Crusaders began to give up their weapons.

The negotiations stopped as soon as the news reached the Sultan – even the ambassadors were made prisoner. The army was now at the mercy of the enemy. Louis, ravaged by illness, was himself a prisoner, although it was quite likely that by morning the Muslims would just have possession of a corpse. It was a time of enormous uncertainty for the expedition. For the humble soldier, survival was now the only priority; thoughts of victory had changed to black idylls of despair long since. For the expedition as a whole, living to fight another day was now all that mattered. From high-water mark, the expedition's fortunes now appeared to be at their lowest ebb.

For the Egyptians, and Turanshah in particular, this was a time of wonderful deliverance. The Sultan wrote a glowing letter to his commander in Damascus, Jamal al-Din, the purpose of which was to 'inform His Excellency Jamal al-Din and all Islam of the victory bestowed by God over the enemies of the Faith'. A remarkable victory had been won because so many had flocked to the cause and sacrificed much in protecting it. Now the Franks had been humbled with 30,000 killed and 'as for the prisoners, it is impossible to count them'. In case there was any doubt about the extent of the victory, this eulogistic epistle was accompanied by the captured scarlet red robe† rimmed with ermine of the French King himself.[7]

The coming days would be a time of transition for King Louis. He would once again resist the disease that ravaged his body; the King possessed a will of iron which was all that enabled him to pull through these regular crises. He was about to enter a new phase of his life. He was ruler of one of Europe's great powers, used to living a life of luxury, surrounded by people who were there to fulfil his every whim. He was the man after all who had built the bejewelled sanctuary of Sainte-Chapelle in Paris, a heady mix of earthly glorification of the power of the King of France and the spiritual extravagance of Heaven. Now he would live life as a prisoner with few luxuries in evidence, although his conditions would generally speaking be infinitely preferable to those 'enjoyed' by his men.

Louis was also a God-fearing man, an individual of immense religious faith. That faith would now be stretched to the limit, as he lived out the next months as a captive, deprived of dignity and material possessions, threatened with torture and even death. Every second it seemed as if a terrible end loomed but through it all Louis would face up to every trial with exemplary courage and fortitude. The history of King Louis was about to take a dramatic change of direction; the legend of Saint Louis was about to begin.

9

Prisoners of War

Whilst King Louis was being taken prisoner on land, the sick being transported by river were trying to make good their escape. A horrifying dash for freedom lay before them, the outcome of which was very far from certain. De Joinville was one of those onboard, by this stage being quite seriously ill. Some knights had been sent with the invalids to protect them, though it appears that they performed this function inadequately, if at all.

The ships that set sail for Damietta soon ran into difficulties. Although they were sailing with the current, the wind was blowing from the north, directly against them. Progress was painfully slow. De Joinville's ship hit problems early on in the voyage. It was blown off course into a small creek branching off the river, and only recovered the main stream with difficulty.

But this was only the beginning of the fleet's problems. Shortly before dawn, the ships of the Christian army ran into the Muslim's blockade. A great fight broke out at once. The Muslim archers loosed an arrow storm at the Christian ships, after having lit them with Greek fire. Poetically, de Joinville described the effect as being as if 'the stars of heaven were falling'.[1]

Despite his poetic turn of phrase, it must have been a terrifying spectacle. Greek fire was deadly in all environments but it was particularly lethal against timber ships, especially when those ships were carrying passengers that were ill and infirm and incapable of doing much to put out any of the fires caused by the clouds of arrows falling on the fleet. The mounted troops that the Crusaders had sent to guard the ships from the riverbanks were equally discomfited. Some small craft had also been deputed to act as guard vessels, but they deserted their charges and attempted to break through the blockade and reach Damietta independently.

Many of the Crusader ships were taken easily. They were manoeuvred to the bank. Already, a horrifying scene was being played out as hundreds of Crusaders, mostly sick, were massacred on the spot and their bodies thrown into the river. Anything valuable that the ships carried was pillaged. Those onboard de Joinville's vessel however stayed in the middle of the stream, judging this the safer place to be. From the shore, the Muslims rained down more arrows on the ship in an attempt to force it to surrender. De Joinville was too ill to take much part in the fight and his comrades put an old jousting harness over him to protect him from the Muslim archers.

The sailors onboard de Joinville's ship were minded to take the vessel to the shoreline in an attempt to save themselves. Although he was very weak, de Joinville called for his sword and threatened to run through anyone who attempted to surrender the vessel. Despite his fever, he could see well enough what was happening to those onshore, and he had no intention of meekly going like a lamb to the slaughter. Therefore, the ship's anchor was dropped so that it would remain where it was.

Shortly after, four Muslim galleys bore down on de Joinville's ship. It was obvious to all aboard that any resistance against these vessels, which bore about a thousand men, would only lead to a senseless loss of life in a one-sided contest. They therefore resolved to give themselves up to the Muslims onboard the galleys, believing them to be a safer bet than those onshore who were putting so many Christians to the sword.

There were a few painful ceremonies to perform first however. De Joinville deemed it unthinkable that his store of holy relics should be taken by the heathen, and so they were deposited over the side along with his casket of valuables. The Muslim galleys were by now on a ramming course with the ship but when they saw that it was offering no resistance, they cast out their anchors nearby and stopped. Then they made ready to board the vessel.

Fortunately for de Joinville, one of the first to come onboard was a Muslim who came from the lands held by the Emperor Frederick in the East. Fearing that the lord would be quickly killed, he came up to de Joinville and advised him to claim kinship to King Louis, and thereby offer the prospect of a sizeable ransom. This was likely to considerably enhance his life expectancy.

Wisely, the friendly Muslim also advised de Joinville to jump over with him to the Muslim galleys as soon as possible, reasoning that those onboard the galleys would be too interested in the lure of plunder from the Christian vessel to take much notice of de Joinville. He did so, although not without nearly losing his balance in his weakened state and falling to his death in the water. He was only saved by the prompt actions of his protector, who managed to grab him before he fell.

There were 300 armed Muslims on the galley and they jumped on de Joinville with knives drawn. For a moment it looked as if the helpful Muslim's attempts to save his life would end in bloody failure but once again he rescued de Joinville in the nick of time. Desperately he interceded with the crew, who were fired up with blood lust, claiming that de Joinville was cousin to the French King and therefore should be spared. Once more, he was successful.

Seeing that de Joinville was seriously ill, the Muslims attempted to ease his condition. The chronicler says that it was out of pity for him, although a cynic might be more inclined to believe that they did not want to lose the chance of a good ransom – after all, not long since they had been all too ready to despatch him on the spot.

They took off his armour and laid a blanket over him. Gripped with fever, de Joinville was now trembling terribly, although he is honest enough to admit in his chronicle that it may have been fear as much as illness that caused him to shake. They brought him a drink. However, when he drank the water they offered him, a large amount of it spewed forth from his nostrils.

When his surviving comrades saw this, they were beside themselves with grief, convinced that this was a sure sign that he was going to die. However, when one of the Saracen knights saw the symptoms, he told them not to grieve, as he knew of a cure for de Joinville. Sure enough, he treated him with some local medicine and within a couple of days de Joinville felt much better.

The Muslim commander in charge of the galleys soon heard of the prestigious prisoner onboard. He sent for de Joinville and interrogated him. He began by asking whether he was really cousin to King Louis. De Joinville said that he was not and explained his reasons for the deception, which the commander agreed were wise. He then asked him whether he was related to the Emperor Frederick. De Joinville in fact had a distant kinship with the Emperor, news that pleased the Muslim commander greatly (it presumably increased the prospects of a good ransom being paid for him).

The men stayed onboard ship for a few days, and it was then decided that they would go ashore. The relatively good treatment handed out to de Joinville so far may have lulled him into a false sense of security. He was soon to be reminded just how parlous was his state, and that of his comrades, especially those who could not command a decent ransom.

A couple of months previously, his priest, John de Voisey, had been a hero when he drove out the Muslim archers attacking de Joinville's camp outside Mansourah. Now he collapsed with a fever. His throat was unceremoniously cut and his body was dumped over the side. Another cleric also collapsed; his brains were dashed out with a rock and then his corpse too was thrown into the river. Any other prisoners that were too weak to walk were met by Muslim guards that had been specially deployed for the purpose: they were run through with swords like sick animals being put out of their misery.

De Joinville was enraged by these events and turned on his captors, berating them for indulging in wicked acts that were completely contrary to Muslim rules of hospitality. The Christians onboard ship had been given food by their Muslim captors, and they therefore assumed the status of guests; tradition demanded that their lives must be protected by their hosts.

It was a strange argument. The armies were in the middle of a bloody war; atrocities were not limited to one side. Richard I had cold-bloodedly massacred 4,000 Muslim prisoners after the siege of Acre during the Third Crusade. Crusaders from the West who had no previous experience of warfare against the Muslims had rather naïve notions of the chivalry of battle. Their innocence was being quickly transformed. In the horrific massacres taking place, cosy notions of honour and glory seemed sadly out of place.[2]

It was in an atmosphere of abject terror that de Joinville was taken ashore. Before he left the ship, he was interviewed once more by the Muslim commander. Mockingly, the latter told him that the sailors onboard his ship had all denied their faith. De Joinville replied that the Muslims should not be too euphoric at this so-called triumph; if a man were a bad Christian, he was equally likely to be a bad Muslim. Coming from a terrified man who was seriously ill, it was a worthy riposte. He then took his leave of the commander and was placed ashore.

With a cruel twist of irony, the captives were taken to Mansourah, the city for which they had fought so hard and for which so many had died. It would have been particularly agonising for the Christians to see once more the place for which great numbers of their comrades had paid the supreme price, all in vain.

De Joinville was not well enough to make his way unassisted, so he was put on a palfrey and led over a bridge of boats into the city. Once he arrived, his name was noted by the Muslim bureaucrats accompanying the Sultan. The Muslim who had protected him so well now had to bid his farewells but before he did so, he handed de Joinville a strange present, the bastard son of a Western knight, whose name was Bartholomew. The knight was then led away to join the other Christian captives of whom there were about 10,000. They were delighted to see him again. No doubt many of them feared the worst, knowing that de Joinville was so ill and having seen what had happened to a large number of the sick.

The Muslims now sought to take advantage of their host of prisoners. Some of those who were fired up by blood lust wished to make martyrs of many of the Christian army but pragmatically the large number of prisoners gave the Egyptians a huge bargaining chip which could be cashed in, for example, to restore Damietta to them without a fight. So others managed to stay the hands of the would-be assassins in the hope of making more positive use of them.

However, Matthew Paris tells us that the Muslims tried to recover Damietta first of all through subterfuge. A large number of them dressed themselves in the armour of the dead or captured Crusaders. They made sure that their force was about the same size as the Crusading army that had originally left Damietta, and they planned to fool the garrison into letting them into the city. They advanced on Damietta, to the initial delight of those inside.

But when they were close enough to be clearly seen, the guards became suspicious. For one thing, these men were riding in isolated pockets whereas Christian armies tended to travel massed closely together. For another, their physical features gave the lie to the pretence to be Westerners. Their dark skin, and their beards, showed them to be men of the East. They were therefore refused admittance. Those inside were beside themselves with grief, knowing that the fact that so many of the Muslims were dressed in very familiar armour told of a great disaster befalling the Christian army.

It is a strange story, and the fact that de Joinville does not mention it may suggest it is a figment of Matthew's fanciful imagination. Yet there is a form of corroborating evidence. The tale is not unique. A few years later, a party of Muslims tried unsuccessfully to gain access to Acre in similar fashion. They were led by the Sultan at the time. His name was Baibars. Did the great man get his idea from the attempted ruse at Damietta? It is at least a fascinating hypothesis.

With this subtle trick exposed before it could come to fruition, the Muslims resorted to other tactics. They approached the mass of the prisoners and asked who should be their spokesman. As King Louis was being kept apart from the main body of the captives who were housed in a courtyard enclosed by mud-brick walls, the Crusaders elected Count Peter of Brittany as their representative.

The Egyptians asked him first of all whether he would demand that the castles of Outremer should be given over to the Muslims in return for the release of the prisoners. The Count replied that he had no authority to make such an offer. He was right. The lands in Outremer officially belonged to Conrad, son of the Emperor Frederick from his short-lived marriage to Yolande, late Queen of Jerusalem.[3] Therefore, any such agreement would have to come from him.

The Muslims next asked him whether he would enquire if the castles belonging to the Templars and Hospitallers in Outremer could be handed over. Again, the Count replied in the negative. When the castles were handed over to a castellan from the Orders, he was made to swear that he would never hand them over in return for ransom. And Peter of Brittany, or even King Louis himself for that matter, had any authority over the Orders. Any such request was therefore bound to be in vain.

The Muslim negotiators were greatly angered by these negative responses. They claimed that it seemed to them that the prisoners had no great wish to save their lives. Ominously, they threatened that if the captives would not listen to reason, they could not protect them from the wilder element of the Muslim army. The prisoners must have been greatly disturbed when, a short time later, a large party of Muslims with their swords drawn descended on the makeshift camp. Fortunately, they seemed to be happy enough just to resort to taunting the Western prisoners who, for the time being, survived.

Shortly afterwards, another party of negotiators came to see the captives. They asked whether the Western leaders would like to see their King once more. They assembled four of their leaders who joyfully went to meet Louis. They were John of Valery and Philip of Montfort and two representatives of one of Outremer's foremost families, Baldwin and Guy of Ibelin.

It was with great joy and relief that these men renewed their acquaintance with Louis. As he had been kept apart from the main body of his men, and as he had been seriously ill, presumably the imagination ran wild when they thought what had become of him. Matthew Paris tells us that for a time the Sultan thought that he should be sent eastwards to the Caliph, the spiritual leader of the Muslim world, there to be kept prisoner as an object of scorn and derision. But it was decided that it would be a pointless waste of a supreme negotiating opportunity if the King were disposed of in so cavalier a fashion. His captors therefore began to bargain with him.

The early signs were that Louis would not be a pliant prisoner. He had refused food for two days. He would not accept the terms later offered to Peter of Brittany. Louis's response had been equally negative, partially for the same reasons and also because of his innate resistance to any kind of negotiation at this stage of his activity. His captors had therefore resorted to threats. They shouted that they would torture him if he would not be compliant.

They threatened him with a crude but brutal form of torture known as the bernicles. These were two pieces of wood, which were joined together with teeth. The torture worked simply; the victim's leg was placed in between the two pieces which were tied together at each end with a length of rope. The torturers would then sit on the wood, until the leg was crushed. The instrument was designed so that virtually the complete leg was mashed to a pulp. Then, three days later, when the leg had swollen up, the torture would be repeated. It was a horrific form of torture but Louis refused to kow-tow to these threats. Another step had been taken down the road towards canonisation.

Louis's stock had reached a real low-point. The Muslims could not even resist taunting him in writing. Ibn Wasil quotes a contemporary,

Jamal ad-Din ibn Yahya ibn Matruh, derisively writing of Louis that anyone visiting the captive French King should upbraid him in the following terms:

> You came to the East boasting of conquest, believing our martial drum-roll's to be a mere breath of wind.
> And your stupidity has brought you to a place where your eyes can no longer see in the broad plain any way of escape.
> And of all your company, whom you commanded so well that you led them into the tomb's embrace,
> Of fifty thousand not one can be seen that is not dead, or wounded and a prisoner.
> God help you to similar adventures...[4]

The threat of torture having failed, the Egyptians then tried a different line of approach. Although many of the army were in captivity, Louis had left a garrison of mercenaries under Oliver of Termes to protect Damietta, and it would therefore still be a tough nut to crack. There were a number of notable figures in the city, such as Queen Margaret and the legate, Eudes of Chateauroux. The Crusaders were therefore hardly likely to hand it over without a fight unless a deal could be struck.

The Sultan suggested to Louis that he and his army should be released in return for a massive ransom as well as the surrender of Damietta. The King demurred, saying that his wife was in charge of the city in his absence and it was her decision whether to pay the ransom or not. This response was disingenuous. It is inconceivable that Margaret would have gone against her husband's wishes in a matter as important as this. Louis eventually conceded that he agreed that the sum demanded (the sum agreed was 500,000 *livres*, about two year's annual income for Louis from all his possessions) was reasonable. The Sultan was so pleased when he heard this that he even agreed a rebate of 100,000 livres against the sum agreed.

The rest of the Franks in captivity were no doubt delighted when they heard this news. As well as the massacres of the sick and infirm early on in their captivity, de Joinville also relates how various members of the army had been offered a choice of conversion to Islam or death. When some opted for the latter, they were promptly beheaded. The imminent escape of the survivors from their trials and tribulations must have seemed little short of miraculous.

Shortly after the deal was agreed, some of the Crusade's leaders were taken towards Damietta onboard Egyptian galleys. De Joinville sailed in the company of a number of important men, including Count Peter of Brittany, and the brothers Guy and Baldwin of Ibelin. After a while, they came to the Sultan's encampment, which he had set up by the banks of the river. It was an impressive structure which, from the detailed description that de Joinville gives, obviously made a significant impression on those who saw it. In front of the structure was a tower made of planks hewn from fir trees. This served as the entrance to the camp.

Close to this main entrance was a tent, where those who were making their way to see the Sultan were required to leave their weapons: a sensible precaution in any circumstances no doubt but perhaps also a clue to the sense of insecurity that Turanshah may have been feeling – there were rumblings of discontent in his camp. After passing through another tent, a larger pavilion was reached. This was where the Sultan had his hall.

Behind the hall was yet another tower through which was the entrance to the Sultan's bedchamber. Beyond a court stood the tallest tower of all which the Sultan would climb if he wished to survey the camp and the countryside round about. A pathway led to the river along which the Sultan would pass if he wished to bathe. The whole encampment was stockaded by a large wooden fence. The walls were draped in cloth so that those outside could not see in, giving the Sultan privacy.

The galleys sailed up to the camp, and Louis was taken off to be accommodated within his own pavilion inside the walls. Everything seemed to be progressing smoothly. The King was even being given some of the trappings of luxury that he must have thought had gone for good. The Crusaders were on their way back to Damietta, the ransom due had been agreed and there seemed to be nothing that would interfere with the handover of the captives. There was however about to be a massive stumbling block placed in the way of further progress.

Turanshah had learnt little since his arrival in Egypt. He continued to favour his own councillors over those who had been in Egypt before he came to the country. This infuriated the Mamelukes, particularly the Bahrites. Their leaders were particularly concerned that, once Damietta was safely in his hands, he would openly turn on them and have them thrown into prison. They were not prepared to meekly let this happen. Accordingly, they began to plot together to depose him. The shades of intrigue and conspiracy began to stalk the camp. There were hushed whispers in the shadows and an air of menace was palpable.

An opportunity presented itself when Turanshah invited the leaders of his bodyguard to dine with him. A disloyal bodyguard is the most dangerous enemy a ruler can have. These men saw very well which way the wind was blowing, and fell in with the plot with little compunction.

After the meal at which they had been his guests was completed, the Sultan took his leave of the men and began to make his way to his chamber. As he did so, one of the guards who carried the Sultan's sword rushed at him and struck him. The sword smashed into his hand, cleaving it up through the fingers as far as his arm. Terrified and in agony, Turanshah pleaded for help from the others in the tent, but their part in the plot was quickly apparent. When he asked for their assistance in saving his life, the answer was clear and unequivocal:

'It is better that we should kill you than you should kill us!' they answered with one voice.[5]

The young Sultan proved surprisingly hard to murder. He ran off, being as de Joinville describes 'young and active', taking refuge in one of the towers. The bodyguard, some 500 mounted men in all, then ran riot (they had taken the precaution of despatching most of the army towards Damietta before they did so, saying that Turanshah had ordered this). They dashed his pavilions to the ground and surrounded him in his tower.

He only had three Muslim clerics with him for protection and the rebels shouted up to him to come down, as they would not take his life. It was of course arrant nonsense to suggest that he would be safe in their hands and Turanshah knew it, so he stayed where he was. He 'opened the windows and called to the people for help, but no one responded, and none of the Egyptian emirs would come to his aid, for he had lost their loyalty completely'.[6] His actions only delayed the inevitable. They set the tower alight with Greek fire. It was made of timber, and was festooned in colourful cloth; it became an inferno in seconds.

Turanshah was ensnared in a death trap if he stayed where he was. He therefore jumped down from the tower and ran off towards the river. It only prolonged his agony. He was protected for a few seconds as the path to the river was surrounded by a fence. However, this only kept off the traitorous bodyguard for a very short time. They quickly broke down the fence and set off after the fleeing Sultan. As they caught him, one of them thrust his spear in his ribs. Turanshah still staggered on and made it to the river.

Here, his brave but futile effort to survive ended in failure. His struggle to live ended in the Nile, his lifeblood staining the water a vivid red. Gradually his struggles lessened, and then stopped altogether. One of his murderers, Faress-Eddin Octay, cut out his heart. According to de Joinville he then showed his true mercenary colours by taking it to Louis and asking him boldly 'what will you give me? I have just killed your enemy who would, if he had lived, have killed you'.

Not surprisingly, Louis said not a word in reply, though whether from fear, shock or just revulsion is not clear. Turanshah was left where he had been slaughtered, the final indignity for any Muslim, as fodder for the jackals, until some passing boatmen took pity on him and gave his decaying corpse the dignity of a decent burial.

This turn of events threatened to change the Crusaders' situation dramatically. All negotiations had been with the Sultan, who was now dead. They might well be back at square one. When Turanshah was killed, his place was assumed by his wife Shajar ad-Durr. She was a Turkish slave, and the appointment of a woman as Sultan was unprecedented in Egypt. Although an innovative step, this was an ominous portent of what was to come.

The installation of a woman as Sultan could only be construed as an attempt to install a ruler who would be pliable in the hands of the real power brokers in Egypt. The involvement of the Mamelukes in her husband's death left little real doubt about their identity. There was certainly no guarantee that the deal to release the Crusaders would go ahead as planned or, if it did, whether the price would remain the same.

The disposition of the rebels towards their defeated enemy was far from clear. Rather than freeing the prisoners, they might be more inclined to finish them off. A short while after the murder of the Sultan, a large party of the rebels was seen coming towards the galleys on which the body of the Crusade was held. Their demeanour looked far from welcoming. Around their necks they carried great battle-axes, and they generally appeared extremely hostile.

When they came onboard the galleys, they forced all the Crusaders down into the holds of the ships. The Crusaders believed that their intention was to call them up on deck one by one and execute them individually. Thrown into a panic, most of those onboard de Joinville's ship laid hold of a priest who was in their company and one after the other made their confession to him. To die unshriven, without due confession to God via a priestly intermediary, would condemn a man to Hell.

It was a terrifying time for the captives but, fortunately for them, this was a false alarm. The rebels were as much enamoured of money as the late Sultan was. The captives spent a long and harrowing night below decks, believing that every second might be their last. However, when the rebels approached them again in the morning, it was to tell that the deal was still very much alive.

The rebels told the Crusaders that Turanshah would certainly have killed Louis, and the rest of the captives as well, rather than go through with the plan. They informed the leaders of the Crusade that many of the rank-and-file soldiery had already been taken back towards Cairo which was specifically against the terms of the agreement made between Louis and the Sultan.

The terms would not be amended either. The ransom to be paid would still be 400,000 *livres*, the same figure that Turanshah had finally agreed on. This was to be paid half before the King left Egypt and the other half when he arrived back in Acre (his next planned port of call once he left Egypt). In return, the Egyptians would look after the sick in Damietta, and the great engines of war and the supplies of salted meat in the city until Louis was in a position to send for them subsequently.

Solemn oaths were sworn that these covenants would be complied with in terms that legal experts confirmed would be the most binding possible. In return, the Saracens made King Louis vow to agree to his side of the bargain in an equally formal and binding manner. There was some debate about the precise terms on which Louis would swear, which were eventually settled to the satisfaction of both parties, although not before the Patriarch of Jerusalem, who had been taken captive by the Muslims when he came on embassy to the camp, was threatened with torture.

At last, the deal was struck. For some time, those held in captivity had lived in mortal fear, not knowing from day to day whether they would see another sunset. Now there was at least the possibility of some relief from their sufferings. The city of Damietta was not far away, and they would soon return to it.

But there was, apart from survival itself, little to celebrate in this outcome. The army had set out with high hopes when they marched towards Cairo, but now they were coming back, not in triumph but in humiliation. Even Damietta itself would be lost, meekly handed back to the Egyptians from which it had been taken in the very recent past. For an enormous outlay of time, money and terrible loss of life, the Crusade was back where it started, having achieved no more than the previous expedition to Egypt had decades earlier.

Louis, at the head of an army of prisoners, journeyed back towards Damietta with a heavy heart, pondering on the severity of God's punishment for those who sinned. It was a long way from the glories of Sainte-Chapelle. Of all the emotions that he felt at this particular moment, surely the greatest was a despairing realisation of how far the mighty had fallen.

10

The End of the Beginning

It was a humbled and shamed King of France who made his way back towards Damietta. He had invested a huge proportion of his country's resources into this expedition and it had achieved precisely nothing. Reflecting on the transience of earthly wealth and glory, his emotions were in turmoil and, in the long weeks of captivity that he had endured, he must have pondered often on his next move.

He was faced with several choices. The first was to return back to France, away from this searing heat and the dust of the desert. When news of his capture was received in France, it generated an emotional response in some unexpected quarters. A number of humble folk grouped together to lead a Crusade with the aim of releasing the King. They were led by a self-styled Master of Hungary and the movement became known as the Shepherds Crusade.

The Master claimed to be inspired by the Virgin who had given him a letter. He castigated the nobility and the clergy of France who he blamed for the debacle. The Crusade reached Paris and were received kindly by Queen Blanche, Louis's mother and the acting regent. Not untypically however, this well meaning but undisciplined group quickly ran out of control. There were riots and violence. The Master was killed and the movement fell apart without achieving anything.

Louis had little stomach for the option of abandoning his Crusade. To return from an expedition that had taken so long to prepare and for which his country had paid so dearly, both in terms of its treasures and the blood of its men, would be a source of great shame. To show only abject failure after such a huge effort might well weaken his grip on the throne in what was still a very volatile era. There were predatory barons back home in the West, who would pounce on any sign of weakness. For these reasons alone, a return to France was difficult.

But for Louis this was not the greatest argument against an immediate return. There was for him a far stronger moral imperative. His vow to take the cross was a personal pact with God. To flee homeward from the East after having brought nothing but shame to the Crusading ideal was a prospect that was anathema to this pious King. He would far rather spend more time in the region, recovering his personal credibility and working for a better outcome to his endeavours, even if he were to die in the attempt.

There were also humanitarian arguments swaying Louis against an abandonment of his Crusading efforts. Many of the army would remain in captivity until the second instalment of the ransom was paid for their release once he had arrived in the kingdom of Outremer. Louis could not return to France whilst they still remained there. To do so would seem to him to be an act of desertion: as a man of honour, he could not countenance this. He felt a great sense of personal responsibility for the position that the captives found themselves in, and he would not meekly abandon them to their fate.

It is easy to forget how dreadful the months of captivity must have been for the people the Crusaders left behind in Damietta. We do not know when they first heard of the news of the army's defeat but clearly they would have realised that something was badly amiss when so many of their supply vessels were intercepted on the way

Left: 1 The Omayyad mosque in Damascus, one of Islam's sacred places.

Below: 2 The walls of Jerusalem, Louis IX's ultimate objective during his great Crusade.

3 Richard I, still an inspiration to the Seventh Crusade.

4 A clash of religions: a Muslim pulpit in the Crusader castle of Krak des Chevaliers.

5 The Palestinian landscape: the view from the castle of Krak des Chevaliers.

6 The effigy of the Crusader William Longspee in Salisbury Cathedral. He was killed in the streets of Mansourah.

7 A Templar chapel from Laon, France: French and Templar fortunes were intertwined during the Crusade.

8 Three medieval monarchs look on from the façade of Notre Dame where Louis IX took his leave of his capital.

9 The struggle of good and evil would have been a symbol for many Crusaders' views of the Crusade: a contemporary piece of architecture from Notre Dame.

10 A riot of colour from the windows of Sainte-Chapelle.

11 Soldiers on the move from Sainte-Chapelle.

12 Christ in glory, from the façade of Sainte-Chapelle.

to Mansourah. Not long after they became aware of these problems, they had been faced with an unmistakable sign that something was wrong when the Egyptians had tried to trick their way into the city.

A little later still, they received the dreadful tidings that the army was captured, and that a huge ransom must be raised if they were to be released. The news had been brought to them by an Egyptian delegation along with four specially chosen knights, accompanied by secret tokens to vouch for the authenticity of the tidings. The Christian leaders still inside the city were thrown into great despair and confusion by this turn of events. According to Matthew Paris[1] they were particularly perturbed because they believed the Saracens to be a duplicitous and perfidious people who would, as soon as the ransom money was safely in their hands, renege on the agreement and kill all the prisoners.

But there was really no choice: the terms must be agreed to if the army, or the King, were ever to be seen alive again. It was an especially awful time for Queen Margaret. Thousands of miles from the relative security and stability of her court she was faced with the dreadful prospect that she would never again see Louis. And to make matters worse, she was pregnant.

The couple had enjoyed a difficult relationship. The strong beliefs of her husband, and the stubbornness of his nature, must have made him difficult to live with. Equally, her relationship with her mother-in-law, Blanche of Castille, was problematic. Blanche was a domineering mother, who exerted an unhealthy influence over her son even when he was a mature adult. De Joinville says that she could not bear to see her son in his wife's company[2], and that the married couple had to go through an almost farcical routine of creeping around secret passageways in order to meet.

There was one particularly terrible incident, when Margaret was close to death after giving birth. Blanche bluntly told her son to leave his wife in peace, despite her entreaties to her husband to stay, as he could do nothing for her. The son meekly obeyed at first, and began to leave the room with his mother. The sight of this was too much for

Margaret who fainted. Terrified that his wife had died, Louis returned to the chamber whilst the Queen's attendants brought her round.

To add to Margaret's anxieties alone in Damietta, she was faced with other immediate problems. By this stage, the Queen was heavily pregnant. She was terrified that the city would at any moment fall to the Muslims, so much so that she suffered from recurring nightmares that they were in her room. To counter this, she asked an octogenarian knight to keep watch in her bedchamber at night. His task was to soothe the Queen when she awoke in a cold sweat, reassuring her that she was still safe from the Infidel.

This devoted guardian was still with her when she gave birth to a son. The state of her mind can best be judged from the name that she christened him with, Tristram, which means 'sorrow'. Shortly afterwards she took the faithful old knight to one side and made him swear that, should the Saracens take the city, he would kill her rather than let the enemy take her. The knight dutifully acceded to her doleful request, having already secretly resolved to himself that the enemy would never take the Queen alive.

The very same day that she gave birth, she received more dreadful news. There was a sizeable contingent of both Pisans and Genoese in Damietta. Their presence was absolutely crucial to the continued defence of the city. The Queen was told that both the Pisans and Genoese had resolved to leave the city. There were practical reasons for their decision. Provisions had been slow to arrive from the West, and there was the threat of famine. The Italians clearly had no wish to starve for a cause to which most of them were more commercially, rather than morally, committed. They would therefore go.

Margaret summoned their leaders to her presence. She begged them to stay, telling them that their decision would lead to the loss of Damietta and, with it, possibly her husband. She offered to buy up as many provisions as they needed, and keep them supplied with food. It was to all intents and purposes bribery but one of the few weapons that she had left in her armoury. They agreed to her request, and the immediate crisis was solved.

Ironically, an unfortunate corollary was that she had to dig deep into the financial resources available to her to find the requisite sum, making it even more difficult to raise the ransom. It was a creditable performance from a woman in fear of her life who had just been through the physically and emotionally draining experience of giving birth whilst her husband was a prisoner. She subsequently took the sensible precaution of sailing to Acre to await the arrival of her husband before the city was handed back to the Egyptians. There was little point in making a present of herself as an easy hostage for the enemy.

Agreement was finally reached on the date for the King's release and the return of Damietta to the Muslims. The galleys carrying the leaders of the army continued their stately progress north, arriving outside of the city during the night of 5 May 1250. They anchored in front of the bridge leading into the city, and a tent was put up to house the King once he had been taken ashore.

The scene was set for the Muslims to re-occupy the city. They were led through the gates by Geoffrey of Sargines, and soon busied themselves raising their banners in all the places of prominence in Damietta. However, euphoric at their success, the spirits of the occupiers were fired up. Events soon spiralled out of control.

According to de Joinville, they found the stores of wine left behind by the Christian army, and quickly became inebriated as they helped themselves to them. They started to smash the Crusaders' siege engines, which they were specifically required by the terms of the treaty to protect. They also seized the stocks of salted meat that were in the city, once again betraying their trust in the process. Worst of all, the sick and wounded soldiers in their possession, whom they had promised to protect, they laid hold of and started to slaughter.[3]

Matthew Paris gives us a different account.[4] In his version of events, the defenders of Damietta were so distraught when they realised that they would have to hand their hard-won conquest over to the Egyptians that they could not bear the thought of also giving up the provisions they had hoarded so carefully. Therefore, rather than let them fall into the hands of the enemy, they set them alight before they left. So infuriated were the Egyptians that they beheaded all the common people of the city, and sent out parties to intercept those Christians fleeing towards Outremer overland. Once these had been caught, they were massacred. Neither account paints a very rosy picture of the atmosphere of death that hung over Damietta at this particular moment in time.

The pall over the city soon assumed a more literal form. The Egyptians formed great pyres composed of the smashed siege engines, the large amounts of pork they had taken and the bodies of those that they had put to the sword. These were then set ablaze. The resulting fires lasted for three days, enveloping the city in a thick suffocating cloud of acrid smoke. The sight, and the smell, must have been truly appalling.

Presumably, those thousands of men still held captive by the Egyptians were very frightened by the way that events had turned out. Fears that their very lives were in danger appeared to be well founded. Rumours reached the captives that many of the Egyptians believed that, now Damietta was safely recovered, the prisoners should be put to death. If the Crusaders were killed, so they reasoned, the country would be safe from any renewed attack for twenty years or more.

It was a morally indefensible position of course, as indeed a number of the Muslim leadership recognised, but it had great pragmatic attraction. For a time, it looked as if the hawks might win the argument. Armed men were seen coming towards the galleys on which most of the captives were still held. Then the anchors were raised, and the galleys turned about. They started to journey back towards Cairo, with all the prisoners still onboard. It looked as if the Muslims were about to ignore the terms of the peace treaty, with awful implications for those held captive.

This was a very long day indeed for the Crusaders. As they sailed southwards away from Damietta and the promise of safety and freedom, the desperation of the prisoners increased with every passing minute. From the heights of exultant expectation, they had plummeted to the lowest depths of despair.

There were however a number of the Egyptians who harboured serious reservations about the course that their leadership had embarked upon. Whether the protesters were concerned on moral grounds, or because of potential political repercussions, is unclear. They may also have reasoned that there was still a large amount of ransom left unpaid. Whatever the reason – and it is unlikely that morality alone was responsible for the change of heart – the order was given once more for the galleys to turn about and head back to Damietta.

The Christian prisoners were both confused and terrified by this stage. No doubt they felt a sense of relief as they headed once more towards Damietta, but this must surely by now have been tempered with a healthy dose of cynicism. After all, the Egyptians had changed their minds with almost monotonous regularity so far, and there was no guarantee that they would not do so again. This was turning into a nightmare of the most dreadful proportions.

But at last, Damietta was regained once more and preparations were made to release the captives. Before they were completed however a surreal ceremony took place. It would be dishonourable to the Egyptian leadership if the prisoners were not properly fed before they were released. Therefore, an impromptu feast was hastily arranged. A few hours after plotting to kill the prisoners, the Egyptians sat them down and watched them eat cheese fritters ('roasted by the sun so that worms would not come therein', according to de Joinville) and hard-boiled eggs. The eggs had even been painted in gaudy colours to honour the Crusaders.

Although it was hard for them to fully comprehend, the moment for which the distraught Crusaders had lived for so long was at hand. The Egyptians led Louis from his pavilion outside of the walls of Damietta, and down towards the river. There was a vast crowd of them in attendance, twenty thousand if we are to trust de Joinville's arithmetic, though numerical accuracy was not a strong point of any medieval chronicler. By the riverbank, a lone Genoese galley was moored. It appeared to be virtually unmanned. Only one person could be seen on deck.

As the King and the entourage of his enemies approached the galley, the lone individual put a whistle to his lips. With one shrill blast of this, the decks were suddenly alive. As if through an act of prestidigitation, eighty crossbowmen appeared arrayed along the decks, their weapons raised with bolts pointed at the Muslims. Even at this late hour, those responsible for protecting Louis still harboured grave doubts over his safety. Alarmed by this sudden aggressive act, most of those Muslims accompanying Louis drew back in a hurry. Only a small group stayed with him and escorted him to the side of the ship.

A plank was placed from the shore to the ship. Gingerly, Louis ascended it, edging away from captivity and towards freedom. Yet this was a bitter-sweet moment for the proud monarch. He was leaving Egypt not as conqueror, but as a humbled man. Whereas his departure from France had been hailed by the triumphant blasts of trumpets and the excited clashing of cymbals, a deadened pall of depression was all that accompanied his departure from Egypt. Expectation had attended his leaving from France; only shame was present when he left Damietta.

To make matters worse, there were still a large number of captives left behind. They would not be released until the ransom had been paid in full. Although one of his brothers, Charles of Anjou, accompanied him onto the galley, the other who had survived the expedition, Alphonse of Poitiers, remained as a hostage pending further payments to the Egyptians. Their ordeal was still far from over.

For the Egyptians of course the emotions felt were completely different. A mighty army had been humbled to an extent that only seemed possible through divine intervention. For the scale of their victory had been so great that it was almost a rout. Their chroniclers noted that this was an even greater triumph than the defeat of the previous Crusade to Egypt 'because of the large numbers of the enemy killed and captured; so many that the prisons of Cairo were full of Franks'.

Their triumphant army began to make its preparations for its return to Cairo. When they eventually arrived there, great celebrations would ensue and 'for many days on end, rolls of drums announced the glad tidings of the Muslim victory over the Franks and the recovery of the province of Damietta, pearl of Islam and frontier of Egypt'. The euphoria was understandable for 'this was the second time that the infidels had taken [Damietta] and lost it again and had fled in defeat in disarray'.[5] This time, there was every reason to hope that the victory had been so decisive that the Westerners would be discouraged from ever contemplating another attempt in the future.

The day after their release, a number of nobles took their leave of the King. For them, their only desire now was to make all speed back to France. They had seen enough of Crusading to last them a lifetime. They believed that they had earned the spiritual benefits which had been offered to them as their reward for participating in the expedition, and had no stomach for any more of this terrible form of warfare.

Unlike Louis, who was to sail to Acre, they had no further wish to stay in the East a moment longer. There were too many bad memories to remind them of the disaster that had befallen the expedition. As far as they were concerned, they had more than redeemed their Crusader vows. No one could expect more in terms of sacrifice than what they had suffered over the past few months.

Louis asked them to stay, at least until he had secured the release of his brother, Alphonse. His entreaties were in vain. They bade their sovereign farewell and set sail towards the west. Prominent amongst these men were the Count of Flanders and the Count of Soissons. Count Peter of Brittany went with them. Personal tragedy was about to overtake him, and he would never see France again. He was taken ill on the journey home and died before his voyage was completed.

Louis was now required to raise the first part of the ransom to obtain the release of Alfonse, which naturally enough he was very keen to arrange. The handing over of Damietta was only a down payment. He organised the collection of the sum required on the Saturday and Sunday immediately following the Friday that he was released.

They finished the counting in the early evening of the Sunday. There was however a problem, in that the sum they collected was a full thirty thousand livres short of that agreed. There was though one Christian organisation in Damietta that was extremely rich. Since its humble beginnings at the beginning of the twelfth century, the Order of the Temple had accumulated immense wealth. It often acted as banker for the richer elements of society, and as a result regularly had large sums of ready cash available.

De Joinville suggested to Louis that he should approach the Templars and ask them if they would lend him the amount still outstanding. However, when the request was subsequently made they were far from happy. The Commander of the Temple, Stephen of Otricourt, berated de Joinville for the suggestion. He reminded de Joinville that the Templars held the funds that they carried in trust, and that when those who banked with them handed over their money, the Templars in return solemnly swore not to deliver the money to any other than its rightful owner.

A violent quarrel broke out, and many harsh words were traded between de Joinville and the Templar. Eventually, a compromise was reached. Another bizarre scene was acted out, as de Joinville approached the chest holding the Templars' funds with an axe. He made as if to hit it but the Treasurer of the Temple told him to stop as, now that de Joinville had threatened him with force, he would open the chest rather than let de Joinville damage it.

The whole incident was a charade. De Joinville never had any intention of striking the box. The mere pretence of force was enough to morally release the Templars from their vows. It was all something of a nonsense as Louis had more than enough money to repay the Templars once he had made the short sea-crossing to Acre but it spoke volumes of the independent spirit of the order.

The ransom money was now ready. Another minor dispute broke out when the Muslims refused to hand over Alphonse until the money was in their possession. There were a number of Louis's council who felt that he should not comply. However, Louis

– showing either great trust or considerable naivety, depending on one's perspective – said that he would comply with the Egyptians' request. The ransom was duly paid and Alphonse was released. With his business with the Egyptians concluded for the time being, the galleys raised their anchors and set sail, away from this land of bitter memories and dashed expectations.

It was a chastened monarch who restlessly roamed the decks of his galley as it made its way eastward. Nothing had been done to cater to the dignity of Louis before the galley left. The bedding was dirty. He had no fresh clothes to change into, and he still wore the same garments that had been given to him by the Sultan whilst he was in captivity. It was all a far cry from the sybaritic delights of the French Court that he had once been so used to.

The journey to Acre took six days, and to add insult to injury it was an uncomfortable crossing. The sea was rough, and many of those onboard were sick. In the quieter moments, Louis and de Joinville exchanged reminiscences. The King told how he particularly grieved for his late brother, the Count of Artois, a man who, despite his reckless manner, Louis held in genuine affection.

He was also particularly unhappy that the Count of Poitiers appeared to show no gratitude for Louis's efforts to release him and that the other brother present, the Count of Anjou, could not be bothered to spend any time with Louis. On one occasion, Louis discovered that Charles was gambling – a vice that he seems to have hated with a passion – and, in a fit of pique, he stormed over to where he was playing dice and threw the game over the side. Even in adversity, the King still retained his pious streak.

Burdened down by his responsibilities for the remaining captives, and feeling betrayed even by his family, the King brooded throughout the voyage. There were still a large number of men left in Egypt who would not be released unless and until the outstanding 200,000 livres were paid over. They were his main concern for the time being. It would be the greatest disgrace should he return to France with them still in captivity.

As the King attempted to control both his dark, depressing thoughts and the nausea he felt due to the incessant motion of the sea, his plans firmed up. He would not journey back to France empty-handed. His mission was as yet unfulfilled. The first part of his Crusade was over, and he must have known in his heart that it had been a disaster. Now a new phase was about to begin, effectively a damage-limitation exercise.

Louis would not go back to France until he had obtained the release of as many of his subjects as he could. Many may have doubted the King's abilities but few, surely, can have questioned his morality. The terrible trials he had endured in Egypt made him assume the trappings of a martyr. Now he would work unceasingly to gain the freedom of those who had suffered so much because of his mistakes. Another page in the story of the transition from man to Saint was about to be written.

11

Louis in Outremer

A new phase of this extraordinary Crusade was about to begin. The land that Louis was about to arrive in was very different than Egypt for Outremer was a Christian kingdom, founded by Crusaders and governed by Western lords using a system based on European values. But it was also a fragile nation, threatened by powerful forces all along its narrow borders.

Despite its very exposed position as a small salient overshadowed by the strong and volatile states around it, Outremer had managed to survive for one and a half centuries. Its moment of greatest peril had been during the dark days after the disastrous defeat at Hattin in 1187. But when Louis arrived in Outremer, the situation facing Outremer ran this earlier situation a very close second given the recent loss of Jerusalem and the catastrophic defeat at La Forbie with so many men of the standing army lost.

There were two small glimmers of hope offering a morsel of comfort. The first hint of relief came from the fact that the Muslim nations surrounding Outremer were bitterly divided. It was a situation that had been seen time and again throughout the short history of Outremer: it was indeed the major reason that the First Crusade had ever captured Jerusalem in the first place. Louis the warrior had failed in his Crusading aims. Now, he planned to play the diplomat, attempting to exploit the situation by playing one side off against the other.

There was another reason for hope. There was a far greater threat to Islam from another direction. The Mongols had been spreading westwards for decades, building the greatest empire the world had ever known, and their sphere of influence collided head on with the Muslim world in the Middle East. Conflict between the two was inevitable.

In the war that followed, the violence and atrocities committed reached levels rarely seen before or since in history. The Mongols' approach equated to genocide. It was an apocalyptic time for the Muslims. A few years hence a crisis point would be reached. Islam would appear to lurch on the very edge of extinction, but it would find a hero for the hour in the shape of a Mameluke warrior, soon to be Sultan, called Rukn ad-Din Baibars.

With an enemy such as the Mongols, the small Christian state of Outremer was almost an irrelevance to Islam, being little more than an irritation compared to the massive Mongol threat. It was as well that these two factors diverted the Muslim world's attention elsewhere, for the condition of Outremer was by now parlous. There was an acute shortage of manpower, with many of Outremer's warriors drawn from the ranks of the Military Orders, Templars, Hospitallers and a number of smaller organisations, all of which had suffered grievously in recent campaigning.

The loss of so many members of the Orders in the disaster at La Forbie was an enormous body blow. The death of so many knights during Louis's campaign in Egypt was another sickening reverse. The Orders could attempt to plug the gap by despatching more knights from the West but this was not a limitless source of supply. In addition, the attraction of crusading had declined since the halcyon days of the First Crusade and recruitment was becoming more difficult as a result. The debacle on the Nile was hardly likely to improve this situation.

The Orders' resources were perilously stretched. Outremer was in fact a collection of city-states loosely united under the King of Jerusalem, with large tracts of difficult to control country between and around them. Its fragile borders were protected by a series of castles – giants like Krak des Chevaliers, perhaps the most majestic fortification ever built or the gaunt, menacing Safed as well as a host of smaller citadels – which formed a protective mesh around the frontier lands. A number of these castles were garrisoned by groups of soldiers led by members of the Military Orders, who therefore played a vital defensive role as well as an offensive one. The demise of the Orders inevitably meant the demise of Outremer.

Now that Jerusalem had fallen, Acre was the major city of Outremer, only rivalled by Antioch, far away to the north. It was crucial to the viability of the Christian kingdom as it provided it with a deep-water harbour, and was by far the best and most important port along the Mediterranean seaboard of the country. It was massively fortified, with two perimeters of very thick and high walls enveloping the city. These walls were regularly interspersed with towers and bastions, the names of which perhaps hint at their formidability; the most famous of them was known as the Accursed Tower.

Inside this imposing exterior however was a vibrant and cosmopolitan city, for Acre was the gateway to the markets of both East and West for both Christian and Muslim traders (it would be wrong to assume that Outremer was perpetually at war with its neighbours: to survive it had to trade with them, a business which was often flourishing).

There were large trading quarters for all the leading Italian maritime city-states, Genoa, Pisa and Venice, who profited from their trade in the Eastern Mediterranean immensely. The streets teemed with merchants as well as warriors; this was a rich as well as a strong city. So wealthy was Acre that, in 1240, Richard of Cornwall, one of England's foremost barons, said (so Matthew Paris relates) that the city's revenues were equivalent to the annual income of the English crown.

As Louis's ship approached the harbour, the people of the city streamed forth to greet him. No doubt they had heard of the trials and tribulations of the Crusade in Egypt, and it must be assumed that they did not welcome him as a conquering hero. A variety of emotions were present amongst the crowds that went to meet him, curiosity for some, hope that he might provide strong leadership in a time of great stress for others, maybe even a sense of gloating aimed at the crestfallen, once proud, King from others.

It was nevertheless with great joy that most people met him, both the citizens and the clergy coming down to the port to bid him welcome. A friendly hand assisted de Joinville on to a horse but he was obviously still far from well. He collapsed whilst on horseback and had to be held on to the horse until he reached his lodgings to stop him from falling off. Weeks of deprivation and stress were taking their toll on a man who had not enjoyed robust health at the best of times.

The Crusaders were taken to the great hall of the citadel in Acre. Here a sumptuous feast was laid on for them. Perhaps it almost took on the appearance of a coronation feast though there was never any question of Louis becoming legal ruler of the emaciated Kingdom of Jerusalem. He was far too fastidious in his approach towards the Emperor Frederick, within whose sphere of influence Outremer was primarily deemed to lie, to even contemplate such a move.

But the fact of the matter was that the rightful ruler of the kingdom, Frederick's son Conrad, had never been near the country in his life, and was unlikely to correct this omission in the near future. The barons of the frontier lands were an independent group, as such men always tend to be. Some of them, such as the Ibelins, were extremely powerful. Yet with the destruction of so much of the Military Orders' fighting strength in Egypt and before at La Forbie, there was a power vacuum in Outremer. Louis had just arrived at the head of a major fighting force; there was never any real doubt who would effectively move into the vacuum, at least for the short term.

De Joinville was amongst those invited to the feast. Whilst he was sitting in the great hall, a servant in a red tunic approached him, and introduced himself. He asked de Joinville whether he knew him, but he replied that he did not recognise the servant. The latter replied that his name was Guillemin, and he came from the castle of de Joinville's uncle. The two men fell into deep conversation. It was apparently a discourse during which the two men developed a warmth for each other, for at the end of it de Joinville asked the servant whose man he currently was. In reply, Guillemin responded that he currently had no master. De Joinville therefore invited him into his service, a request to which the servant was delighted to accede.

It looked as if the relationship might be short-lived, for de Joinville still exhibited signs that he was far from well. Shortly after the feast, he was given a bath to wash the muck and grime off which still clung to him stubbornly after the squalor of captivity. Whilst he was in the bath, de Joinville collapsed again. He was quickly put to bed; an old knight, one Peter of Bourbonne, took the young lord under his wing and nursed him back to some degree of health. He also took steps to provide him with new clothes, something that was desperately needed as those he wore were virtually falling off of him by this stage.

A few days later, de Joinville's health had improved enough for him to return to the impromptu court that Louis had set up in Acre. The King chastised him because he had been away from his court for a few days, which suggests that either the King was not very well informed about his subjects and did not know of de Joinville's illness, or was a very difficult man to please. He commanded de Joinville to ensure that he regularly sat at his table from now on, until the King had decided whether or not the army should return to France (at this stage, Louis had been silent about his plans for the future).

De Joinville told the King of a dispute that he was involved in. He had given the Templars money to bank for him, but they were now denying that they had ever received it. Kindly, Louis told him that he would repay the money that was lost from his own resources.

The problem became a difficult one, with the new Master of the Temple, Renaud of Vichiers, incensed at de Joinville's accusations, which he believed painted the Templars as little more than common thieves.

It was presumably an embarrassed Master who admitted a few days later that all the aggravation had been caused by an administrative blunder; the man with whom de Joinville had deposited the money had been posted elsewhere in Outremer, and the record-keeping of the Templars had in his absence malfunctioned. They had now found the man, who confirmed that de Joinville had indeed handed over the money as he had said he had.

The stress of this financial difficulty was too much for de Joinville's constitution, for he once again fell seriously ill. His life was despaired of once more. He relates a moving story, which is not only of personal interest but also hints at the general health of the army at this time. His lodgings were in a priest's house, which was attached to a church. There was a connecting door from de Joinville's sick chamber to the church itself. The sick lord was constantly reminded of his own mortality because every day he could hear the funeral service being recited for some poor comrade or other who had expired.

He confessed frankly that it terrified him almost witless, and the sound of the priest's chanting constantly inspired him to offer up a heart-felt and desperate prayer to God that he would make him recover. It is a haunting scene, the sound of footsteps processing slowly only the other side of the door, with the priest chanting 'libera me, Domine' in solemn, doleful tones.

But it is the number of times that it happened that is most striking. De Joinville tells us that there were never less than twenty occasions each day when he heard this grim ritual in progress. Assuming that other churches in Acre were also called upon for such rites, the mortality rate amongst those in Acre must have been particularly high. Whether it was an outbreak of some vicious epidemic, or merely the result of strain, deprivation and wounds incurred in a hot climate in which disease could run wild, is not known. Nevertheless, it was clearly both a blow to morale and a further weakening of the army's fighting state that so many men were being lost.

Fortunately for both the chronicler and future historians de Joinville recovered his health. However, when he was back to something like his old self, he was to receive another disappointment. He asked Guillemin, his newly acquired servant, for a statement of the funds that were available to him. When he subsequently investigated the results, it was only to find out that something was awry. There was less money in the account than the lord thought there should be.

On cross-examining Guillemin, the latter confessed that he had helped himself to some of his lord's funds, although, naturally enough, with every intention of paying them back. De Joinville was forced to dismiss him. He was reluctant to do so, for he genuinely seems to have liked him and gladly wrote off the amount missing, but he could not trust the servant not to embezzle any more funds in the future.

The true story of Guillemin then came out. He was what might be called, to use a modern colloquialism, a likeable rogue. If any told him that they were short of some item or other, Guillemin would go and steal it for them. He appears to have made little for himself, but however good his intentions may have been, he was obviously not a man to trust with financial matters.

The life of the court in Acre soon settled down to something like normality. The King's brothers were particularly well known for their gambling habits, and Alphonse of Poitiers especially enjoyed playing dice. He soon became famous in the city for his frequent gaming. He was however extremely generous and when he had enjoyed a particularly successful night, he would open the hall where he had been playing to all those who wished to come in. He then delighted in sharing his winnings with them, which we must assume increased his popularity no end, though no doubt all of this was to Louis's great mortification, given his dislike of gambling.

However, the normality suggested by this way of life was really little more than a hollow charade. The Crusade could not stay where it was indefinitely. It was time to consider whether the army should return to France or, if not, how it could be best used to bring about the release of the great host of men who still languished in captivity.

Louis called together the leading men of the army to debate what the next move should be. He was in no position to dictate to others how they should act. Involvement in a Crusade was not something that could be ordered by Louis, or any other earthly ruler for that matter. Participation was a question of individual conscience, and men would choose to return home when they considered that they had adequately fulfilled their vows to an extent that they qualified fully for the spiritual benefits on offer.

After what they had all been through, it would be churlish to fail to recognise the great sacrifice that most of them had already made. As well as being involved in great battles against the Infidel, many had suffered wounds, life-threatening illnesses and incarceration in very poor conditions in the searing heat of a desert land. All this reflected a great deal of trauma on the part of the Crusaders and, if many of them wished to return to the relative tranquillity of France, few could blame them.

To compound their problems, a large number of them had virtually extinguished their funds. Crusading was an expensive business, and few men ever made money from it, even in successful campaigns. Most men would be heavily in debt as a result of taking part in such an enterprise, a trend that was presumably exacerbated in this particular campaign because anything portable of valuable would have been captured by the Egyptians. If Louis wished men to stay, it was likely that he would be required to dig deep into his own pockets to pay them.

There were other reasons for Louis to consider his position. He had received news from the Regent of France, his mother, Blanche of Castille, that the English were making threatening overtures again. Attacking France whilst the King was away fighting God's battles might be morally reprehensible, and might even draw down the wrath of Pope Innocent on Henry of England's head, but that made such an act none the less likely.

Taking advantage of a monarch's extended absence was a frequent feature of the medieval landscape (the roles had been reversed during the Third Crusade, when Philip Augustus of France had caused trouble in Richard I of England's territories whilst he was away on Crusade, and had subsequently been imprisoned on the way home). It was always recognised that Louis's involvement in a Crusade did little to help the stability of France, and it was clearly high time to re-evaluate the future strategy of the expedition in the light of Blanche's news.

Louis accordingly summoned a meeting of the great men in his Council to formulate the future strategy of the Crusade. When they were all assembled, he told them all of the news from France. He related the Regent's tidings, saying that 'my kingdom is in great peril, seeing that I have neither peace nor truce with the King of England'.[1]

However, against that the Crusaders had to consider the effect that their departure would have on Outremer. If Louis were to leave, 'all those who are in Acre will follow after me, none daring to remain when the people are so few'. If this were to happen, 'this land is but lost'.

In his simple assessment of the situation, there is a glimpse of the mental torture that Louis was enduring at this time. He held a sacred duty towards the country that he ruled, and as such he was deeply troubled by the news from France. But Outremer was no ordinary land. It was God's land; within or around its borders many of the events that shaped the religion that he held so dear had taken place.

Louis had been commanded by God to lead an expedition to the region that would restore its old boundaries, but his Crusade had achieved exactly the opposite result. Not only was there little chance of cities such as Jerusalem being restored to Outremer, there were now real and serious questions about the viability of what remained of the Kingdom. His military leadership had been a disaster, whether through poor judgement or plain bad luck was an academic debate that held little interest for Louis. From what we know of the character of the King, we may assume that he berated himself personally for the fix in which Outremer now found itself, and as such he would have been suffering great pangs of conscience about abandoning it to its fate.

These were weighty matters for all those present to consider. They clearly rated deep self-examination before any definitive opinions were expressed. Louis therefore commanded those present to adjourn for a period of reflection. They were to return in eight days time, when the matter would be debated again once they had all taken time to evaluate their options. No doubt Louis commended them to pray about the issue: there was no question that he himself would not do so.

It was a time for a great deal of soul-searching to take place. De Joinville was one of those who pondered long and hard on the decision he had to make. During this period of reflection, the Papal legate, Eudes of Chateauroux, approached him. Eudes told him frankly that he believed that Louis should return to France, obviously convinced that he had contributed more than enough to the cause of the Crusade.

He also suggested to de Joinville that he ought to return with the King. The chronicler was not sure that this would be possible. There was first of all a pragmatic reason why this might be an issue for him. He had lost all his money whilst he was in Egypt and a passage back to the West would be expensive. Therefore, he could not as things stood afford to go.

But there were other issues to consider too. Before he had left France, one of his cousins had spoken to him in depth about his involvement in the Crusade. He had told de Joinville bluntly that it would leave an indelible stain on his character were he to return to France if there were a large number of what he described as the 'meaner folk of our Lord' in captivity. De Joinville was haunted by those words, which were so clearly of great relevance to the current situation. He was a man of honour as well as one who was currently financially embarrassed; he would not be returning home. The legate disagreed with his views, but was powerless to do much to change them.

After the prescribed time had elapsed, the Council met again. Louis asked those present to express their views. They replied that they had chosen one of their number, Guy of Mauvoisin, to act as their spokesman. He quickly moved to the crux of his arguments. The King had left France at the head of 2,800 knights; there were now barely 100 left in Acre. The King could not, with honour, stay in the city, with such a paltry army. Therefore, Louis should return to France and recruit another army, and sail back to Outremer when this new army had been raised.

Although this might appear at a casual glance to be a sensible course of action, Louis knew that if he were to return to France it would be years before a new army could recruited, and by the time that it had been adequately prepared and provisioned, there might be no kingdom of Outremer left to sail to. Even that pessimistic analysis might be excessively sanguine in assuming that he would be able to recruit a new army. After the disasters of the current expedition, the attraction of Crusading would be less than ever, and the ideal already had less power to attract men to the cause than it had say a century previously. Even Louis, for all his energy and resources, might find it impossible to lead another expedition to Outremer.

It appears that Louis was looking around for alternative views, for he did not rest at accepting Guy of Mauvoisin's words as being representative of everyone present. He next turned to his brothers, Charles of Anjou and Alfonse of Poitiers, for advice. They agreed with the views of Guy and all those whose opinions he represented. He passed on to the Count of Flanders to ask for his opinion, with the same result.

There was a different opinion presented however by Count John of Jaffa. When he was asked for his views, he initially demurred from giving them. He was, he said ingenuously, a local baron who clearly had a vested interest in the King staying in Outremer and as such he did not feel that he could offer an objective opinion. Louis nevertheless pushed him for an answer. Encouraged to speak out, the Count said that he believed that even if Louis were only to stay for another year, he might win himself great honour by so doing. However, for a time he appeared to be a lone voice. After he expressed his opinion, a number of others were asked for theirs, and they unanimously replied that they wished to return to France.

It came to de Joinville's turn to speak. He said that he agreed with the views of the Count of Jaffa. This caused much debate; after all, it was largely expected (even at the Count's own admission) that John of Jaffa would argue for Louis remaining in Outremer a while longer, whereas de Joinville was of a different ilk altogether. Eudes of Chateauroux asked him bluntly what good it would do for Louis to stay where he was when he had so few men left to him.

De Joinville openly admits to being annoyed by the attitude of Eudes. He replied that the King still had, by rumour, an amount of money that he had not yet spent, even after ransom payments had been allowed for. He could use this to buy the services of men who wished to stay, or indeed join him from elsewhere. He could send to the Latins in Greece for reinforcements.[2] He could offer good money to those who joined him, which was likely to attract enough men to allow him to remain in Outremer for at least a year.

Their presence should be sufficient to pressurise the Muslims into releasing those good Christian men that they held in captivity, of which there were so many. Many of these pitiful wretches were well known to those involved in the present debate. De Joinville's words evidently moved many of those there. It was true enough. All of those in the Council could form a mental image of someone who, even now, languished in some dirty, squalid Egyptian prison. No one reproached him for his views. In fact, some of them openly began to weep tears of both grief and perhaps shame.

De Joinville's words appeared to be on the verge of encouraging others to speak out in support of staying longer in Outremer. The Marshal of France, William of Beaumont, said that he thought that he had delivered an excellent speech and was about to say why when there was a sudden, violent interruption. His uncle, John of Beaumont, exploded in rage when he heard the Marshal's supportive words: he was convinced that the army should return to France. In a rage he shouted at his nephew, 'What have you got to say, son of the filthy tongue? Sit down and keep quiet.'[3]

The King asked his Marshal to carry on, despite this impolite interruption, but he would not do so. After he had been shouted down, only one other agreed with de Joinville's arguments. It appeared the debate had been lost. The King thanked them for their frank presentation of views, and told them that he would consider their arguments for another eight days, and then let them have his decision.

After the debate, de Joinville went back to his quarters, no doubt deflated at the course of events and the fact that there was so little support for his opinions. He became something of a pariah amongst those who disagreed with him. When they met, they sarcastically told him that the King must be crazy not to consider his views rather than those of the entire council. Louis asked de Joinville to sit next to him when he ate, but he said little to the lord. De Joinville detected a slight frostiness to the atmosphere, and assumed that Louis was angry with him because he had had the temerity to suggest that the King had not yet spent all of his money.

Eventually, the sense of depression became unbearable. Whilst the King was hearing grace, de Joinville despondently inched his way out of the hall. He found a little corner near a barred window. He looked longingly through the bars and pondered his future. If Louis were to return to France, he would not go with him. He was on good terms with the Prince of Antioch and he would go and serve him whilst the captives taken in Egypt remained enslaved rather than return to France in disgrace.

As he stood there, lost in these deep, lowering thoughts, he felt a pressure on his shoulders and then two hands placed around his face from behind him so that he could not see who was responsible. Angrily, he told the man behind him to leave him alone. He assumed that it was Philip of Nemours, one of the members of the Council who had been teasing him mercilessly all day for having the nerve to advise the King against the rest of his advisers. Even as he turned to face him however he saw a huge emerald ring on the man's finger. He knew that only one man in court possessed so magnificent a jewel: the King himself.

Louis spoke to him in hushed tones so that no other would overhear. He asked de Joinville why one so young had the boldness to stand virtually alone against others far more experienced than he. As humbly as he could, he responded that he spoke in this manner because he thought that if Louis were to return to France and leave so many captives behind him, then he would be doing a great wrong.

Louis then asked whether, if he were to stay in Outremer, de Joinville would also be prepared to stay behind. De Joinville responded in the affirmative. The King closed this clandestine conversation by asking de Joinville not to mention its contents to anyone else, and to await the next time that the council met to see in which direction Louis was minded to go. Nevertheless, he dropped an enormous hint to de Joinville by telling him that he was well pleased with his advice. Although he mentioned the discussion to no other man, de Joinville was naturally enough uplifted by the King's reassuring words and stood his ground much more confidently when the other barons continued to chide him for his intransigence.

The next Sunday, the council reassembled to make a momentous decision. The King thanked those present for their advice, both those who had recommended his return to France, and those who advised against it. He had of course weighed up his options very carefully. Weighty decisions rode on his deliberations, and he could not afford to make the wrong one. He knew that there were pressing reasons for his return to France, but was equally well aware that Outremer desperately needed his presence at this particularly dangerous time. There were compelling reasons to adopt either course but he could not be all things to all people. He needed to decide which region needed his personal presence the most.

Having assured his audience of the careful deliberations that he had made to come to his decision, he proceeded to the heart of the matter. In his view, France was in no great danger whilst it was in the hands of his mother, Blanche of Castille, in whom he had great trust. However, if he were to leave Outremer, the outcome would be much gloomier, 'for the barons of this land tell me that if I depart hence, the kingdom of Jerusalem is lost'.[4]

Therefore, he had no real choice. He would stay in Outremer until it was safe to go back to France. He had come, in his own words, to guard and reconquer the kingdom, and his job was hardly started, let alone completed. To leave the country in this state would be tantamount to betrayal. Those who wished to stay with Louis would be rewarded generously. The King needed an army and the more that stayed behind in Outremer, the better for the Crusading cause.

A stunned silence descended upon the assembled barons. Some were openly moved to tears. Many were undoubtedly bewildered, convinced in their heart of hearts that the wrong decision had been made. However, although it is not recorded, few probably argued against Louis's resolution. They knew their King well. He was a stubborn man, who would not lightly alter course once he had set his stall out.

Louis's men were free to make their own decisions, as they always had been. Many would cut their losses, and escape from this dreadful part of the World as quickly as possible. The land of milk and honey had been an illusion, a mirage that promised glory and reward, but brought only shame and disappointment. For them the Crusade was over, a shattering experience that most probably wished they had never been involved in. But for their King, a new mission was about to begin.

Louis the Diplomat

Despite Louis's decision to stay in Outremer, many other knights decided to leave. The morale of the army was plainly worse than the King had believed and many were disillusioned at the way the Crusade had gone so far. When the dust had settled and those who had opted to go had departed, Louis was left with barely 1,500 men, hardly a force likely to terrify his enemies. In the light of this, a long and extended military campaign was less likely than ever. If the remaining Crusaders wished to make any gains then diplomacy was going to be key.

Louis's brothers were amongst those deciding to return to France. On the feast day of St James, 25 July 1250, Louis summoned another meeting of his council. A month had gone by since he had announced his decision to stay and he had as yet seen little sign of any men at all committing themselves to serve in his army. At the council, he was told that many were desperate to go home.

Louis summoned de Joinville into his presence, recognising in him a potential ally. The baron made his way into the hall and knelt before him. Louis told him to rise. He asked him why de Joinville had not committed to stay in Outremer. De Joinville's answer was simple. His response mirrored that of many other knights with Louis. He had lost everything that he had brought with him in Egypt and he had no resources to call his own. When Louis asked what he wanted, he said that for a sum of 2,000 *livres* he would agree to serve Louis until the following Easter.

Louis wanted to know what he would get from this bargain. De Joinville told him that he had already approached three knights with a view to them joining his service. They would cost 400 *livres* each, and that would only leave 800 *livres* for de Joinville himself. With this sum, he would have to equip himself with new armour and a new horse, as well as providing food and other provisions for the knights that served with him. He asked Louis whether this seemed an unreasonable request. The King replied that, on the contrary, the bargain seemed very sensible and he would happily accede to de Joinville's suggestion. He was duly accepted into the King's service. His wish to stay in Outremer rather than return home with a reputation besmirched with dishonour had been granted.

Shortly after this, those who had opted to leave Outremer made their preparations to sail. Alphonse of Poitiers borrowed jewels from some of the other great men who were returning with him, and freely distributed them amongst those who were to stay behind so that they might be able to provide for themselves better.

Both Alphonse and Charles of Anjou, Louis's other brother, told de Joinville to take good care of the King. The moments during which the brothers bade farewell were particularly harrowing. As they gathered for one last embrace on the dockside, the scenes of emotion became almost too much to bear. Charles of Anjou particularly was grief-stricken and wept profusely when he took leave of the King.

But despite his obvious affection for Louis there was no last minute change of heart. Charles had given all that he could to the cause and had nothing left to offer. Ponderously, as if wishing to stay close to his brothers for as long as possible, his emotions overwhelmed by the solemnity of the occasion, he crossed from the dock to his ship. The sails were unfurled and, within a short time, the vessel taking him back to France, along with many others, disappeared over the horizon.

Acre seemed empty with them gone. The hall in which Louis feasted daily was much the quieter without his brothers. Perhaps he even missed their gambling which, sinful though it might have been in his eyes, injected a dash of gaiety and fun into the everyday formal rituals of court life. For all their faults as men (and they do not stand out as sinners when compared to other men of the day) they were Louis's flesh and blood, and he loved them dearly. All of a sudden, Louis felt dreadfully alone.

Shortly afterwards, Louis received envoys from the Emperor Frederick, who had a great deal of influence in Outremer. They arrived too late to be of use, for they carried with them letters to the previous Sultan suggesting that the Egyptians should release King Louis. If nothing else, it illustrated well the problem of communication in this period. Seeing that their mission was superfluous, the envoys made polite conversation with Louis and his court and then left.

However, an opportunity was soon to present itself to Louis to help in dividing the Muslim world. He received representation from the Sultan of Damascus, an-Nasir Yusuf, seeking an alliance against the Egyptians, in return for which Jerusalem would be returned to the Crusaders. In response, Louis sent an embassy of his own to Damascus, led by a priest, Yves le Breton, who could speak local languages. The envoys saw many strange sights in what was to them an exotic city but made little progress in forming an alliance. The problem for Louis was that strategically he could not push the prospect of siding with the Damascenes too far as the Egyptians still held the whip hand because they had so many Christian prisoners in their possession.

This army of captives offered great potential to the Egyptians as hostages. Louis eventually responded to the Sultan of Damascus that he felt unable to co-operate with him until he knew for sure whether the Egyptians would fulfil the requirements of the treaty or not: their track record had not been overly impressive to date. If they did not, he assured an-Nasir Yusuf that he would not hesitate to help the Sultan of Damascus to avenge the murder of Turanshah.

This interlude merely presaged a frenzy of diplomatic activity. For a time, it seemed that every major power in the region was attracted to the court in Acre like bees to a honey pot. A delegation was received next from one of the most mysterious groups in the region. In the Nosairi Mountains, in the hinterland of Syria, were the headquarters of a fanatical religious party of Ismaili Muslims. This particular form of Islam was inimically opposed, both doctrinally and politically, to the Sunni Muslims who ruled Syria.

Adopting the old maxim that 'my enemy's enemy is my friend' the group had several times approached the Crusaders in the past with a view to advancing what they saw as their mutual interests. There was one feature that distinguished this group from all others. They welcomed death in the course of religious struggle as they thought that, by such martyrdom, they bought their place in paradise, which was for them a land of luxury and sexual delights.

Like the Bedouins, they believed that a man could not die before the time that Allah had appointed for him, and they wore no armour, deeming it to be irrelevant, as whether or not a man died was God's will alone and armour made no difference. Their devotion to their leader, a mystical and penumbral figure known evocatively as 'The Old Man of the Mountains' was legendary. Whatever he ordered, they would obey.

This usually involved the murder of his political enemies, which was normally a suicide mission for those picked out for the task. They were, later legends were to claim, helped on their way by being doped with hashish, though whether they actually did so is dubious. This supposed proclivity for drugs was responsible for the name given to them. Their fingerprint on history was so great that their name lives on as a word for political murderers that remains an everyday part of modern language. They were known as *hassishiyin* – the Assassins.[1]

They liked to make an impression when they first introduced themselves to any with whom they wished to do business. When the Assassin envoys arrived in Acre, Louis was, typically enough, otherwise engaged at mass. Once he returned, they were shown into his presence. A young emir sat at the front of the delegation of three representatives. He was well-dressed and striking in appearance. In his hand, he bore three knives. If the King rejected any of his master's proposals they were to be presented to Louis as a mark of defiance.

Another representative who sat behind him carried a winding sheet. This was to be given to Louis if he refused to accept the proposals so that he could shortly after be buried in it. It was hardly a subtle approach, but the message of the knives and the shroud at least had the virtue that the recipient was in no doubt where they stood.

Louis bade the well-dressed emir begin. The envoy commenced by asking Louis whether he knew his master. Louis replied that he had never met him but he knew well of his reputation and standing in the region. The emir pushed the point. He was surprised to hear that Louis knew his master. If this was the case, why had the King not sent him any gifts to buy his favour?

Apparently, many others had done so, including the Emperor Frederick, the Christian King of Hungary and the Egyptian Sultan. They did this, the envoy said, because they knew that only by so doing would they keep their lives. Everyone, even the greatest men in the World, only lived by the sufferance of the Old Man of the Mountains. If Louis did not wish to make a monetary gift to the Old Man, there was something else he could do for him. The Assassins paid an annual tribute to the Templars and the Hospitallers. It would be appreciated if the King could use his best efforts to have this requirement remitted.

The King listened to the request dispassionately. A man of his character would not take kindly to the threats implicit in the envoy's message. He bade the delegation leave him and return later in the afternoon. When they did so, Louis was accompanied by the Masters of both of the great Orders. The King asked the envoy to repeat his request. The emir was initially reluctant to do so, haughtily refusing at first to repeat his words of the morning. After his initial rude rebuff of the King's request however he eventually acceded and told the Masters of his lord's requirements. They replied that he should come back the next day for their reply.

Louis may have known of the Old Man, but it is clear that the knowledge was not entirely reciprocated. Whatever might be said of Louis, he was no coward. He had been much more directly threatened when a captive in Egypt and had not given in to bullying tactics despite the very real and immediate threat to his life. He also felt keenly the importance of his position as God's own anointed.

The arrogance of the emir was an insult not only to him personally, but also to the French monarchy. As a result, when the self-assured emir returned the next day for an answer, he got rather more than he had bargained for. The Masters of the Orders submitted the envoy to a verbal assault the like of which he had rarely if ever experienced before. His arrogance towards the King was unforgivable.

He was told that it was only the fact that he came as the messenger of the Old Man that had dissuaded Louis from throwing him into the seas off Acre. If the Old Man wished to have Louis as a friend, there would be no blood money forthcoming from the French King. On the contrary, the envoy should return to his Master. He should re-visit the Crusaders fifteen days later. If he wished to be forgiven his arrogance, he should make sure that he returned bearing gifts as an expression of his remorse.

Humbled, the envoy returned to his master with the message that normal tactics were clearly not appropriate for King Louis. At the appointed time, he returned with a delegation from the Old Man of the Mountains. His stance on this later occasion was somewhat different than that employed formerly.

His first act was to present King Louis with The Old Man's shirt. It appears an odd gesture perhaps but it was deeply symbolic, evidencing as it did the wish of the Ismaili leader to present to Louis that which had been nearer to his body than any other thing. We might assume that Louis was more interested in the more tangible manifestations of goodwill that accompanied this strange gift. There were a number of precious objects of much value that the Old Man had sent with his ambassadors.

There were for example jewels of elephants made of crystal and 'a beast called a giraffe' made of the same material. There was a chess set and other gaming tables. The peace offerings of the Old Man were wrapped in ambergris and tied together with thread finely woven from gold. When the well-carved caskets that they were carried in were opened, the delicate perfumes from inside permeated the room with warm and beautiful odours.

This was a much more acceptable approach as far as the King was concerned. He needed allies badly, and it was sensible to overlook the hostility and arrogance of the Assassins' earlier approach. The point had been well made; Louis was no pushover and demanded to be treated in a way that was appropriate to a great monarch. Now that the Assassins had been taught this particular lesson, it made sense for the Crusaders to swallow their pride and foster amicable relations with them as they might prove to be very useful allies.

The loyal Brother Yves was again deputed to lead a delegation, this time to the headquarters of the Old Man of the Mountains. The priest was a trustworthy man, who clearly did not lack for bravery either. He spent much of his time when he arrived at his castle trying to convince the Old Man of the perceived doctrinal errors implicit in his creed but with no success.

The leader of the Assassins made a great impression on the Crusaders. They were particularly impressed by the way that his progress was announced when he travelled around. In front of him, a bodyguard carried a great Danish axe, capable of cleaving a man's skull in two. This already intimidating weapon was made doubly impressive by the knives that protruded from its haft. As the bodyguard walked he shouted to those around, 'Turn aside from before him who bears in his hands the death of kings.'[2]

This diversion aside, the King wished to increase the stakes with the Egyptians. Anxious to secure the release of the captives that they still held as soon as possible, he sent a delegation to Egypt under the leadership of John of Valenciennes. He boldly went on to the offensive. He demanded that the Egyptians should make reparations for the wrongs they had committed in breaking the terms of the treaty. For their part, the Egyptians said that they were willing to do so provided Louis joined them in an alliance against the Sultan of Damascus. John said that he did not have the authority to agree to this on Louis's behalf but that it would clearly help their case if they were to release the prisoners that they still held.

John's embassy ended with considerable success. When he arrived back in Acre, he had with him 200 knights that the Egyptians had freed. He also carried a more solemn burden. One of the great knights of the Crusade who had died in Egypt was Walter of Brienne. As a token of respect, the Egyptians sent his remains back with John. He was subsequently buried with great pomp and ceremony in the Hospitaller church in Acre. In an appropriately subdued and reverent atmosphere, the bones of the Count were interred.

Amongst the prisoners that were released and came back with John of Valenciennes was a party of some forty knights from Champagne. They came from the same region as de Joinville and it was therefore not a surprise when they asked him if he would take them into his service. There was not universal agreement to this; some felt that the King's finances were too severely stretched to assume the responsibility of paying for these men, as he would be bound to do because de Joinville did not have enough resources of his own to cover their costs.

De Joinville was infuriated. He told those that were against the appointment that thirty-five knights from Champagne had lost their lives in the campaign to date. Therefore, these new recruits only restored the balance. Further, the King was in desperate need of more men. The latter point was particularly telling. The heavily armoured horsemen were the shock troops of all Crusader armies. They were the warriors feared more than any other by the enemy. If Louis were to be successful in his ambition to recover anything from the Crusade, such men were vital to his cause and he needed more of them.

De Joinville felt his frustrations well over, so much so that he began to weep. Moved by his obvious emotion, as well as the logic of his arguments, Louis told him not to fret. The men would indeed be taken into service. No doubt overjoyed at his decision, de Joinville prepared to enrol the men in his battalion, duly kitted out in surcoats of green cloth.

The Egyptians had released these captives as a gesture of goodwill. In return, they continued to press for an alliance against the Sultan of Damascus, an-Nasir Yusuf. The situation was developing perfectly as far as Louis was concerned, as one Muslim party bid against the other for the support of the Crusaders, whose reputation as fighting men had obviously not been too catastrophically dented by their humiliation in Egypt.

Louis sensed that he could take further advantage of this situation. He clearly enjoyed being in the position of power broker. Therefore, he sent John of Valenciennes back to Cairo asking for further concessions. One of his requests had a touch of the macabre about it. Ever since the campaign that culminated in their victory at La Forbie, the Egyptians had removed the heads of the Crusaders that they had killed in battle, or executed after the event, and draped them round the walls of Cairo. It was a humiliating reminder to the Crusaders of the terrible happenings of the last few years, as well as being an insult to the memory of men who were effectively regarded as martyrs in the Christian cause.

Louis asked that the Egyptians should remove all these remains and return them to Outremer so that they could be interred with due respect. He also asked for the return of all the Christian children that had been taken captive and forced to convert to Islam, as well as full remittance of the 200,000 *livres* that remained outstanding from the ransom. It was a very tough position for Louis to take, and probably represented his opening gambit in what he expected to be an extended round of negotiations but it also evidenced his increasing confidence.

Shortly afterwards, he demonstrated further his heightened ambition. Partway between Acre and Jerusalem stood Caesarea. It was in an important strategic location and it had been destroyed by the Muslims. Louis felt that it should be re-occupied and fortified as a means of exerting pressure on the enemy by threatening the approaches to Jerusalem. Much to the marvel of de Joinville, who wondered how the Crusaders had managed to avert an attack from the Muslims whilst they were in such a weakened state, the King set out with a force to rebuild the fortifications of the city. Whilst he was there, another delegation arrived. This particular embassy had undertaken the longest journey yet.

It seemed like a lifetime since the King had despatched an ambassador to the Mongols, although it was in fact only a couple of years since Louis had sent an embassy, along with the beautifully-embroidered chapel in the form of a tent, to the Great Khan. Louis's life had turned topsy-turvy since the heady days of expectation in Cyprus that preceded the attack on Egypt. The envoys that he sent then had initially made the short crossing to the great city of Antioch. From here, they had ridden hard across Asia to seek an audience with the Great Khan.

Some idea of the challenge posed by the journey can be gauged from the fact that, despite the fact that they rode for 30 miles a day, it took them a full year to reach their final destination. On the way, they saw some horrifying sights. They passed near a number of cities that had been taken by the Mongols or, more accurately, what remained of what were once-great conurbations. In places, the country resembled a wasteland the most prominent feature of which was huge piles of human bones.

It was an apocalyptic landscape that met their eyes. With an increasing sense of horror, the truth of the Mongol's request for an alliance slowly dawned on them. As they advanced further into the heart of Asia, they became ever more acutely aware of the reality of the Mongol menace. For the Great Khan, 'the lord of earth and heaven', nothing less than complete submission would suffice. All men – including King Louis – must accept his suzerainty or perish.

Even now, centuries later, it is impossible not to feel a sense of admiration for Louis's ambassadors. The prospect of an audience with the man who led the people responsible for such savagery must have been truly terrifying, yet the envoys persisted with their mission. When they finally reached the camp of the Great Khan, they realised more than ever how terrible was the threat posed by the Mongols, for as well as their prowess in war and their violence in victory, they appeared to be as numberless as the sands.

The Great Khan's encampment was enormous. The ambassadors were particularly struck by the number of 'chapels on wagons' that were in the camp. There were 800 of them in all, catering for the large number of Nestorian Christians amongst the tribes. In addition, there were vast numbers of Muslims. This division of loyalties was fully exploited by the Mongol leaders, who tried to use Christian warriors in wars against Muslims and vice-versa.

The strange habits of the Mongols made a special impression on the ambassadors, not least their attitude to food. A Mongol's greatest asset was his horse. It was what gave him mobility: the greatest threat of the Mongols came from their ability to move quickly in vast numbers and pounce suddenly on an unsuspecting enemy with overwhelming force. However, it not only provided him with a form of transport, it also acted as a source of nutrition.

The favourite drink of the Mongol was mare's milk flavoured with honey.[3] His favourite food was horseflesh, prepared by soaking the meat in brine and then drying it, so that it looked like black bread. The tribesmen (and women, many of whom accompanied the Mongols on their expeditions) tenderised the meat by riding with it between their bodies and their saddles. The meat was eaten raw, and if it could not be consumed immediately, it would be placed in the pouches that the Mongols carried and taken out later when a meal was to be eaten.[4]

When the envoys had offered their gifts and greetings to the Great Khan – which he fortunately received favourably – he summoned a number of other people into his presence. He had the tent that Louis had sent as a gift erected, and showed it to several Kings who had not yet submitted to his rule, meaning to impress them. His interpretation of what the gifts meant was clear enough. He turned to those who, as yet, resisted his claims to supremacy and exclaimed, 'Lords, the King of France has sued for mercy and submitted himself to us and behold here is the tribute he has sent to us.'[5]

Clearly he believed that the sumptuous gift that Louis had sent was more than an expression of friendship towards the Mongols; rather, it was a plea for mercy from the great arbiter of life and death and an expression of obeisance. The Great Khan used the tent to intimidate others into submission. According to de Joinville, the strategy was very successful.

Nevertheless, the interpretation placed on the gift by the Mongols was very different than that intended by Louis. The Great Khan gave the envoys letters to deliver to Louis. They left the camp and made their way back towards Outremer, no doubt eager to put as much space between them and the terrifying Mongol hordes as quickly as possible. These letters were duly presented to Louis. There was no attempt at subtlety, as the Mongol Khan told Louis bluntly that the only way to hope for peace was to submit absolutely to his authority.

The letters went on to demand that Louis should pay over a yearly tribute to the Mongols, comprising gold and silver, if he wished to retain their friendship. They ended with a flourish, saying that 'if thou wilt not do this, we will destroy thee and thy people'. Louis listened with an increasing sense of dread as the letter progressed. When it ended, he realised how completely he had misjudged the intentions of the Great Khan. With wonderful understatement, de Joinville tells us that 'it repented the King sorely that he had ever sent envoys to the great King of the Mongols'.

Louis received more welcome visitors in the shape of a group of knights from Norway. It is easy to forget that Crusaders came from all over Europe and at various times there were expeditions great or small from virtually every Catholic power on the continent from Ireland to Hungary.

The Scandinavian party arrived whilst Louis was away re-fortifying Caesarea. They were led by Alenard of Senaingan. They had endured a difficult voyage and to attempt it at all spoke volumes for their Norse sea-faring heritage. They had constructed the ship back home in Norway, 'at the world's end' according to de Joinville, and had sailed down past Spain, through the Straits of Gibraltar and along the north coast of Africa.

It was a dangerous journey, and to survive it at all may have seemed like a miracle in itself to many of those involved in the expedition. Alenard proved a popular man, and he was recruited into Louis's army along with some of his knights. He was a particularly entertaining storyteller (another old Viking characteristic) and kept many amused with stories that to them were virtually unbelievable, such as how night never arrived in Norway during the summer.

They were also reckless. There were many lions in Palestine. The Asiatic version was smaller than its African cousin, but was none the less deadly for all that. These beasts were prized as sport amongst the Crusaders. The Norwegians approach to hunting was risky to say the least. They would shoot arrows at the lion. When it sprang back at them in anger (one arrow was never enough to mortally wound it), they would drop a rag at its feet. Confused, the lion fell on the cloth and ripped it to pieces, thinking that it had in its jaws its assailant. Whilst it did so, another hunter came up behind it and fired another arrow. The lion would then attack the second hunter, and the ruse would be repeated. This cruel ritual would continue until the lion, pierced all over with arrows, fell exhausted and dead to the ground.

There was one other significant visitor to arrive at the court of King Louis at the end of this busy season, and he was most welcome. This was Philip of Toucy, Louis's cousin. His sister was married to the Latin Emperor of Byzantium. The French had a special place in their hearts for the Byzantine Empire that had been created by the Fourth Crusade some forty years previously, as they thought of it as essentially an extension of the French court. Louis was delighted to greet his cousin and enlisted him into his army, along with nine knights, for a year. At the end of that time, he returned to Constantinople.

Whilst he was with Louis, Philip talked much of affairs in Constantinople. The Latin Empire had always been vulnerable, surrounded by enemies from its birth. It was now seriously under threat from a rival Greek Emperor, John Vatatzes. Since Constantinople had fallen to the Crusaders, there had usually been at least two rival Greek Byzantine kingdoms, one centred around the ancient city of Nicaea and the other in the north-west of Greece in the Epirus region. Vatatzes had changed all that. He had defeated the ruler of Epirus and re-united much of the old Byzantine Empire. This meant that the Latins in Constantinople were surrounded and dangerously exposed.

In such a situation, difficult realities had to be faced. There were a number of barbarian tribes in the region of the Balkans and its immediate environs who were traditional foes of the Greek Byzantines. One group in particular, the Cumans,[6] were well known for their ferocity in battle and general savagery. They were excellent horsemen, of Turkish stock originally, who were extremely useful light cavalry. They were particularly renowned as horse-archers – a traditional strength of most Turkish forces – who could charge in to the massed ranks of the enemy, loose their arrows and charge out again before their foe had a chance to re-organise. They would be very useful in battle against the Greeks, but they had many traditions that were very alien to most men from the West.

For example, when two parties agreed to enter an alliance together, the Cumans insisted that their friendship should be sealed by a ceremony especially designed for such an occasion. The Latin Emperor of Byzantium came to their camp to go through this unusual ritual, which required that he and his Cuman counter-part both cut themselves with knives and let their blood flow into a silver bowl. Others from both sides followed suit. The blood was then mixed with water and wine to form a distinctly unappetising cocktail. Men from all parties then drank from the bowl and were deemed to be blood brothers.

Neither was this the end of the rituals. A dog was forced to pass between the two parties, who slashed at the poor creature with their swords until it was cut to ribbons. The point of this particularly barbaric ceremony was that any man who broke the terms of the treaty between the two parties could expect similar treatment to be meted out to him.

Whilst Philip, who had accompanied the Emperor, was in the camp of the Cumans, he saw another strange ritual take place. One of the great Cuman knights died, and the Latins were present at his funeral ceremony. A large grave was dug in the earth, and the dead Cuman warrior was sat up in it in a chair. One of his squires was then dressed in a scarf of gold and silver. The dead man's horse was also brought forward.

Both horse and squire were then put in the grave, the squire carrying a letter written by the Cuman King that he was to present to the spirits he would meet at a later stage, telling them that he (the squire) had lived a good life and had been loyal to his master. Both the squire and the horse were then buried alive, to serve their master in the world that was to come. Wooden boards were placed over the grave, which was finally covered with a huge mound of earth. Those that were left alive drank to the memory of the dead warrior long into the night. These were strange bedfellows indeed for the Christian Latins, but desperate times called for desperate measures.

These diplomatic manoeuvrings show that there was more than martial glory involved in Crusading in the East. The disparity in the strength of the respective forces involved in the region meant that a range of approaches needed to be adopted to ensure that any such enterprise achieved as much success as was possible under what were usually unfavourable circumstances. Louis must have pondered much on the tales related by Philip of Toucy: this was a strange part of the world indeed.

Louis was not the first Western monarch to discover that politics was needed to plug the gap where military enterprise had failed – no less a Crusading legend than Richard the Lionheart had discovered the same during the Third Crusade. As the stories of Philip of Toucy illustrated perfectly, all sorts of unusual alliances must be sought if a

Crusading kingdom of any description were to survive in the region. It was a lesson that Louis, after the disastrous debacle in Egypt, had started to learn well.

Taking stock of the situation, Louis would have been pleased at the progress made since arriving in Outremer. In contrast to the military disaster of the Egyptian campaign, his diplomatic efforts promised to achieve much more. Most importantly of all, he was being wooed by both the Sultan of Damascus and the Sultan of Egypt. Further, the eagerness of the Egyptians to ingratiate themselves to him had led to the release of a sizeable number of prisoners with the promise of more to come.

Although there were still a great number of men in captivity, there was now genuine hope that they too might be released. Louis's stock had risen as a result of these events. When he arrived in Acre from Egypt, it was as a discredited, defeated monarch. Now, although the Muslim world hardly trembled in fear at the threat that he and his forces posed, he was at least thought of with respect. It was not much of an achievement perhaps but for Louis everything was relative. His attempts to limit the damage caused by the debacle in Egypt had started well. He now had to ensure that he made the most of the limited opportunities that were to come if his great Crusade were to achieve anything at all.

13

Consolidation and Disappointment

Although the Crusaders were not strong enough to significantly threaten either party in the ongoing dispute between Damascus and Cairo, they were nevertheless in a position to tip the scales of the balance of power. For this reason, both Sultan Aibek of Egypt and Sultan an-Nasir Yusuf of Damascus were eager to have the Crusaders supporting their side in the continued confrontation. It was an advantage that Louis had to reap the maximum benefit from if he were to achieve his aim of improving the situation in Outremer.

For most of the rank-and-file in the army, their continued presence in Outremer was a source of both adventure and anxiety. They were hemmed in on all sides by hostile parties, who would not hesitate, if the political tensions between the Muslim parties in the region eased, to drive the Infidels back into the sea. Lofty politics meant little to most of those of Louis's army who were not directly involved in the ongoing higher-level discussions. Survival and a long-term future (which for many would hopefully include a return to France) were of far greater relevance.

Few men remaining with the army had independent means to support their existence in Outremer, and most were consequently in the pay of the King. De Joinville had covenanted the year before to stay with Louis, in return for which the King would subsidise him financially. The time was fast approaching when the agreement would need to be reviewed as Louis had only undertaken to underwrite his costs until Easter, a time of year that was now rapidly approaching.

Louis was well aware of this, and asked de Joinville to share his future plans with him. De Joinville replied that he did not wish to enter into a bargain with the King in the same way that he had previously, 'because,' he said, 'you are angry when one asks you for anything.' This hints at the King's state of mind, which must often have been one of extreme agitation, required to balance the affairs of his realm with those of Outremer and also to find ways to finance what was a very expensive stay in the East.

So de Joinville offered to serve the King provided that, in return, Louis should not be angry with him if de Joinville should ask for help at any time during the next year. The King laughed and, thinking that it was a fine bargain, he readily assented to enter into it. Then he led de Joinville into his council chamber, where he announced that a bargain had been struck. The council and the legate were all delighted to hear this news because, as de Joinville himself immodestly said, 'I was the man of most note and substance in the host'.

This was a jocular little exchange of views but it suggests a deeper concern. Louis was rich but he had invested hugely in the Crusade so far and the ongoing support and maintenance of many of the men left in Outremer was a strain on even his considerable resources. If Louis was becoming irritable because men were always asking him for financial support, it was probably because he himself was running short of resources. Even the purse of the King of France was not bottomless.

De Joinville spent four years in Outremer after Alphonse of Poitiers and Charles of Anjou left Louis for France. His chronicle tells us much about life in Outremer, although we should also be careful to avoid over-romanticising such an existence as de Joinville was undoubtedly amongst the more privileged elite of society's hierarchy – for most people, life would have been much tougher. In addition, the fact that he wrote years after the events to which he referred would hardly have helped his accuracy.

As an illustration of the resources available to him, de Joinville had in his company two chaplains to attend to his spiritual needs. De Joinville's day began with one of them reciting mass at dawn. The other waited until the knights and other men in de Joinville's entourage were awake, and then said mass with them. Once de Joinville had started the day in this religious fashion, he left his pavilion and went to see Louis. Often, he and the King would then ride together. On many occasions, messengers would make their way to the King whilst he was out riding with de Joinville, which meant that the Seneschal had great insight into political matters.

There were other more worldly distractions too. Whilst men were away from their wives for so long, it was inevitable that they would be tempted to stray. In a spiritual sense, it was vitally important that men avoided such dalliances. It was not that such *affaires de cœuer* were stigmatised by society. They were commonplace even when men were living in France. But if a man were to reap the full spiritual benefits on offer from his involvement in the Crusades, then he should abstain from participating in sexual practices whilst he was Crusading. If he broke this vow, then the supreme efforts he had made to take part in the Crusade would be wasted, as the spiritual benefits offered by Indulgences would be ineffective.

De Joinville therefore made sure that he laid out his pavilion in such a way that anyone who entered could see that he lay in his bed alone: he did this 'so that there should be no ill suspicion as concerning women'. Evidently, not only was it important to be scrupulous in his dealings with the opposite sex; it was also important that he was seen to be so.

The fact that de Joinville had a large retinue with him was something of a double-edged sword. On the one hand, it meant that de Joinville had many of his needs attended to by others, which obviously made life much more pleasant for him than for those amongst the Crusaders who were less well off. But on the other hand, it meant that he had to provide not only for himself but also for those of his company. De Joinville ended up with fifty knights in his division. These men all had to be fed, as well as the squires that supported them.

Meal-time was a great ritual, partly because it was the part of the day that men most looked forward to; not only could they feast, they could relax, they could jest, they could discuss tactics and future plans. Therefore, much was made of it. The knights were sat on mats grouped around de Joinville. Wine was served with the meals, along with jugs of water.[2] Each knight could therefore add water to the wine to suit his own taste. The less important men in de Joinville's retinue did not have this privilege; their wine was watered down in advance.

There was an inverse relationship between the importance of the social group and the amount of water in their wine; the lowlier the social status of the individuals consuming the wine, the greater the volume of water in it. On important festivals, de Joinville made a point of laying on sumptuous feasts to which all men of note were invited, so much so that on occasion Louis had to 'borrow' some guests from de Joinville because there were not enough men of note attending on him.

Outremer as a community was dangerously vulnerable because it was a salient in the midst of hostile enemy states. As a kingdom, it would not have been viable without its strong maritime links with Western Europe and Italy who effectively provided part of its life-support system. It relied on the trade routes that had developed for provisions, and also reinforcements of men, to be shipped in. The importance of the maritime strength of the great Italian city-states to the continued survival of Outremer cannot be overstated. The galleys of the West criss-crossed the Mediterranean with great regularity, and for a time the sea was largely the domain of the West (although there were a number of pirates who made the crossing hazardous for anything except a well-protected fleet).

The seasonal nature of the crossings meant that men like de Joinville had to stock up with supplies before winter came. Otherwise, they would run short and, even if food were obtainable during these months, it would be inordinately expensive. He took measures to deal with this. He brought pigs for his sties, as well as sheep, flour and wine. He brought wine a hundred tuns at a time. Like many self-respecting Frenchmen, he seems to have been a connoisseur, noting that he always drank the best wine first.

Louis proved himself to be a stern disciplinarian in Outremer, much as he was in France. At Caesarea, he gave a number of judgements that give a fascinating insight into the problems of life in Outremer. Some were everyday issues: immorality, petty brawling, rights of property for example. Their very ordinariness reminds us that Outremer at this time was to some extent an extension of Western Europe. Despite the partial assimilation of local cultures and practices from those who had lived in Outremer for a time, this was still a society based on Western values.

For example de Joinville tells of a knight who had been caught in a brothel. Prostitution existed as much in Outremer as it did anywhere else in the world. For a knight caught with one in such a compromising situation, local custom demanded one of two remedies. The first was that he should be led through the Christian camp by the harlot he had been caught with, dressed only in a shirt and tied up with a rope. The other men in the camp could then see what a despicable Christian he was.

His shame would be unbounded. If he wished to avoid this very public stain on his honour, his alternative was to hand over his horse and arms to the King, and leave at once. It is an interesting insight into the code of honour amongst the knights of the day that the guilty man in this case handed over his weapons and his horse rather than endure the disgrace of the first option. This was a hugely expensive option for him to choose.

However, this brought about a problem of a different kind. A horse was a very valuable commodity in Outremer. De Joinville knew of a poor knight with the army who did not have a horse of his own, and he asked the King, who by law now owned the horse, to donate it to this disadvantaged warrior. Louis would have none of it. The horse was worth 80 livres, far too valuable a prize in his view to hand over in such a fashion.

De Joinville had the temerity to remind the King of the latter's covenant with him and had the effrontery to imply that Louis had broken the terms of the bargain by displaying his displeasure. Louis laughed his complaints off. He was not angry with de Joinville at all, he assured the Seneschal. Nonetheless, the horse was not handed over. Louis was not always as even-handed in his dealings as his subjects would like. The ease with which he ignored the agreement that he had previously made with de Joinville suggests a King absolutely convinced of his divine right to total authority over his kingdom and his subjects.

There were other practical matters requiring justice too. Hunting rights were much prized, and a dispute broke out between some Hospitaller knights and part of the army. De Joinville was right at the heart of the confrontation. Some of his knights were out hunting gazelle when they were set upon by a group of Hospitallers who drove them off. There were many who believed that the Military Orders had too much power for their own good, and complaints against them were not uncommon.

De Joinville took the matter up with the Master of the Hospital. The Master appears to have handled the problem in an absolutely scrupulous fashion. Finding that his men had exceeded their authority, he made them all sit on their cloaks when they were eating. This seems a bizarre punishment but was regarded as something of a disgrace in Outremer. The guilty knights were to sit this way until they were raised from the ground by those they had wronged.

A short time later, de Joinville visited the Master whilst he was dining. He saw that the wrongdoers were still being made to sit on their cloaks whilst eating. He felt that they had been sufficiently punished and asked the Master to command the brethren to stand up. The Master refused point-blank. The men had, in his view, been guilty of a great crime which might discourage pilgrims from travelling to Outremer. They should therefore be punished for longer before mercy was shown. De Joinville believed that the point had been well proved and felt that the Master was going too far. He told him bluntly that he would sit with the guilty knights whilst they ate himself until they were forgiven. Feeling that his hand was forced, the Master reluctantly assented to pardon the knights forthwith.

Another problem that involved de Joinville personally might have had a much more brutal outcome. One of the King's sergeants man-handled one of his knights. It was not a serious offence and did not go beyond some low-key jostling. But De Joinville was infuriated. He took the matter up direct with Louis. The King suggested that the Seneschal was overreacting. However, de Joinville hinted at his strong sense of principle by telling Louis bluntly that, if the King's men were allowed to push anybody around in such a fashion, he would leave the King's army at once.

Perhaps concerned at the loss of such a loyal supporter, Louis agreed that the knight should be punished. The offending sergeant was led before his 'victim' barefoot, clothed only in his shirt. In his hand, he held a sword. Fearfully, he approached the knight that he had wronged. Kneeling before him, he pointed the point of the sword towards his body and handed it over. He then admitted his offence. He agreed that he had laid hands upon de Joinville's knight. By rights, the offended knight had the right to cut off his assailant's hand. Fortunately, good sense prevailed. De Joinville asked his knight to forgive the sergeant, a request that he assented to.

Another incident that de Joinville relates had potentially much greater political consequences than the others described. Of all the Orders, the greatest were the Templars. But not only were they very powerful, they were widely regarded as being more arrogant than the other Orders. The history of Outremer is littered with examples of when the Templars or the Hospitallers went their own way; on occasion they even ended up fighting each other after allying themselves with different Muslim factions.

On one occasion, the Master of the Temple sent one of his knights, Hugh of Juoy, to negotiate a settlement concerning a land dispute with the Sultan of Damascus. The Templars claimed sole ownership of it but the Sultan of Damascus wished to have part of the land. As a result of the negotiations, it was agreed that it would be divided into two, with one half going to the Templars and the other to the Damascenes. This bargain was made subject to confirmation by Louis.

Louis was extremely annoyed when the deal was put to him. His major concern was that, not only did the deal signify the intention of fostering good relations with Damascus – something he would be anxious to avoid if he wished to further ingratiate himself with the Egyptians – but also Louis felt that the Templars should not be dealing with anyone without his knowledge.

It was a moot point whether Louis had any authority over the Templars. In a legal sense, they were a separate entity who were not answerable to any monarch, only to the Pope himself. However, pragmatism dictated that, if Outremer were to recover from its recent series of body blows, there needed to be a coherent strategy in place. If the Templars had not breached any laws in negotiating separately with Damascus, they had nevertheless been myopic in their decision to conduct such discussions without reference to any wider strategic considerations. Their actions could compromise Louis's attempts to play off one party against the other.

Louis decided to prove a point with the Master. Bluntly, he told him that he had overstepped the mark in undertaking such delicate discussions without first referring them to him. He demanded reparations. The Master agreed to comply with Louis's judgement, a surprising turn of events which suggests that the Master, who was still relatively new in the post, was lacking in confidence. It may also reflect the fact that he was a Frenchman who had no wish to fall foul of Louis.

The terms of the judgement were humiliating. The Master was to make his way barefoot through the camp, with all the Crusaders assembled and watching. He would be accompanied by all his knights, also barefoot, in the style of penitents. When they had processed through the camp in this fashion, the King commanded the Master to sit on the ground in front of him, seated next to the envoy of the Sultan of Damascus who he had also summoned to attend.

Louis then turned to the Master, and told him to tell the envoy that he had exceeded his authority in making the agreement with his Sultan. The Sultan was to hold himself discharged from all obligations under the terms of the agreement, and any sureties he had handed over were to be returned. The Master complied with the command, and a written statement was handed over to the envoy so that he could take it back to his lord as proof of what had happened. The Master and his knights were then made to rise and kneel once more to beg the King's forgiveness. The Master then handed over the end of his cloak to the King to show that he was in Louis's power. Louis completed his punishment by exiling Brother Hugh, he who had made the agreement, from Outremer forever.

There was one aspect of the affair that presaged the greatest danger for Outremer. The Templar Grand Master, Renaud de Vichiers, was a Frenchman and in his capitulation before Louis we can see the actions of a man who did not wish to upset his monarch. It is inconceivable that virtually any other Master would have allowed this humiliation to take place. The balance of power changed radically with this surrender of Templar powers.

Although this may have been to the short-term advantage of Louis, the long-term effects were disastrous. Louis was a strong King but he was only a visitor. When he left, there would be no one to assume his mantle of absolute authority in Outremer. However hard Louis might find it to digest the fact, strong Military Orders were far more important to the long-term viability of Outremer than he was. They provided the manpower that was all that stood between the Kingdom and oblivion. But many of the Templars must have been incensed when they saw their Order humbled in this way. It was an act of the gravest significance for Outremer. As a result of it, Templar morale – and therefore their ability to continue to defend the kingdom – was weakened.

Such concerns were not of immediate concern to Louis, who received marvellous news from the envoys that he had sent to Egypt. They had returned from Cairo with the offer of a treaty, under the terms of which Louis was to travel to the port of Jaffa. The Egyptians were to journey to Gaza and formally hand over to Louis's representatives much of the Kingdom of Jerusalem that was currently in Egyptian hands. In return, Louis would help the Egyptians in their battle for supremacy against an-Nasir Yusuf, the current ruler of Damascus. It was tremendous tidings for the Crusade, as it offered great tangible gains from the expedition. However, such hopes proved to be a mirage.

News of the alliance reached Damascus, where it generated genuine concern. Should Louis side with the Egyptians, then the war might go against Damascus. Such an eventuality could not be allowed to come to pass. Further, the Caliph, spiritual head of the Muslim world, was most unhappy that the two halves of Islam were fighting against each other when they were faced with danger from the Crusaders and, even more so, from the terrible Mongol hordes. He therefore attempted to broker a deal with the two parties so that their differences could be healed.

Whether Louis was aware of these discussions is an impossible point to prove, although both Christians and Muslims had some access to information through spies in the camp of their respective enemy. Louis nonetheless marched towards the city of Jaffa. The Count of Jaffa decked the city walls out as well as he could, hanging a shield from each of the battlements so that it looked like a formidably defended place. The army encamped around the city walls and outside the castle, which stood right next to the sea. Louis thought that he would keep himself busy whilst he was there, and decided to strengthen the city defences. He himself personally took part in the digging, so that he might gain the rewards of an Indulgence in return.

However, he was soon to suffer a severe blow. The Egyptians did not turn up at Gaza as promised. They did fulfil other parts of their bargain. The heads that had adorned the walls of Cairo for so long were returned to the Christians for burial. A number of the children who had been forced to convert to Islam were also sent back to Outremer. They even sent an unusual, exotic gift to Louis: an elephant, which the King subsequently had shipped back to France.

They did not call off the agreement. They asked Louis for more time and agreed to meet at Gaza at a later date. Unable to do anything other than agree to this unhelpful suggestion of a time extension, Louis kicked his heels in Jaffa. The only light relief came when a local emir came too close to the city. A small party of Crusaders was despatched to intercept him, and in the ensuing skirmish the emir was run through with a lance.

Whilst in Jaffa, the young Prince of Antioch, a sixteen year-old boy, visited Louis. Antioch was a separate principality from the Kingdom of Jerusalem. From its early days[3] the principality had normally run its own affairs, often virtually autonomously, forming alliances with a range of peoples, particularly the Armenians in Asia Minor.

The young man, named Bohemond,[4] was intelligent, likeable and ambitious. His mother, Lucienne, was Regent of the city and would officially remain so for another four years. He sought Louis's help to inherit his rights and powers early. The King was impressed by the youth and agreed to help him. As a bonus, he personally dubbed him a knight. Bohemond subsequently returned to Antioch and claimed his inheritance. His presence at Jaffa however was most welcome. He had with him a small entourage including some Armenians. They were making their way to Jerusalem on pilgrimage.[5] They were multi-talented entertainers, being both fine musicians and excellent acrobats who kept the Crusaders enthralled for hours on end.

The waiting was agonising for Louis. Whilst the Egyptians delayed, his plans to redeem the Holy Land for Christianity hung in the

balance. He well knew that he simply did not have the manpower
to effect a military conquest of the country, and that he had to rely
on his powers of negotiation if he were to achieve anything at all.
The lure of the ultimate prize hung tantalisingly close, but just out
of reach.

An-Nasir Yusuf had not been inactive. His first thought was to
resort to force. He took his army to face the Egyptians at Gaza. The
two forces came to blows, with the Egyptians having rather the
better of the confrontation. An-Nasir Yusuf was wounded in the fray,
suffering blows to both his head and his hands. He made his way into
Gaza to recuperate.

Whilst he was there, he received a delegation from the Egyptians.
Their message was simple. Continued confrontation served the
purpose of nobody save the enemies of Islam. Far better that the
two parties should make their peace and face the common enemy
together. An-Nasir saw the merits of their arguments, particularly as
he had had the worst of the recent battle. A truce was agreed, and
Damascus and Egypt patched up their differences. There would be
no alliance for Louis with the Egyptians, and no handing over of
Jerusalem to him.

The bottom must have dropped out of Louis's world when he
heard this. All that he had worked for was ripped from his grasp at
the last moment. His temper was not improved by news of a frivo-
lous and costly skirmish. One of his knights heard of a large caravan
passing Ramleh, some ten miles away. Without conferring with the
King, he saddled up and led a small group of men towards this tempting bait. He was successful enough in capturing a large amount of
booty but he posted an inadequate guard. A force of Muslims fell on
him and, catching him unawares, overran his small contingent. Only
four men escaped.

The knight was one of the few to escape. Panic-stricken, he spurred
his horse back to Louis. He roused the camp, telling them of the disastrous skirmish. Louis quickly ordered a force to be assembled to go
out and see what, if anything, could be recovered from the debacle.

De Joinville was one of those who took part in this counter-attack, along with a group of Hospitallers and Templars.

They arrived in the valley where the skirmish had taken place. This time, it was the turn of their enemy to be caught unawares. Their men were stripping the bodies of the dead of anything of value when the Crusaders fell upon them. There was a violent fracas, during which the crossbowmen with the Christian force in particular did great damage. The Muslims were driven from the field after losing several of their men.

In one incident, two knights, one Muslim, the other Christian, charged at each other with great force. They collided so violently that both were simultaneously unhorsed. Whilst they were lying dazed on the ground, a Crusader sergeant came up and took away their horses. Planning to steal them, he crept away in the shadow of the city walls of Ramleh. His ruse might have gone undetected had he not stepped on an old water cistern. It gave way under his weight and, in a cloud of dust, he fell through the roof. The noise of its collapse attracted the Crusaders attention. They saw the knight trapped below and they dug him out. Fortunately for him, he was uninjured.

This particular incident did not end up as badly as it could have done. All of the relieving force made their way back to camp. It could however not sweeten the bitter disappointment that the Crusade now felt. All the planning and diplomatic manoeuvring was in vain. The alliance between Damascus and Egypt was the worst of all conclusions. They had lost their last negotiating card, and there was little likelihood that the lost lands of Outremer would now be restored by this expedition.

The reality of the situation was graver still. Now that the two local Muslim super-powers had buried the hatchet, there was nothing to stop them, either individually or collectively, using their resources to attack Outremer instead. In his moments of solitude and meditation, Louis's visions were now haunted by the depressing vision that his ambitions were destined to be unrequited. It was a major blow for a proud King who had lost so much in search of his ambition. His men would not stay with him for ever and his country needed him to return soon. For Louis, time was running out.

14

The End of the Dream

Within a very short time of the agreement being made between Damascus and Egypt, the Crusaders were involved in a battle. The context of the Crusade had moved from the diplomatic sphere to warfare with worrying rapidity. An-Nasir Yusuf had ordered his army to return to Damascus from Gaza with him. They decamped from the coast and made their way back towards the hinterland of Syria.

There was, de Joinville tells us, a huge force arrayed with 20,000 men from Damascus and 10,000 Bedouins involved. They ventured very close to Louis's army, being only about 5 miles distant, but they did not show any immediate intention to attack. Nevertheless, they could obviously not be left unobserved in case their intentions were hostile. The master of the Crusade's crossbowmen took his division to watch them closely. They stuck limpet-like to the enemy for three full days.

On the morning of St. John's Day, 6 May 1253, Louis attended mass as was his normal custom. The King was listening to the sermon when there was a disturbance. A sergeant strode breathlessly into the King's presence, knelt before him and frantically told Louis of the reason for his interruption. The master of the crossbowmen was surrounded by the Muslim force which enjoyed a massive numerical superiority. De Joinville was with the King and immediately asked for permission to mount a rescue bid. Louis assented, and within minutes the chronicler was rushing headlong from the camp at the head of 500 men. The Muslims saw them coming, and moved away towards a nearby hillock.

A fight quickly ensued. It began when the Muslims launched an attack on the crossbowmen. The Crusaders fought back fiercely and for a time their enemy appeared to be getting the worst of things. An emir who was close at hand and had been watching developments intently committed more men to help his hard-pressed Muslim troops. These in turn started to push the Crusaders back, who then committed more men of their own.

It showed all the symptoms of becoming a classic battle of attrition and, as they were outnumbered, this would almost certainly end badly for the Crusaders. Fortunately, back in the Crusaders' camp many of the leading knights were worried at the Crusaders' involvement in a battle against a much larger force and they prevailed on Louis to recall all his men to the camp. The King saw the sense of their arguments and messengers were sent to summon the men back.

De Joinville and his men, as well as the crossbowmen, returned to camp, little the worse for their adventure. However, many of the Crusaders were confused that they were not subject to a far more intense assault from the Muslims, something that they could only put down to the fact that the latter had been away from Damascus for some time and their horses were tired.

This was just a precursor of things to come. The Saracens passed by Jaffa where the Crusade was camped and northwards along the coast towards Acre. They were confident of their ability to intimidate the Crusaders and when they approached the environs of Acre, they sent envoys to the citizens to demand money in return for leaving the city unmolested.

In particular, they threatened to destroy the gardens outside of the city. This was no idle boast. The gardens were an important part of the food supply of the city. The Muslims must therefore be beaten off. The latter approached very close to Acre, so near that they were within bowshot of the walls. A force was quickly assembled by the defenders to resist them. They formed up on a hill just outside the city. As the Muslims came in range, they started to bombard them with arrows and crossbow bolts.

The man in charge of the defence of the city, the Lord of Tyre, was suddenly distracted. He noticed that a large number of unarmed civilians had issued forth from Acre so that they could enjoy the spectacle. But they had ventured too close to the action and were in danger. He deputed one of his knights, John le Grand, Genoese by birth, to go to these people and escort them back inside the walls. John carried out these orders but, whilst he was accompanying the citizens back to the security of the city, events took a sudden, dramatic turn.

Nearby there was a group of Muslims. One of them mocked the Crusaders for fleeing. He also challenged John le Grand to a joust. John was not about to pass up on the opportunity to win himself personal glory. He couched his lance and started to ride towards the insolent Muslim. As he did so, he noticed to his left a group of eight Saracen warriors on horseback. They were obviously enjoying the spectacle of the joust that was about to begin, but they were about to become more involved in it than they wished.

For John veered off towards them and rode headlong at the first knight in the group. He was so off guard that he barely knew what was happening before John was on him. The Crusader ran him through with his lance and he dropped to the ground, stone dead. As John started to make his way back towards the civilians he was supposed to be defending, the remainder of the Muslims present in the small party fell on him in a fury. One struck him a glancing blow with his mace. It made little impression on the Crusader knight's steel helmet. As the mace glanced off, John struck his assailant with his sword, knocking his turban to the ground.

The next opponent charged at full pace towards the knight with his lance levelled. At the last moment, John skilfully manoeuvred out of the way and, as he passed, struck him with full force with his sword on his arm, sending his spear flying to the ground. The rest of the group thought better of taking on this colossus and let him make his way unmolested back to the party of civilians that he was escorting. They were led without further incident back into Acre where they all marvelled at the prowess of John le Grand.

Whilst all this was happening, Louis had sent a party to repair the fortifications of the important port of Sidon.[1] So far neither Jaffa nor Acre had been seriously attacked as they were defended by a reasonable number of Crusaders. Sidon was however a different matter. The defences were not in good order, and there were insufficient men to defend the city.

When he knew that a Muslim army was headed in his direction, Sidon's commander, Simon of Montbeliard, felt that he did not have enough resources at his disposal to resist. He therefore withdrew to the castle, which was in a very defensible situation as it jutted out into the sea and was only approachable via a causeway. He took as many of the citizens with him as he could but the castle was simply not big enough to accommodate them all.

The citizens of Sidon were largely left to their fate, which was to be an awful one, characterised by bloodshed and plunder. Finding the city undefended, the Muslim army embarked on an orgy of destruction. They struck down the citizens mercilessly, slaying more than 2,000 of them. Then they took away everything of value that they could carry back to Damascus.

Louis was enraged when news of the events at Sidon arrived. But there was little that he could do immediately to avenge the outrage though the local barons did manage to turn the massacre to their advantage. Louis had planned to re-fortify an old castle fifteen miles inland. The local warlords advised against it as it would be difficult to re-provision and anyone taking supplies to the garrison would be dangerously exposed to ambush. When news of the destruction of Sidon came in, they prevailed on Louis to repair the shattered city instead of the old (and, to them, useless) castle. Accepting the wisdom of their arguments, Louis agreed to do so.

Whilst he was still at Jaffa, Louis received word that an-Nasir Yusuf would extend to him and any of his entourage a safe conduct if he wished to visit Jerusalem. As a deeply pious man, he felt deeply ambivalent about the offer. Part of him wanted to visit the place where Christ had died and to pay homage to the King of Kings.

Yet Louis was, after all, of flesh and blood. But he had human emotions in the same way as every other man. To visit Jerusalem on the sufferance of a Muslim lord would be deeply humiliating. Louis wanted to enter the city as conqueror, not as an invited visitor. His emotions were pulling him in two contradictory directions.

In an attempt to resolve this conundrum, Louis summoned his council. They referred to a strong precedent. Sixty years earlier, Richard I of England had led, with Philip Augustus of France, the Third Crusade. His avowed aim was to reconquer Jerusalem. Despite his best efforts, it became obvious to Richard that he was not going to achieve this objective. One day, out hunting for game he spurred his horse to the top of a hill. As he reached its summit, there in the distance he spied the minarets of the mosques inside the Holy City itself. Instantly, he averted his gaze. Then, his eyes smarting with fresh tears, he rode back to his men. If he could not take Jerusalem, he did not wish to even look upon it.

The Council referred back to the example of King Richard, who appears to have been – even to the French – something of a paragon of Crusading virtue.[2] They reminded Louis of Richard's claim that, should he accept the invitation he had received from the Muslim lord Saladin to go to Jerusalem as a mere pilgrim, then all Christendom would be happy to follow suit. Richard had argued that he would be failing in his duty to inspire others to fight to regain Jerusalem if he accepted an offer similar to that now made to Louis, allowing him to visit the city as a pilgrim rather than a conqueror. This was a strong precedent as far as they were concerned. They therefore recommended that Louis should take a leaf out of his book and refuse the offer. Louis did so.

He instead turned his attention to Jaffa. The fortifications of the port needed strengthening and he set to this task with great vigour. He spent over a year in the city, arriving in May 1252 and not leaving until June 1253. His energy was impressive. He erected twenty-four towers around the perimeter of the walls and deepened the moats around the city. The two moats were cleared of debris and mud to make them more formidable. Three gates were also inset into the fortifications at immense expense.

As a result, Jaffa was far more likely to fight off future attacks. In the event, these achievements were not especially long-lasting. Count John of Jaffa would find it difficult to find enough finance to adequately provide for its defence and successive Popes would have to regularly appeal for funds to maintain the city. It played a valuable strategic role as the southernmost point of Outremer's defence and various raids, including several involving Geoffrey de Sargine's French regiment that Louis would leave behind when he left Outremer, would start out from there. But the city would attract the unwelcome attentions of Baibars who perceived it as a threat and it would eventually fall to the Muslims in 1268.

Louis's achievement at Jaffa merely whetted his appetite. Conscious of his pledge to the local barons to re-fortify Sidon, Louis made preparations to set out for the city. As he started on his journey towards Sidon, he camped before the castle of Tyre.[3] He suggested that the army should make a detour and take the ancient city of Samaria. All those with him, the Templars, the Hospitallers and the other local barons advised that Louis ought not to go in person and attempt to capture the city, as if he were to fall in battle the damage would be incalculable.

The barons may have been genuine in their advice, as Louis was clearly a great friend to the Crusader cause. By the same token however they would have reasoned that a strong Sidon, strategi-cally placed on the coast, was far more important to Outremer than Samaria, probably indefensible in the longer run as it was in a far more exposed position. Ruefully, his dreams of glory and honour once more dashed, Louis agreed to return to his original plan, the far less glamorous task of rebuilding the walls of Sidon.

He travelled on up the coast, stopping once more at Acre. Whilst he was there, a party of Armenian pilgrims entered the camp. They had been travelling to Jerusalem. The Muslim authorities there normally welcomed pilgrims, as they were a source of financial gain for the merchants of the city. Such pecuniary considerations may well have been the impetus behind the Muslims' recent offer to Louis to visit the city.

These Armenian pilgrims now had another objective in mind. They approached de Joinville and asked if they could see the 'saintly' King Louis. De Joinville relayed the message verbatim. The King was beside himself with laughter at the way they appeared to be worshipping him, but agreed to see the pilgrims anyway. There is something of the apocryphal about this story. It reminds the reader that de Joinville wrote his chronicle many years later at the end of his life, and there is maybe a degree of hindsight in his relation of this particular tale (Louis was already canonised when he wrote it). However, it hints at the image of the virtuous King that was already current during Louis's lifetime.

The army moved on and the next day camped by a stream of very good water. It flowed past fields of sugar cane for which the area was famed. There was a quarrel over the ground that the men were to camp on. Within moments, fists were flying. A brawl developed which was only stopped when de Joinville personally intervened. One of de Joinville's knights, who had started the fight, was dismissed from his service.

The King again hatched a plan for the army to make a diversion. He suggested that they should raid the city of Caesarea Phillipi[4]. Here was the place where the Jordan had its source, flowing forth from two streams that merged as one near the city. Although the barons with the army saw some merit in the scheme, they again felt that Louis should not personally lead such a dangerous expedition. The debate rumbled on for some time before Louis was talked out of his declared intent to accompany any diversion against the city. Although Louis was eventually dissuaded, the force that subsequently set out nevertheless had some extremely important men in its ranks. There was for example Giles de Brun, the Constable of France, the Masters of the Templars and the Hospitallers along with many of their men and a number of prominent local barons from Outremer itself.

The force left camp just after nightfall. Riding through the night, they found themselves on the plain outside of Caesarea Phillipi as dawn broke. It was decided that an attack on a number of fronts offered the most hope of success as the defending garrison would be confused by having to resist a series of assaults at the same time. The King's men, who included de Joinville and the faithful Geoffrey of Sargines, were to take up position between the castle that protected Caesarea Phillipi and the walls of the city itself.

The local barons were to attack from the left whilst the Hospitallers were on the right. In accordance with the machismo that was an integral part of their image, the Templars would attack the city head on. It was an ambitious plan, requiring good co-ordination if it were to succeed, otherwise the defenders could drive back the Crusaders – who had of course weakened their forces by dividing them – piecemeal.

The battle did not start well. De Joinville and his men moved forward to find that their progress was soon blocked. It was imperative that his men took up their required position as quickly as possible to protect the men advancing on the city itself from a dangerous counter-attack.

This task however was much easier said than done. A landscape that was a nightmare for cavalry stood between them and the place where they were supposed to take up position. There were at least three sets of dry stone walls blocking their way, the land was so steep and rugged that horses could only cross it with great care if they could cross it at all and, worst of all, their progress was barred by large numbers of the enemy.

The foot soldiers with de Joinville's party frantically began to dis-assemble the dry-stone walls with their bare hands but progress was still difficult. De Joinville watched as one of his horsemen crossed the rubble. The mount of this horseman lost its footing, and fell on its rider, crushing him badly. Heeding the warning from this incident, de Joinville dismounted and led his horse gingerly by the bridle rather than risk riding.

Despite their difficult situation, the advancing knights still presented an intimidating sight. The defenders were disheartened when they saw that the seemingly impregnable men in armour continued their advance up the hill. Their will to stand and fight evaporated. As one, the defenders abandoned their positions and fled away as quickly as they could. De Joinville's men continued their advance to the top of the hill. When they reached the summit, they found that there was a sheer drop down into the city on the other side.

De Joinville's success temporarily demoralised the enemy. Thinking that any further defence of the city would be futile, they abandoned it to its fate and hurried to the nearby citadel, the castle of Subeibe. This fortress was positioned partway up a mountainside. It was fairly new, having been built only in 1220 and strengthened soon after with the addition of rectangular towers.

It was not an excessively large fortification but its position, on the rocky crags behind Caesarea Phillipi, gave it an evil and menacing appearance. The approaches to it were strewn with rocks, making it look an even more intimidating edifice. The Crusaders pursuing the Muslims from the town advanced a little way up the hill towards the castle, took one brief look at it and decided that they would leave the fleeing enemy forces well alone.

The Muslims were panicking badly, convinced that they would imminently be run down by the pursuing Crusaders. However, when they saw that the Western knights were no longer at their backs, they took fresh heart. They turned about and started to launch a counter-attack. The Crusader horsemen, picking their way downhill through rocky and broken ground, were in a dangerously exposed position. Unable to escape quickly, they found themselves attacked by agile Muslim foot soldiers who clambered over the rocks and beat the knights around the head with their maces. They also clutched at the saddles and reins of the cavalry, threatening to pull them off.

All of a sudden, the nerve of the Crusaders seemed to crack. The cavalry became ever more frantic in their attempts to escape. Behind them stood de Joinville and his men. His sergeants were terrified and wanted to flee. Conscious that what had seemed to be a great victory only a few minutes before was on the point of disintegrating into a disaster, de Joinville refused to budge.

His foot soldiers said that his decision was unfair. De Joinville was on horseback and could easily escape if needed whereas they, on foot as they were, would soon be overtaken and killed. His response was brave and decisive. He sent his horse away so that he too was on foot. He would stand and fight, with or without them. The perilous nature of his situation was perfectly illustrated just moments later when one of his knights, John of Bussey, was struck in the throat with an arrow and dropped dead at his feet.

News of impending disaster reached some of the army gathered below who could not see what was happening higher up in the hills. When one of the knights, John of Valenciennes, wanted to go to de Joinville's aid others said that it was pointless as he was by now surely dead. Nevertheless, a force set out to rescue de Joinville, hoping that was still in the land of the living.

They fought their way up the steep hillside. Reaching the top, Oliver of Termes, who led the relieving force, was relieved to find that de Joinville was still alive and well. However, unless a quick retreat was engineered he would not remain so for much longer. The direct route down was already difficult, as more and more Muslims, encouraged by the obvious discomfort of the Crusaders, made their way towards the enemy. The lower slopes of the hill already teemed with them.

Oliver of Termes hit on a plan. They should make their way along the ridge towards Damascus, as if they were about to attack the Muslims from the rear. Then, with the enemy caught off guard, they should suddenly run for their lives in the opposite direction towards the plain. Their only hope lay with a rapid skirting of the city walls back to their own lines.

The plan lacked dignity or glory but such concerns counted for little when the situation was so precarious. It worked like a dream. The Crusaders advanced menacingly. Then, suddenly, they made a dash for safety. Thrown off guard by the initial aggressive manoeuvres that they had been making, the Muslims were slow to react. By the time that they did so, de Joinville's men were already back on the plain.

They made sure of their escape by taking hold of some sugar canes and using them to set fire to the fields behind, blocking any attempt by the enemy to interfere with their withdrawal. De Joinville and his men made their way, weary, bedraggled but relieved, back to the Crusader camp. The ultimate indignity was to be experienced when they arrived back in the Crusaders' camp only to find that most of their comrades were already disarmed and relaxing, blissfully unaware that de Joinville was even absent.

Given the ignominious nature of their retreat, and the fact that the raid achieved precisely nothing in terms of results, it was presumably an embarrassed raiding party that eventually arrived at Sidon to rejoin Louis, who had made his way separately to the city. His first job when he arrived had been to clear the putrefying corpses that lay dotted about, unceremoniously lying where they had been recently slaughtered.

Although the smell of death and decay hung heavy in the air, Louis personally took part in carrying the cadavers from the places where they had fallen to the trenches that had been dug to act as mass graves. Although the smell was so bad that most of those burying these unfortunate wretches had to hold their noses, the awfulness of their condition did not seem to shock the King, who carried out his part of the task with great reverence whilst not showing any sign that the scene nauseated him.

With this sad task completed, Louis moved on to more positive matters. He summoned as many workmen as he could find to Sidon and put them to work on restoring the walls of the city. No expense was spared. Great walls were erected, regularly interspersed with strong towers. The King's energy was praiseworthy. He even laid out the camp so that when the raiding party returned they all found that the spot at which they were to pitch their tents had been painstakingly marked out for them.

The men appeared to be in good spirits. However, on occasion something would happen to cause them to panic, suggesting that subconsciously they were always on edge. One particular morning, de Joinville made his way to see Louis at the break of day when the King was to hear mass. Afterwards, they rode out together into the fields around Sidon. They chanced upon a priest singing mass inside a humble church. The King's appetite for such holy rituals was seemingly unquenchable. Eager to hear the service through to its completion, he told de Joinville that he wished to enter the church. The chronicler dutifully accompanied him into the church.

When they entered, de Joinville quickly became nervous. He noticed that the cleric assisting the priest was an intimidating looking man, 'big, black, lean and shaggy'.[5] Immediately suspicious that such an uncouth looking individual could truly be a priest, de Joinville intervened when the time came for the host to be delivered to Louis during the Communion service.

Rather than let the assistant hand over the sacred bread himself, de Joinville took it from him. De Joinville had convinced himself that the assistant was really an Assassin, who would not hesitate to plunge a dagger into the King when he was close enough. When the service was over, the King and his party left the church. Louis was angry that de Joinville had been so suspicious and refused to accept that he had been in the right, even though de Joinville clearly felt that he was acting in the King's best interests.

There was an opportunity whilst still at Sidon for one more act of diplomacy. Another delegation came to visit Louis. This time they were a party of Byzantines. They had come from a small enclave of the Byzantine Empire, separately governed, based on the city of

Trebizond on the Black Sea coast.[6] Anxious to win as many friends as possible for their tiny state, they brought many precious jewels as gifts for Louis.

They also asked a favour. They would be grateful if the King would provide a wife for their Emperor. It was not an unusual suggestion for the time but Louis replied that he had no suitable bride available to fill the role. He suggested that they should approach the Latin Emperor in Constantinople instead, hoping by so doing to improve the stability of the frail Latin territories in Byzantium by forming a useful new alliance.

The Queen arrived at Sidon soon after. She had just given birth to another child, a daughter tactfully named Blanche after her mother-in-law. She had then travelled by sea to rejoin her husband. De Joinville met her from the port and led her to the castle. He then went to tell the King that his wife and daughter had arrived. Louis asked after their welfare and de Joinville replied that they were well. It suddenly struck the chronicler that this was the first time in five years that he had heard the King talk about his immediate family. In words that are more critical of Louis than most that he wrote, de Joinville noted that 'it was not seemly to be thus a stranger to one's wife and children'.[7]

Jerusalem was not the only place that Christian pilgrims visited in the Holy Land, and de Joinville wished to travel to Tortosa, a town many miles to the north and a place much revered by all Christians. It was here that the first known shrine to the Blessed Virgin had been erected. Many miracles had been performed there.

Louis granted permission for him to go. He also told him to buy large quantities of camlet (expensive light cloth, a speciality of the region) so that he could make a present of it to the Franciscan friars when he eventually returned to France. The request cheered de Joinville no end. It was the first time that the King had ever hinted at returning home.

De Joinville's enthusiasm for the Crusade had long since waned, and his initial enthusiasm to stay in the region had been extinguished.

There was little to be gained by staying in Outremer for much longer. The pilgrimage was duly made, and the camlet purchased. De Joinville returned to Sidon with his spirits lifted by the trouble-free pilgrimage and the gracious welcome that he had been given by the local barons who had hosted him on his way to Tortosa.

The time spent at Sidon was a profitable one. The fortifications were rebuilt, and the city was defensible once more. The temper of the army was good. There was much to interest them. On one occasion a stone was brought to Louis which, when cracked open, had the perfectly formed fossil of a fish that looked like a tench inside.

But crushing news was imminent. One day, a grim faced messenger made his way into Louis's presence. Bowing obsequiously before the King, he delivered his message. As he did so, all the colour drained from Louis. With disbelief, which soon turned to grief, Louis heard the terrible news that his mother was dead.

Blanche had told Louis when he left that she would never set eyes on him again in this world, a prediction that had clearly proved all too accurate. Overcome with grief, Louis withdrew into a world of his own. For two days he would see no one. He blankly stared through any who approached him with eyes glazed over with tears. After this time, he sent a servant to fetch de Joinville. Pathetically, he held out his arms towards the knight. As if de Joinville did not know already, the King cried piteously, 'Seneschal, I have lost my mother!'

Louis was shocked almost senseless by the news. He had been dominated by Blanche all his life and now the strongest individual influence on him had been removed from the world. His grief at his mother's death contrasts vividly with his lack of concern for his wife, a trait that modern psychologists would have a field-day with. De Joinville, his loyal subject and, as much as a subject could be also his friend, took his courage into his hands. The time for plain speaking had come.

He reminded Louis that Blanche was human and all humans are one day destined to die. He was surprised at Louis's reaction. For Louis was a King, a great and wise man, and the excessive manner of his mourning caused his enemies to rejoice and his friends to suffer. It was not becoming and it was not helpful. The duty of a sovereign was to put the responsibilities of the King before the desires of the man.

These were bold words but they needed to be said. Louis had to pull himself together, for the sake of his men, his kingdom and, indeed, the kingdom of Outremer. Pondering on these words and heeding de Joinville's admonitions, the King considered his options. He had been away from France for five years. He had left Aigues Mortes with high hopes, with a proud, large fleet, pennons flying boldly in the breeze. At the head of a great army, he had carried with him the hopes of Christendom. Early on, disaster had struck him and his Crusade when his men were hopelessly beaten in Egypt.

Since that time, Louis had fought unceasingly to recover a lost situation. He had expended huge amounts of money on rebuilding as well as he could the shattered infrastructure of Outremer. He had fought with every weapon at his disposal, diplomatic as well as military. But his army was small and its chances of achieving much more in the East were limited. Louis had given everything in the cause of Outremer, in the service of the cause that he believed in so passionately, but he had nothing else left to give.

He also had to remember that he was the King of a great country, a land that had been forced to survive without him for half a decade at a time when it was threatened by many enemies. The situation in Europe was still volatile, although there had been some significant changes since Louis left France. In 1250, Frederick, Emperor of Germany, 'the greatest of the princes of the earth, wonder of the world and admirable innovator',[8] had been summoned to meet his maker for what, judging by the unorthodox events of his life, may have been an interesting conversation. Europe was probably a safer, although undoubtedly much less colourful place, for his passing.

But his son and successor, Conrad (titular King of Jerusalem), picked up his mantle and continued to plot against the Papacy, although he himself died in 1254. And Henry III of England was as avaricious for French-held lands as ever and it was likely that, in the vacuum left by the death of Blanche of Castille, Regent of the country, he would try to benefit from the continued absence of Louis. Louis pondered these thoughts constantly in his mind. Tired, dejected, defeated and distraught he gradually reached an inescapable conclusion. The unthinkable must at last be faced. It was time to go home.

Homeward Bound

The death of Blanche forced Louis's hand. He was now determined to return home. The last great Crusade to the Holy Land was about to come to an unsatisfactory close, its aims unfulfilled, its hopes dashed, its soldiers disillusioned. So much effort, so many lives, so much money, so little to show for it all. All this had a knock-on effect for future Crusading prospects. Men would think long and hard before committing to such a brave but risky enterprise again.

The refortification of Sidon was now almost complete. Louis ordered a great procession to make its way through the Crusaders' camp with the legate, Eudes of Chateauroux, at its head. Once it had completed its progress, the legate was to offer up fervent prayers to God so that Louis might make the right decision. The procession duly made its way reverentially through the camp, and earnest invocations for divine guidance were then made. The King then retired to privately consider his options.

Shortly afterwards de Joinville was summoned into the King's presence. He walked away from the barons that he had been talking to and was led to the nearby King. Louis had few men with him but he had obviously discussed his plans with the legate, for it was Eudes who relayed his decision to de Joinville.

It was the legate who started the discussion. Louis had reached a decision. The army would return to France next Easter. The death of Blanche of Castille was undoubtedly a major part in the decision (a modern commentator wrote that 'Louis had been free to operate in the East only thanks to the presence of his mother at the head of the kingdom'[1]), but there were other pressing reasons as well.

The Crusade had cost a fortune. And the resources of even a wealthy man like Louis were not limitless. He had done well, given the vast efforts he had made to provision the Crusade properly, to stay solvent but by this stage he was forced to borrow heavily from Italian bankers to finance his expensive activities. The Crusade was becoming a major financial drain on his resources. As well as spending heavily on refortifying Jaffa and Sidon, he had also taken a number of men into his pay. The simple economic facts of the situation were that he would run out of money if he stayed for longer than one more year.

De Joinville then retired to a private apartment to discuss the matter further with the legate. It turned out to be a particularly emotional interview. Eudes was overjoyed that Louis had decided to take the army back to France. The King had done all that could be expected of him, and much more besides, and the Crusade could return with a clear conscience.

But then, without warning, the legate completely lost his composure. Weeping bitterly, he bewailed the fact that he himself would have to return to the Papal court in Rome. It was, in truth, an awful prospect. Conrad, the son of Emperor Frederick, had inherited all of his father's vices with none of his virtues. He continued the war that Frederick had waged against the Papacy.[2] Italy was as much in turmoil as ever. Eudes would be thrust right into the middle of this awful situation.

It was an unappetising prospect that faced the legate but he had devised a plan to deal with the problem. He would stay at Acre for a year after the rest of the Crusade left, and spend all the money that was left to him on strengthening the defences of the city. He reasoned that if he were in penury when he returned to Rome, then all 'the treacherous people who are there' (his words to de Joinville) would quickly lose interest in him and leave him alone.

The conversation then wandered onto other matters. The legate told de Joinville that Acre was a city that was full of sinners. Many great offences had been committed by the citizens and God would surely punish them in the future. He related his concerns to de Joinville, predicting that an apocalyptic day of reckoning was at hand. In his view, 'Acre [will] be washed clean in the blood of its inhabitants, and other people will come hereafter to dwell there'.[3]

The oracular powers of the legate were remarkable; within a few decades the walls of Acre would come crashing down and what remained of Outremer would be washed away in a sea of blood. But it should be noted that de Joinville might have once again been writing with the benefit of hindsight as he wrote his memoirs long after Acre had fallen.

Soon after, Louis summoned de Joinville to him. He wished him to undertake one final mission by escorting his wife and children down the coast to Sur. It was a heavy responsibility. The Crusaders were after all at war with the forces of Damascus and Egypt and the group would have to travel right across Muslim territory. De Joinville was constantly looking over his shoulder during the mission, particularly when the group stopped to eat, rest and light their fires to cook their meat. Fortunately for him, his fears were groundless and the journey was completed without incident.

Soon afterwards, the barons of Outremer and the Patriarch of Jerusalem came to see Louis. They thanked him with sincerity and generosity for all that he had done for the country. They listed his achievements; the fortification of Sidon, the strengthening of the defences of Jaffa, the work he had done at Acre. Considering all that he had achieved, they were unanimously agreed that the King had more than played his part in securing the future of the country.

Their advice was that the King should return to Acre and prepare to return to France, as he wished, at Easter. No doubt gratified that he left the country with their blessing, the King thanked them for their kind words and recommended them to God, praying that He would watch over them and protect them. Soon after, the King journeyed down to Sur, where he was reunited with his wife and family. Together, they completed the rest of their passage down the coast to Acre.

Preparations to return to France now began in earnest. In contrast to the massive armada that had accompanied Louis on his way to Outremer, only thirteen ships and galleys were needed for the return trip.[4] But the dangers facing the King were by no means over. The sea could be a fierce enemy. The sailors waited patiently for the wind to turn in the right direction for the journey home. At last, on 24 April 1254, the wind was favourable. It was time to leave Outremer.

The small fleet sailed out of the protective waters of the harbour at Acre into the wide expanse of the Mediterranean. Louis's thoughts at the time of departure are sadly not recorded but it is not difficult to speculate what these might have been. Surely, above all else, he felt a burning disappointment that he was leaving behind the kingdom of Outremer in almost as fragile a state as it was when he set out.

Although its cities might be stronger now, thanks to the work that Louis had financed on their defences, the Military Orders, the standing armies of the kingdom, had been devastated by his expedition into Egypt. For all that, he had given five years of his life to the country. His efforts had been at times almost superhuman. Even at the end of his time in the East, he was thinking of the future and he left behind him a small force of 100 knights to help to garrison Acre. It would stay there until Outremer itself died.

Apart from refortifying some of its cities, this 'French regiment' was Louis's lasting contribution to Outremer. Geoffrey de Sargines was left in command of it, and would also achieve high office in the country during the extended period that he subsequently spent there. The regiment would provide sterling service. Just a few years after Louis left it helped to fight off a Muslim attack on Jaffa. A raid in 1263 injured Geoffrey, though not seriously. He died in 1269, still in Outremer.

But the regiment stayed on. It made a very useful contribution but given the imminent demise of Outremer it was largely an irrelevance. It was involved in action on a regular basis. At the end, when Acre itself fell, the regiment was given the Tower of the Legate, at the south-east corner of the city, to defend. They fought heroically but in vain. Some escaped but many paid with their lives in a last vain but valiant gesture.[5]

De Joinville personally felt relief, both for himself and for his King, at leaving behind 'that perilous land'. The first stopping off point for the fleet would be Cyprus. It was only a relatively short crossing from Outremer, but even before they reached the island, the fleet ran into difficulties. A thick mist descended on the sea as they drew close to Cyprus during the hours of darkness. In those days, navigational aids were limited, a particular problem when visibility was poor. The sailors onboard were unsure of their position when the mists descended and were much closer to shore than they realised. They believed that they were far out to sea and were therefore careless.

Suddenly, without warning, the progress of the ship that carried the King and de Joinville was abruptly halted. With a sickening thud that shook the ship to the base of its timbers, the vessel ground to a halt. Fortunately for them, they had stuck on a sandbank rather than rocks, as the latter would have caused the ship to founder. But the situation was still serious.

The initial reaction of those onboard though was that the ship was in great danger. Cries of despair went up from many who were convinced that they were all about to drown. De Joinville, who was lying down when the ship struck, rushed up to the forecastle to see what was happening. There was a Templar onboard, Brother Raymond, who commanded one of the sailors to throw a line overboard so that they could see how deep the water was. It became obvious that they were stuck hard aground. When this news was relayed back to the Brother, it caused him much distress.

There were four galleys nearby. Those onboard the King's ship shouted across to the galleys to come across and rescue the King.

The galleys refused to budge, probably afraid that the vast numbers onboard Louis's ship (some 800 in all according to de Joinville) would swamp the much smaller galleys when they came over to take the King off to safety.

Louis himself reacted in a quite amazing fashion. He lay himself prone in the shape of a cross on the deck in front of the mast and lay there silent, as if supplicating the Almighty to succour him.[6] However, it appeared that the panic onboard was unnecessary. When shortly after the line was dropped over the side again, it was apparent that the ship had cleared itself and was in deep water once more.

However, no one could assume that the ship was still sea-worthy after the collision. With the advent of daylight, four divers were sent over the side to swim underneath the ship to confirm the extent of any damage. In the cold light of day they also saw the sharp rocks that they would inevitably have struck if they had not grounded on the sandbank.

When they returned, they were interviewed individually so that their version of the damage would not be swayed by each other's accounts. All of them told the same tale. Some 20ft of the ship's keel had been removed by the collision. Louis assembled the master mariners accompanying the fleet and asked them for their assessment of the situation. They were all of one mind in recommending that Louis should transfer to another vessel and complete his journey. In their view, the integrity of the ship had been seriously compromised by the accident.

Crossing the Mediterranean was a serious obstacle at the best of times but if a bad storm were to hit the ship in its current condition it must in their opinion founder. They offered the evidence that, on the journey west to Outremer, another vessel had suffered a similar accident. When it continued on its way, it subsequently ran into heavy weather. The ship was broken apart by the heaving seas, and of its entire complement only one woman and her child were saved.

Louis then asked his political advisers for their views. Their number had of course been seriously depleted since he set out but those that were still with him, people such as Giles le Brun, his Constable, all advised that Louis should follow the advice of the mariners for they, after all, understood technical matters better than any other men onboard ship. However, he seemed unhappy with these answers. He turned once more to the master mariners and asked them if they would abandon the ship if they themselves owned it. They replied that they would not, as they would rather run the risk of drowning in the damaged vessel than have to find a small fortune to replace the ship.

Louis asked them why, if they answered in such a fashion, they then recommended that he should desert the ship and find another back to France. They retorted that the King's life was worth far more than theirs, and had a value beyond measure in terms of silver or gold. It was a very logical argument. Louis had a responsibility not only to himself. His foremost duty was to his kingdom. If his life were lost, the effect on France, coming close on the heels of the death of his mother the Regent, could be disastrous.

There is a fine line between bravery and foolhardy recklessness, and Louis was about to cross it. The King imperiously concluded the argument by giving his final decision to his advisers. There were hundreds of other souls onboard ship with him. If he were to leave it, they too would be almost certain to follow suit.

However, it was impossible to transfer them all to other ships in the small fleet – there was simply not enough room for them all. Therefore, their only option would be to go ashore onto the island of Cyprus. If they did so, it could be months, or even years, before they found transport back to France. They could therefore be doomed to a life of penury in exile due to his decision to abandon the ship.

Louis concluded that he would rather risk his life, and that of his wife and children, rather than sentence so many people to such an uncertain fate. Louis's morality could not be questioned, nor his valour. It was nevertheless a decision that was fraught with great risk. To many, the odds appeared simply too high to be worth taking.

The decision only makes sense when one recognises the immense personal faith that Louis had. In his eyes, his life was in the hands of

God and, if He wished Louis to make it back to France safely, His divine protection would make certain that this happened. It is hard to understand from a twenty-first century perspective but it exemplifies perfectly the abandonment to fate (or the will of God) that was at the heart of Crusader theology. It also perhaps indicates the state of mind of a man who desires to become a martyr.

Louis's point though was proved when Oliver of Termes, who was also onboard, could not face the prospect of the dangerous journey ahead and chose to land on Cyprus instead. He would not return to France for another eighteen months as a result. De Joinville points out correctly that this was not through lack of money, as he was a very rich man. It merely reflected the difficulty in finding ships prepared to make the long journey across the Mediterranean to France. As the chronicler correctly notes, if Oliver, who was a man of substance, had so many problems how much more difficult would it be for those with no wealth of their own?

There were few attempts to persuade the King to change his mind – based on past experience even if anyone was brave to enough to do so, they were almost certainly doomed to fail when faced with the obdurate nature of Louis. Accordingly, preparations were made to continue the voyage.

However, the accident was merely the beginning of the troubles facing the fleet. Shortly afterwards, a strong wind blew up, threatening to push the ships onto the rugged coastline of Cyprus. The great anchors of the King's ship were thrown over the side to stop the vessel from being pushed onto the rocks, but the wind and the seas were so strong that it took five of them to arrest the ship's movement.

Louis had erected a tent onboard as a form of cabin for him but the wind was so strong that this had to be disassembled. Queen Margaret came to see her husband, but he was not there. She found de Joinville and Giles de Brun instead. She was frightened out of her wits. She had heard some of the sailors talking and they had said that in their view all those onboard were doomed to perish in the storm that was rising.

De Joinville suggested that she should follow her husband's lead and seek divine intervention to overcome the problem. He recommended that she should vow to have a ship made of silver which she should take to the shrine of Saint Nicholas, the patron saint of sailors, at Varangeville in France if they arrived safely.[7] The queen, agreeing to this, asked de Joinville to be witness to the sacred covenant, a service that he was happy to perform.

Shortly afterwards, the sea and the winds began to abate, and the violent motions of the ship started to lessen noticeably. The Queen gave thanks: true to her word she would deliver a silver ship to the shrine. In fact, she subsequently sent the ship to de Joinville to deliver to Varangeville in person. It was a remarkable piece of work, containing models of the King, the queen and the three children accompanying them made of silver. Even the sails were sewn with silver thread.

Fortunately this was the last alarm for the fleet whilst it was off Cyprus. The ships restocked with fresh water and set out into the open sea once more. After a few days, they came to a small island. They landed there to take on whatever supplies they could find. There were a good number of rabbits on the island and many of them were trapped and taken onboard ship. Fresh meat during a voyage was a rare luxury.

There was also an old hermitage on the island. It was set in a garden that sounded as if it would not have been out of place in the original Eden. In it were olive trees, figs, vines and other fruits. There was also a stream of sparkling, refreshing water running through it. There was a little chapel at the far end of the garden, a whitewashed edifice that was part of a cave. A cross had been marked out on the floor with red earth.

There was another cave nearby. Its contents were somewhat disturbing. There were two bodies lying there, neatly laid out facing the east. The flesh was long since decayed and the hands were neatly folded across the breasts of the bodies. Apart from this macabre discovery, the island was a beautiful spot. One of the sailors fell under its spell. When the crew were counted, there was one missing. It was widely believed that he had decided to stay on the island and live the life of a hermit. Three bags of biscuits were left by the crew to help him along his way.

They passed near another island with a Muslim population. The Queen was desperate for some fresh fruit to be brought to her children and asked whether some could be collected. It was a foolhardy request. By sending men ashore to collect the fruit, the King was exposing them to great risk. They could easily be spied by the local population.

Nevertheless, the King went along with the suggestion. Three galleys were sent to the shore where they disappeared out of sight in a small anchorage hidden amongst the surrounding hills. A long time passed and still there was no sign of the galleys returning. Those onboard ship wanted to wait no longer. Situated where they were, they were exposed to Muslim pirates. Louis though would not budge. The Queen meanwhile was inconsolable, blaming herself for the problem. But then, just as the ships were about to make for the shore, the galleys were spotted coming back towards them.

As the galleys drew alongside, Louis asked the mariners in charge of them why they had been so long. They replied that the delay was no fault of theirs. There were some young men onboard, sons of some of the leading merchants of Paris, and they had enjoyed the fruit that they had found in the orchards so much that they could not be made to hurry back to the ships. Instead, they had glutted themselves on the wonderful fresh food that they had found.

This was a very irresponsible act. It had been a risk for the men to go ashore at all, but to tarry unnecessarily was stupidity. Yet no harm had come about as a result of the escapade, which largely seems to have been the result of some bored and immature young men showing excessively high spirits: hardly unique in the annals of history.

Most men would have let the incident pass with no more than a rebuke. Louis was not however like most other men. He determined to teach the youths a lesson. Larger ships of the time towed a barge behind them, which served a variety of purposes. One of them was to keep thieves and captured pirates safely confined whilst the ship sailed over the seas.

Louis told the youths that they would complete the journey back to France confined in this barge. They were beside themselves with grief. It was a mark of great shame to be treated in such a fashion and in an era when honour was highly prized that was the greatest punishment of all. But there were other practical concerns as well. If crossing the ocean was an ordeal in a large ship, then it was doubly so undertaking the same voyage in a small barge. Such a journey would be both extremely uncomfortable and, at times, downright terrifying.

Seeing that the youths were so distressed, virtually everyone onboard begged the King to change his mind. Even the queen asked him to do so. But Louis would not be moved. His decision, once made, was final. The youths were accordingly placed in the barge. They endured a journey from hell for the rest of the trip. When the seas were high, the waves washed right over the barge, soaking them to the skin. They dared not stand up in case the wind blew them off their feet and over the side.

It was, to be frank, a complete overreaction on the part of Louis, and endangering the lives of these foolish young men demonstrated a darker side to his character. There was a world of difference between being a disciplinarian and being a tyrant, and Louis did himself little credit with this misguided demonstration of his power. Possibly his actions reflected his mood. After all, God had been a hard judge with him; why should he be any less stern an arbiter?

Nerves were not to be made any calmer by another incident. It occured late one evening when the queen was put to bed by her maidservants. One of the maids, either tired or just careless, took the scarf that the queen had been wearing and placed it unthinkingly on top of the stove. There was a candle still burning on this. The maids retired to their cabin below the queen's quarters for the night, leaving the candle to burn on. As the ship slept, the flame from the candle caught hold of the scarf which was alight in seconds. The fire that resulted leapt across to the Queen's bedclothes.

Fortunately, the smoke alerted the Queen to the danger before it was too late. Fire precautions onboard these primitive vessels were virtually non-existent and the incident could have resulted in a conflagration that was uncontrollable. Alerted just in time, the Queen rushed naked from her bedchamber and threw the scarf over the side. She then hurried back to her cabin and beat out the smouldering fire that was threatening to engulf her bedclothes.

Ironically, the only people other than the Queen to witness the immediate danger were the miscreants being towed in the barge. They shouted 'Fire! Fire!' but in voices that were not loud enough to wake those onboard (cynics might conclude that they, relatively safe in their barge, might have concluded that a fire onboard his ship would serve the King right).

The commotion eventually woke the ship. De Joinville half-dressed himself and looked over the side quickly enough to see the offending scarf, now far away in the wake of the ship, still alight on the water. In the interim, Louis had come looking for de Joinville hoping to discover what all the noise was about. Finding him absent, he was now looking for his wife.

The incident passed without serious consequence but it shook Louis. The next day, the King delegated to de Joinville the task of going round the ship last thing at night to ensure that all the fires onboard had been extinguished. Louis told him that he would not sleep until de Joinville had come to his cabin every night from now on and confirmed that all the fires were out.

One last exciting interlude was to disturb the monotony of the journey back to France. One of the knights onboard another ship was asleep in the vessel when he was awoken by the full blast of the early morning sun striking his face. Grumpily, the knight instructed his squire to cover the opening through which the sun shone so that it would no longer annoy him. The squire reached over to do so but as he stretched he lost his footing and fell over the side.

In most cases, such an accident would be fatal. Many men could not swim and it could be ages before the squire was noticed as missing. Even if he were seen falling overboard, it would take a while for the ship to manoeuvre into position to pick the fallen man up. It was incredibly fortunate for the squire that there were other ships close at hand and one of the galleys escorting the King's vessel was able to pick him up.

His rescuers were particularly curious to find out why he had not cried out when he fell overboard. The squire answered that he had not done so because he was never in any danger. The instant he hit the water he saw the Blessed Virgin next to him and she held him up by the shoulders until he was rescued. To the cynical modern mind, this might appear as a classic case of hallucination caused by a blow to the head or a case of half-drowning. The psyche of medieval man was, however, very different. To many, the incident seemed like a genuine miracle. De Joinville was so impressed by it that he had a window made for his chapel in his chateau in Joinville commemorating it.

The Crusade was nearing journey's end. His ships were soon close to the coast of France. Louis wished to land at Aigues Mortes, the port that he had virtually created especially for his Crusade. However, this meant extending the voyage by sea for a few days longer. The peregrination across the Mediterranean had clearly damaged the nerves of many of those onboard ship who had been at various times threatened with drowning, incineration and an imagined imminent assault by pirates.

They had had enough. They wished to set foot on dry land, especially French land, at the earliest possible moment. For two days the King argued against his councillors on the matter but they were so insistent that even he, stubborn as he was, agreed to land at the nearby port of Hyeres, which was in the lands owned by his brother, Charles of Anjou.

With laconic understatement, de Joinville records the fact that 'the King accepted the advice we gave him; whereby the queen was greatly rejoiced'.[8] The queen, a largely silent and statuesque figure in de Joinville's chronicle, was clearly a woman who suffered much due to the idiosyncrasies of her husband.

Shortly afterwards, the ships sailed into the harbour and ropes were thrown to those ashore so that the ships could be tied up. Planks were then placed from the gunwales of the ships to the dockside. Gingerly, still giddy from the constant movement of the poorly stabilised boats, those onboard stepped back on to French soil once more.

This was no triumphant homecoming, though. Little tangible could be shown for the great exertions of Louis's crusade, financed significantly by taxes on his people. Yet, if the King was no conqueror, he already had about him something of the hero. In Louis's case he even now possessed the aura of a martyr for his faith, one who had suffered much for what he believed, and had on many occasions been on the edge of losing his life for it.

The King was back at last, returned to prepare his armies afresh against an enemy closer to home, King Henry III of England. His people could rest safe in the knowledge that his crusading days were over. The debacle in Egypt had been such a horrific ordeal that logic decreed it inconceivable that the King would ever crusade again.

But logic meant little to Louis. One thought above all others still haunted his waking hours. He had set out to reconquer Jerusalem and he had failed miserably. He could not rest until this stain on his character was expunged. There would be one last twist before the story of Louis the crusader was at an end.

Few were aware at the time that for Louis the crusading obsession was as much alive as ever. His failure had merely fuelled his ardour. And no one had a chance to discuss such matters with their King in the immediate aftermath of his disembarkation at Hyeres. The King was not to be disturbed because he had been introduced to a great holy man who was in the town, and he had weighty doctrinal matters to dispute with him. With King Louis, some things never seemed to change.

The Last Crusade

So Louis's Crusade was over, ending in failure and bitter disappointment. All that now remained was for his army to disperse, and for the participants, both great and lowly, to make their way back to their homes and their loved ones.

De Joinville started out with his King on the road to Paris. They passed through the fecund and beautiful region of Provence. True to form, Louis heard about a local shrine, in the city of Aix, where it was said that the body of Mary Magdalene lay. Naturally, Louis could not pass over the chance of visiting a holy site connected with such an august member of the Christian pantheon. There was a cave, way up in the mountains, where it was said that the Magdalene had lived for seventeen years.

The diversion was a pleasant distraction for Louis, but the sight-seeing could not last indefinitely. The party eventually arrived at Beucaire, in the heartlands of Louis's kingdom. Here de Joinville took his leave of his sovereign. The chronicler does not say much of the emotions that were exhibited by the two men when the time came to say *adieu*.

It must have been a moment of supreme poignancy though. The two men had shared much together, from the euphoria of the

Crusade's early days to the terror of captivity in Egypt through to the hard days of endurance in Outremer. Louis felt a great bond with de Joinville, who had been one of the few leading men to stay with him in his long exile overseas. For his part, the chronicler's affection for his sovereign is clear from the way that he writes of him.

At last it was time for de Joinville to return home to the wife and family that he felt so deeply for, the same kinsfolk who were responsible for that terrible feeling of emptiness that he felt in the pit of his stomach when he said farewell so many years ago. Theirs is an unwritten story and at this far remove it is difficult to relate to the gamut of emotions that they must have felt over the years of de Joinville's absence. But there must have been relief at his safe return, sorrow for so many men lost, regret at the lost years. Out of touch with what had been going on for months at a time, receiving so many items of bad news, the ordeal of de Joinville's family must have been profoundly distressing.

When he eventually did arrive back then the homecoming must have been a very moving occasion. Great feasts would be held in his honour, and many an hour spent by the fire in his hall whilst he regaled his audience with tales of all he had seen. Neither would spiritual matters be forgotten. Prayers of thanksgiving, earnestly uttered and keenly felt, would have been offered up in remembrance of this wonderful reunion of the family with its head once more.

Shortly after Louis left Outremer, momentous events were to take place in the East. The crisis point in the conflict between the Mongols and the Muslim world was about to be reached. In 1256, an immense Mongol army made its way towards Syria like a pack of hungry wolves about to tear its prey to shreds. Its aim was a simple one: the Muslim world presented a formidable barrier to further Mongol conquest and must be eliminated, as much of it already had been. The time for one final decisive battle was at hand. The Mongol army despatched towards Syria had one objective in mind. It was to participate in an act of untold ferocity, the aim of which was to cow Islam into submission.

It was the start of a great terror. In 1258, the entire Muslim world was shaken to its very foundations and pushed it to the brink of a dark and deep abyss. Baghdad was the greatest of all Muslim cities, the spiritual centre of the Islamic world. It was besieged by the Mongols and taken after a few weeks. The massacre that followed was appalling even by the dreadful standards of the Mongols. It is estimated that 80,000 people, mostly defenceless civilians, died in the bloodbath that followed its capture.

Women were raped in the streets and plunder of unbelievable value was taken. The Mongols were assisted in their excesses by a number of Christian allies. The Caliph, head of the Muslim faith, was to suffer a special fate. He was tied up in a felt bag and then ridden over by thousands of Mongol cavalry. In the 600 years that had passed since Islam was founded by Mohammed, this was its worst moment. It appeared that the Muslim world teetered on the edge of oblivion.

The Mongols pushed on into Syria. An-Nasir Yusuf's attempt to surrender Damascus to save himself was ignored, and the city was put to the sword after a brief siege. Some of the tortures inflicted on the victims of the Mongols were beyond comprehension. The ruler of the city of Mayyafaraqin choked on his vomit when he was force fed with chunks of his own flesh. Reports of these atrocities must have reminded Louis of his foolishness in believing that he could achieve an alliance of equals with these people, although he would continue to receive the occasional envoy from the Mongols for the rest of his life.

It was Islam's darkest hour. The whole Muslim world appeared to be consumed in flames. A pall of smoke hung over the East. But just as it appeared that Egypt, one of the last bastions of Islam, was about to be attacked, the fickle hand of fate intervened. At the crucial moment, news reached the general of the Mongol army, Hulagu, that the Great Khan, his brother Mongka, had died thousands of miles away. Inevitably, there would be a succession dispute and Hulagu, who was likely to be the leading contender to succeed his brother, could not afford to be absent when it took place. He rode back to Central Asia, taking most of his army with him.

It appeared to be a miraculous deliverance. Devout Muslims saw the hand of Allah in these great events, but it was inconceivable that the Mongol threat was gone forever, merely that the final confrontation with Egypt had been postponed. Sure enough, the next year, in 1260, the Mongols despatched envoys to the Sultan of Egypt, Qutuz, demanding that he surrender his country to them. The Sultan's answer lacked subtlety but clearly told the Mongols what he thought of their ultimatum. The envoys were promptly sliced in half.

But Qutuz knew what he was doing. At his side he had a military genius. When the Mongol and Egyptian armies subsequently met at the Battle of Ain Jalud, one of the decisive battles of world history, his commander outmanoeuvred and outfought the Mongol generals. Once again Rukn ad-Din Baibars proved himself to be a man of exceptional military ability, and the Mongol threat was destroyed once and for all.

Shortly afterwards, Baibars tired of playing second fiddle to the Sultan and murdered him. As Sultan, he would be a ruthless opponent of the Crusaders in Outremer, perhaps the most dangerous foe that they had ever faced. Baibars launched a series of raids into Outremer, on one occasion reaching the very walls of Acre itself.

But these raids were just a precursor to the biggest shock to strike Outremer since the capture of Jerusalem by Saladin nearly a hundred years before. Now that Jerusalem was long lost to the Crusaders, the greatest city that they held was Antioch, far to the north. On 18 May 1269, Baibars' army stormed the city. The entire population was either massacred or dragged off into captivity. News of this dreadful defeat shook the West. Rumours that another Crusade was imminent began to circulate.

Inevitably, these rumours centred on the court of King Louis. As a man who had already led a Crusade, it was known that he had a great love for the Holy Land with its sites of supreme religious significance. The disappointing outcome of his Crusade did not diminish his interest in the Holy Land. The French treasury paid out 4,000 pounds tournois per annum in support of initiatives in the East, mainly on the upkeep of the French force in Acre.[1] And tales that a new Crusade was imminent pre-dated the fall of Antioch – news of its loss would only add fuel to a fire that was already well alight.

During the period of Lent in 1267, Louis summoned all his barons to Paris. De Joinville was one of those asked to attend on the King but he offered his apologies as he was suffering from a fever. Louis insisted. He told de Joinville that he must attend on him, promising him the services of his best physicians. Not wanting to offend his sovereign, de Joinville duly went to Paris. He was not aware of the King's plans, until he had a vision in which he saw Louis put on a chasuble[2] of scarlet. When he told one of his priests of his dream, he offered the opinion that it meant that Louis was shortly to take the cross once more.

The next morning de Joinville heard Mass at dawn. He then went to find Louis. He was, as was his common practice, in his chapel. He was looking through his vast collection of relics. Amongst these, he had a fragment of the True Cross. This was a small piece of wood that was supposed to be taken from the cross on which Christ was crucified.

A number of his knights, hearing this news, knew what Louis had in mind. Such sacred relics held a prominent place in Crusader iconography – a fragment had been carried into battle and lost at the cataclysmic defeat at Hattin nearly a century before. Using such relics to whip up Crusading fervour was an obvious tactic. They were in no doubt that Louis was about to embark on another Crusade. Ominously, there was little enthusiasm for such a scheme. The following morning, Louis decided to put an end to the speculation. He was indeed planning such a venture.

Initial reactions were not favourable. Much of the enthusiasm for Crusading had now dissipated after the series of reverses that had been suffered in the Holy Land during the preceding decades. De Joinville refused point blank to accompany Louis and told him bluntly 'that all those who advised the King to go on this expedition committed mortal sin'.[3] The kingdom was at peace but its security would be threatened if Louis were to leave it once more. There was also the health of Louis himself to consider. He was not well, and when de Joinville escorted the King on a visit to a nearby abbey of Franciscans shortly afterwards he ended up carrying his sovereign.

But, as Louis well knew, such an undertaking could not be started overnight. Intensive preparations were required. Simon of Brie was given the task of preaching the Crusade although he would be replaced in 1268 by the Bishop of Albano, Raoul Grosparmi. In all likelihood, Louis had been corresponding in secret with the Papacy for months before he announced his plans to Crusade. In keeping with the chivalric spirit of the times, a number of minstrels also wrote ballads exhorting their listeners to 'take the Cross'.

Allies were sought to assist in the Crusade. A surprising supporter was Prince Edward of England, son of Henry III, an ambitious young warrior who was keen to christen his sword with Muslim blood. There were also expected to be contingents from Scotland and the Low Countries. Steps were taken to raise the requisite finance and ships were obtained, primarily from Genoa and Marseilles. The French Church contributed a tenth of its income towards the Crusade and a tax of a twentieth was also promised by the dioceses bordering France. Alphonse of Poitiers, Louis's brother, contributed 100,000 pounds tournois towards the expedition.[4]

Louis's Crusade was again very well organised. He agreed contracts with a number of leading men to supply him with a certain number of troops for the duration. These 'divisional commanders', as they have been termed, comprised Alphonse of Poitiers, Guy of Flanders, Robert of Artois and Prince Edward of England. It was their responsibility to supply the number of men that they had contracted for and this led in some instances to them entering into sub-contracts with others so that they could fulfil their obligations.[5]

There was also a significant contribution from Aragon. King James I sailed from Barcelona on 1 September 1269 but the start of this particular part of the expedition could not have been more inauspicious. Appalling weather battered his fleet so badly that the King and many of the men accompanying him returned to Spain and did not set out again.

The rest of the Aragonese expedition fared no better. James's two sons, Ferdinand Sanchez and Peter Fernandez, made their way to Acre. When Sultan Baibars appeared before the walls with a sizeable force soon afterwards, they had no option but to stay put behind the walls whilst the Egyptians paraded around outside, mocking the Crusaders for their weakness. Seeing that they could contribute nothing effective or long-standing to the welfare of Outremer, the two Spanish princes returned home with nothing achieved for their efforts.

When the preparations were complete, Louis announced his intended destination. Given the chaotic state of Outremer, there seemed no doubt that Egypt or the Holy Land would be the chosen target. The loss of Antioch was a hammer blow, which seemed to threaten the beginning of the end for the Crusader kingdom of Jerusalem. It was, therefore, a profound shock when Louis announced that he planned to take the expedition to Tunis.

It was an incredible decision. Tunis was peripheral to the Muslim world, and its capture would aid the Crusaders in Outremer hardly at all. Further, the Emir of the city was well disposed towards the West and had been on good terms with Christendom for years. But Louis believed that he was ripe for conversion to the Christian cause and that the expedition's subsequent arrival before his city would give him the final impetus needed to convert him to Christianity.

Even commentators who are generally well disposed towards Louis agree that it was a bizarre decision. Richard, generally very supportive of Louis, describes it as 'a strategic aberration'.[6] The strangeness of Tunis as a target is exemplified by the debate that has raged amongst historians concerning why it was chosen. Some see in it the hand of Charles of Anjou, who was at the time in frequent contact with Baibars. Supporters of his view hold that Charles did not wish to see a Crusade going to Egypt, because that would jeopardise his good relations with Baibars.

But Richard sees it as an attempt to convert the Emir of Tunis to Christianity. There is insufficient evidence to prove any particular

case. But although there may have been some strategic benefits resulting from the fall of Tunis (the region had provided supplies and men
to Egypt in the past), the rewards of the city's capture were out of
all proportion to the effort involved in taking it and the risks that it
entailed.

Louis sailed with his army[7] from Cagliari on the south coast of
Sardinia on 15 July 1270. The wind was favourable and the crossing
was made in only two days. Great attention had been paid once more
to the accumulation of supplies, preparations that were apparently
so meticulous that Sicily, one of the main sources of grain in the
region, was bled dry and there were significant shortages elsewhere
in Europe as a result.[8] It was an excellent start to the campaign, but it
was almost the last thing to work in the Crusaders' favour.

Louis laid siege to the city, setting up camp on the site of the
ancient city of Carthage, the connotations of which would not be
lost on the Crusaders. But a fortnight or so after his arrival Louis
fell ill. The symptoms described sound suspiciously like a recurrence
of dysentery. For several weeks Louis fought against the ailment.
The camp suffered dreadfully from the ravages of the disease. Louis's
youngest son, John Tristan, the child born in Damietta, was one of
those to die. There was for him a neat symmetry about his life. Born
amidst the wreckage of one Crusade in North Africa, he died whilst
another was about to collapse in the same region.

Louis's health worsened and it became apparent that his life was
once more in danger. His eldest son, Philip, was with him, and Louis
talked often to him of what would be expected of a King of France.
He extolled Philip to be a protector of the Church and to defend its
rights against those who would harm it. He was also to be a defender
of his people against all that would harm them, both physically and
morally, exhorting him to ensure 'that your subjects live under you
in peace and righteousness'. He was to exercise justice, although
with a firm hand. He must 'maintain the good customs of your realm
and abolish the bad'. Of particular relevance to Louis's attitude to
the Crusading movement was his admonition to Philip to 'beware

of undertaking a war against any Christian prince without great deliberation'; for Louis, such actions were an affront to God.

As time went on and Louis did not improve, it became clear that on this occasion there was unlikely to be a miraculous deathbed recovery. Louis's time on earth had run. The King was dying and was himself well aware of the fact. For the medieval Christian, the manner of death and dying was as crucial as the way that life was lived as far as the eternal welfare of the soul was concerned.

Louis's priests were therefore called to his tent. His condition continued to deteriorate. The sacraments of the Church were brought to him, which he took as reverently as he could in his debilitated state. Despite his infirmity, he was conscious and very aware of what was happening around him, although for a time he could not speak. This was important, as an understanding of what was happening during the last rites (in which the dying man or woman was expected to be an active participant) improved the prospects of dying well. Louis was anointed with oil, a common practice at the time which, amongst other things, ensured that the corpse would not be used by the Devil for evil purposes. Religious readings were then said over him.

He was by now in a shadowy world between life and death. Most of the last rites had been administered to him, and all that remained was to wait for Louis to die. The King himself was fully aware that the end would not be long in coming. Several times he called out for the help and protection of the saints, to St James and St Genevieve amongst others.

In the quietness of these sacred last moments the King was seen to mouth something. Those who were at his bedside claimed that he whispered the words 'Jerusalem! Jerusalem!' To the end, the Holy City was the dearest of all things to him.

Shortly afterwards, the King asked to be placed on a bed of sackcloth. On it was sprinkled a cross of ashes. This was traditionally the way that the corpse of a Christian was laid out signifying their humility and penitence. For one of the great Kings of Christendom, it signified his utter obedience to God and his complete impotence when faced with the omnipotent power of his Lord. Then he crossed his hands over his breast and prepared himself to leave this world behind him.

De Joinville notes the end with moving simplicity. He says simply that 'on the day after the feast of St Bartholomew the Apostle (25 August 1270) did the good King Louis pass out of this world'. The priest who confessed Louis for the last time was insistent that his last words were 'into thy hands I commend my spirit', an echo of the words that Christ uttered on the Cross. He noted the time of death as 3 o'clock in the afternoon, the same time that Christ himself died.

It was a model Christian end for a model Christian King. The same day, Charles of Anjou, his brother, arrived. He had been late in departing for the Crusade and when he found his brother dead he was inconsolable. He wept like a baby when he visited his brother's corpse in his tent. But he was a man who was, like Louis, aware of his responsibility. He composed himself before he left the tent, not wanting to harm the fragile morale of the army. With Louis's death, he was now the most experienced military leader with the Crusade and could expect to inherit its leadership. He needed to set an example.

Louis's son Philip, who had also been ill but had recovered, assumed the crown. Messengers were sent to France with news of the King's death along with his will (at this period in history these were often not written until the writer knew that they were dying).

In the meantime, the Crusade had to be continued, regardless of Louis's death. The camp had already been under fierce attack whilst Louis was ill. Soon after his death, a fierce counter-attack drove the Muslims back and captured their camp. But no one's heart was in the fighting any more. The skirmishing became desultory and then stopped altogether. Soon after, negotiations began. The Emir agreed to pay a large tribute, in return for which the Crusade would leave him alone. A substantial part of it would go to Charles of Anjou who was the subject of some criticism for the profit that he appeared to be making from his involvement in the Crusade.

Prince Edward of England arrived late, in November 1270, and was infuriated to find that the Crusade was over, and that he was not even to have a share of the tribute paid. In a fit of pique he sailed away towards the East. He would eventually arrive in Outremer, where he would be shocked to find the state of morale in the country and the bitter infighting that was then infesting it, with Venetians fighting Genoese, and Hospitallers fighting against Templars. His army was so small that it had no chance of changing the military balance of power.

Edward's Crusade was short-lived and unmarked by any military triumph, although his presence did encourage Baibars to enter into a truce with the Crusaders which at least bought Outremer some time. Edward's presence and bearing however clearly disturbed Baibars, who arranged for the Assassins to eliminate him. Edward was attacked with a poisoned dagger but survived the assault. Disillusioned with the Crusading movement, he returned to England where, as King Edward I, he was destined to earn greater fame as the man who finally subdued Wales and who was such a fierce enemy of the people of Scotland that he earned the sobriquet 'Hammer of the Scots'.

Edward was lucky in more ways than one. Shortly after he left Tunis, heading for Palermo in Sicily on his way east, a violent storm battered the Crusader fleet. The timing could not have been worse as the army was onboard, about to sail back to Europe. Fortunately, the new King, Philip, and his wife went ashore rather than stay onboard ship at the dubious mercy of the sea. Others were not so fortunate.

The fleet was devastated by the storm that broke. Forty ships, and hundreds of men, were lost. There had been talk of another Crusade in the following spring, but this finally put paid to that hope. Louis's dynasty was to suffer several major blows after his death. On the way back to France, King Philip's wife, Isabella, was killed in an accident. The following year, Alphonse of Poitiers announced his intention to Crusade once more but Charles of Anjou talked him out of it for the time being. Alphonse however only delayed his plans rather than cancel them. He made his way towards Genoa looking for a fleet. On his way he died on 21 August 1271, the day after his wife. But

Charles of Anjou lived on for a decade or more, to live a life that was increasingly characterised by intrigue, plot and counter-plot.

Louis's mortal remains were placed in a casket and shipped back to France. They were interred in the great church of Saint-Denis, where Louis had wished them to lie. But this was not the end of the story of Louis. The outpouring of grief that followed his death was accompanied by a large volume of anecdotes concerning the holiness of his life.

Eudes of Chateauroux, old friend and confidante of Louis, received a letter from the late King's son-in-law, Thibaud of Navarre, telling him that the 'king had died a saintly and most devout death'. There were already stories of miracles being performed in the presence of his mortal remains, which were even now assuming the status of holy relics. The Crusade refused to be parted from Louis's bones when they were carried home, across Italy, where the Crusade made landfall, and up through France. A great procession followed his remains all the way back to Paris.

By 1272, Pope Gregory X asked Simon of Brie to conduct an investigation into the miracles that had already been attributed to Louis. Over the next twenty years, various other Papal investigations were launched into his character but for a number of reasons they did not lead to more formal recognition of the sanctity of the late King. But in 1297, Pope Boniface VIII formally started a process the objective of which was to evaluate whether or not the King was worthy of sainthood.

There was a huge amount of information available; virtually everyone of note seemed to have an anecdote that attested to the King's piety and humility. A wide range of witnesses was called including de Joinville. After examining all the evidence they had collected, Louis was recommended for sainthood. The Pope confirmed their view, judging that there was incontrovertible evidence that Louis was an exceptionally devout man. When the news of his decision arrived, all of France rejoiced.

His formal canonisation was accompanied by a moving ceremony when his mortal remains were exhumed and carried to a platform that had been raised in the church. There, in the presence of their King for one last time, a great congregation of the greatest men in France listened as a sermon was preached, extolling the virtues of Saint Louis, King of France, Crusader and man of God.

At the conclusion of the service, the coffin was carried reverently back to its vacant tomb, to rest in eternal peace. But Louis still seemed to inherit the realm of the living, at least in the world of dreams. One night, an elderly man, asleep in the comfort of his bedchamber, was visited in his dreams by a familiar face long since gone from the world. There, in this netherworld of visions and shadows from the past, King Louis told his friend de Joinville how glad he was to see him once more.

The next morning, when he woke, Jean de Joinville, friend, adviser and chronicler of King Louis reflected on the dreams of the night and resolved to build a shrine to his old master in his chapel at Joinville. Once met, Louis was a man never forgotten. De Joinville would remember his King to the end of his days. Thanks to the efforts and lucidity of this octogenarian chronicler, witness to great men and great events, we too can glimpse briefly what a remarkable man this King of France really was. And we can understand, even now, just how momentous were the events of that last, great Crusade to Outremer.

Postscript

Louis was the last King to lead an army to Outremer on Crusade. Prince Edward's expedition was a small scale affair that did not engage in a major battle and achieved very little. Louis's interests in the Crusading movement as a vehicle for earning spiritual reward were already, to some extent, an anachronism. Although religious motives were still important to many in the West, other motivations were becoming ever more crucial. The development of the concept of chivalry within the aristocratic society of Western Europe led to a search for glory that was inspired as much by earthly as heavenly recognition.

The ease with which Indulgences were now granted meant that much less dangerous and costly acts were now required to earn spiritual benefits than had been the case in the preceding centuries. This led to a devaluation of the Crusade as a source of spiritual rewards. 'Spiritual inflation', as the effect has been termed, diluted the attractiveness of involvement in the Crusade to individuals considerably.

The very term 'Crusade' had developed a wider meaning. Once used as a term applied to a pilgrimage to the Holy Land, a man could now Crusade against pagans in the lands bordering the Baltic Sea, against the Moors in Spain, or even against heretics in his own country. Crusades were increasingly called against political opponents of the Papacy too.

Allied to a constant stream of bad news from Outremer the potential of Outremer to attract Crusades to go its aid plummeted and then fizzled out completely. Men reasoned that if Saint Louis, whose qualities as a man far outshone any other Western monarch, found nothing but disappointment in Outremer then God no longer had any interest in the kingdom.

Outremer would only outlive Louis by just over twenty years. In 1291 a rabble of newly-arrived Crusaders from Italy (poor people from the cities of northern Italy, with hardly any arms, they merited the status of little more than a mob) massacred a group of Muslim traders in Acre. The families of the murdered men sought vengeance from the most powerful court in the Muslim world, throwing the bloodstained robes of their kin on the floor of the mosque in Cairo and demanding retribution.

On 5 April of that year, the land around Acre was filled with the noise of beating kettledrums and the war cries of fired-up warriors. A fierce siege followed with a huge Muslim army battering away at the city. The defence was desperate but hopeless. Six weeks later the defences of this mighty city, fortified by the Crusader King Louis of France, were finally breached by the Egyptian army.

In the battle that followed, Templar and Hospitaller knights, often in the past bitter enemies, fought and died side by side. They fought heroically but their resistance was in vain. Outmanned to the last, they could not stop the irresistible Muslim tide that engulfed them, swallowing them up without pity. Thus Outremer was washed away in a sea of blood, with its citizens massacred in their thousands. Only the mercenary fleets, Genoese and Venetians, saved themselves, sailing to safety accompanied by the rich citizens of Acre, who they charged extortionately for the privilege.

The pitiful remnant of Outremer that remained was lost soon after, the last fortresses falling after the merest pretence of resistance or just being abandoned altogether without a fight. It was the fulfilment of

Baibars's dream, though the mighty warrior was not there to see it, having died over a decade earlier, reputedly from poisoning. Having been heavily implicated in the plot against Turanshah and other rulers, in his case he who lived by the sword truly died by it.

After the sparks of hatred for the Crusaders were ignited into a raging inferno by the genocide of the Mongols, the Crusader state could no longer be allowed to live. It had survived for over a century after the disaster at Hattin, most often by the sufferance of the Muslim lords in the lands around it who were too occupied by internecine warfare to worry unduly about them. Perhaps the Muslims felt that the kingdom no longer posed a threat. But Baibars had seen the mighty Crusade that Louis had led against him and took note. Once the Mongol threat had been driven back, the kingdom could no longer be allowed to exist.

The pitiful survivors of Outremer made their way back to the West. There would never be another Crusade journeying to Outremer. Crusades had traditionally been called by the Pope as an expression of his power, a statement of intent in the ongoing war between the Papacy and secular rulers. The battle fought by Innocent IV and many others for so long against the Emperors and Kings of the world was going against the Papacy.

Only a few years after the fall of Acre, when many of the Templars had returned to France, their order was brutally suppressed by the King of France, a man of dubious morality with the ironic title of Philip the Fair. The last Master of the Order was burnt at the stake in Paris. The Pope, little more than a puppet in the hands of the French King, meekly did as he was told throughout most of the affair. It was the clearest sign yet that the Papacy had conceded that it had lost the fight for power. An efficient administrator with a ruthless edge to his character and a strong affinity with religion, it was as if, through Philip, Louis had been reincarnated with the darker side to his character exaggerated.

No more would men journey to the East. Other things would occupy their minds. Within half a century the vicious war known to historians as The Hundred Years War would break out between England and France. Although, perhaps he would not be surprised given the problems that he experienced with Henry III, Louis would nevertheless have despaired that Christians once more waged war on other Christians.

In the East, Europe was pushed ever more on the defensive as the vacuum caused by the terminal decline of Byzantium was filled by the Ottoman Turks, Muslim warriors who conquered all who dared resist them. In 1396, a French army embarked on the last and, in terms of its size, perhaps the greatest Crusade. It was fought not in Outremer but in Bulgaria; the battlefield on which the Crusades were fought was moving inexorably westwards.

Charging wildly into battle without discipline or order, the flower of French chivalry was crushed on the field of Nicopolis, broken against the impenetrable defensive barrier created by their Turkish opponents. Prominent amongst the knights who argued that the Crusaders merely had to charge the Turks for the enemy to break and flee was a man with the eerily familiar title of the Count of Artois, although his Christian name was Philip rather than Robert. Few would have understood the desolation of this awful defeat better than Louis, King of France and Crusader Saint, who had given his all for the cause he held so dear and had, in return, achieved so little.

No more would Christian Kings set sail for the Holy Land, at the head of large armies and great fleets. Jerusalem was gone forever, not to be in the hands of a Christian army until the First World War. Soon after the day that it fell in 1917, at the Temple Church in London, a solemn ceremony was held commemorating the men, Templars and others, for whom the Holy City had been an inspiration centuries before. It was a touching memorial but it was also an anachronism. The world had changed beyond recognition. There was to be no lasting glory in possessing Jerusalem, only blood, toil, sweat, tears. The Last Crusade had long passed into the dim and distant recesses of faded memory, in a land peopled only by ancient and largely forgotten heroes.

Suggested Further
Reading

The foremost primary source for Louis's crusade is, of course, that by de Joinville. The version used and referred to throughout this book is Marzials, Sir F., *Villehardouin and de Joinville: Memoirs of the Crusades* (London, 1908), (reprinted 1957). Also in print, and easily accessible, an English translation of de Joinville's chronicle may be found in Shaw, M.R.B., *Joinville and Villehardouin – Chronicles of the Crusades* (London, 1963).

There are several versions of Matthew Paris's chronicles available. The version on which the quotes in this book are based is Vaughan, R. (ed.), *The Illustrated Chronicles of Matthew Paris* (Stroud, 1993). Although this only covers the earlier years of Louis's Crusade, it has the virtue of being easily available and also well illustrated.

Brief extracts from primary sources discussing Louis's Crusade and the events immediately before and after it may be found in Brundage, J.A., *The Crusades: A Documentary Survey* (Milwaukee, 1976); Gabrieli, F., *Arab Historians of the Crusades* (London, 1969); Hallam, E. (ed.), *Chronicles of the Crusades* (Guildford, 1996). There are several works available which examinine the life of Louis, the best of which is Richard, J., *Saint Louis* (English translation published in Cambridge, 1992).

The reader may also wish to refer to Guizot, M., *The History of France from the Earliest Times to 1848* (translated by JB Alden) (New York, 1884); Jordan, W.C., *Louis IX and the Challenge of the Crusade* (Princeton, 1979); Pernoud, R., *Blanche of Castille* (English translation, London, 1975).

There are a number of general histories of the Crusades available, of which the following are easily accessible: Bartlett, W.B., *An Illustrated History of the Crusades* (Stroud, 1999); Mayer, H.E., *The Crusades* (English translation, Oxford, 1990); Richard, J., *The Crusades – c. 1071–1291* (English translation, Cambridge, 1999); Riley-Smith, J., *The Crusades* (London, 2001); Riley-Smith, J. (ed.), *The Oxford Illustrated History of the Crusades* (Oxford, 1995); Riley-Smith, J. (ed.), *The Atlas of the Crusades* (London, 1990); Runciman, Sir S., *A History of the Crusades*, 3 vols (reissued by Harmondsworth, 1992); Setton, K., *A History of the Crusades* (Madison WI, 1975); Tyerman, C., *England and the Crusades* (Chicago and London, 1988).

A brief but illuminating outline of what the Crusades were may be found in Riley-Smith, J., *What were the Crusades?* (Basingstoke, 1992). The story of the Albigensian Crusade is considered in Oldenbourg, Z., *Massacre at Montsegur* (English translation, London, 1997); O'Shea, S., *The Perfect Heresy* (London, 2001); Sumption, J., *The Albigensian Crusade* (London, 1978).

A number of studies of life in Outremer have been published including: Benvenesti, M., *The Crusaders in the Holy Land* (Jerusalem, 1970); Boas, A.J., *Jerusalem in the Time of the Crusaders* (London and New York, 2001); Boase, T.S.R., *Kingdoms and Strongholds of the Crusaders* (London, 1971); Jotischky, A., *Crusading and the Crusader States* (Harlow, 2004); Prawer, J., *The Crusaders Kingdom – European Colonisation in the Middle Ages* (London, 1972); Prawer, J., *Crusader Institutions* (Oxford, 1980); Richard, J., *The Latin Kingdom of Jerusalem* (English translation, Oxford, 1979); Smail, R.C., *The Crusaders in Syria and the Holy Land* (London, 1973); Tibble, S.,

Monarchy and Lordships in the Latin Kingdom of Jerusalem 1099–1291 (Oxford, 1989).

For a historical perspective of the Mongols, the following works are suggested (Curtin's book is of course somewhat archaic in its style and some of the views contained in it have been revised as historical science has moved on, but it is still nevertheless a very readable history); Curtin, J., *The Mongols: A History* (Boston, 1908, reprinted 1996); Morgan, D.O., *The Mongols* (Oxford, 1986).

For the 'Assassins', see Bartlett, W.B., *Assassins – The story of Medieval Islam's Secret Sect* (Stroud, 2001); Daftary, F., *The Assassin Legends* (London and New York, 1995). Lewis, B., *The Assassins* (London, 1999 edition).

For background perspectives to Europe at the time of the Crusade, readers may wish to refer to Fossier, R. (ed.), *The Cambridge Illustrated History of the Middle Ages*, vols 2 and 3 (Cambridge, 1997); Holmes, G., *The Oxford Illustrated History of Medieval Europe* (Oxford, 1988).

For an examination of the castles of Outremer see Kennedy, H., *Crusader Castles* (Cambridge, 1994). The chivalric background to the period is considered in Barber, R., *The Knight and Chivalry* (London, 1974).

The Military Orders are considered in Riley-Smith, J., *Hospitallers – The History of the Order of St. John* (London, 1999); Robinson, J., *Dungeon, Fire and Sword* (London, 1991).

The ultimate demise of the Templars is covered in Burman, E., *Supremely Abominable Crimes* (London, 1994).

The military background to the Crusades, and the period generally, is considered in Bradbury, J., *The Medieval Siege* (Woodbridge, 1998); Finucane, R., *Soldiers of the Faith* (London, 1983); Hooper, N. and Bennett, M., *Cambridge Illustrated Atlas of Warfare: Middle Ages 768–1487* (Cambridge, 1996); Keen, M. (ed), *Medieval Warfare: A History*, (Oxford, 1999); Koch, W.H., *Medieval Warfare* (London, 1978); Marshall, C., *Warfare in the Latin East, 1192–1291*, (Cambridge, 1992); Nicolle, D., *The Medieval Warfare Source Book*, vols 1 and 2 (London, 1996); Oman, Sir C., *The Art of War in the Middle Ages*, vol. 1 (reprinted London, 1991).

A valuable insight into the impact of the Crusades on the Islamic world can be found in Hillenbrand, C., *The Crusades – Islamic Perspectives* (Edinburgh, 1999).

For the religious background to the Crusade, see Brundage, J.A., *Medieval Canon Law and the Crusader* (Madison, Milwaukee, 1969); Purcell, M., *Papal Crusading Policy: 1244–1291* (Leiden, 1975).

Notes

Introduction

1 Riley-Smith, J., *The Crusades*, p.254.

2 The quotation, and the idea of the three major events shaping the year 1250, may be found in Richard, *The Crusades*, p.332.

3 Setton, p.487.

Chapter 1: The Vow of King Louis

1 Routledge in *Oxford Illustrated History of the Crusades*, p.107.

2 For support of the theory that Isabella may have had a strong influence on Louis, see Riley-Smith, J., *The Crusades*, p.157.

3 For the background to the Albigensian Crusade, see Oldenbourg, Zoë, and Sumption, 'Massacre at Montsegur' in *The Albigensian Crusade*.

4 De Joinville's *Chronicle*, p.154.

5 As well as being a poet, Tibald had a long-standing family interest in the Crusading movement. He led an expedition to the East in 1239 – which achieved very little – and his father, Tibald III, was the first leader of the ill-fated Fourth Crusade, which sacked Constantinople, although he had died before that expedition ever left France. His uncle, Henry of Champagne, had been uncrowned King of Jerusalem. He provides an excellent illustration of how important family history sometimes was in inspiring individuals to set out on Crusade.

6 Simon was the father of Jean de Joinville, the chronicler of Louis's crusade.

7 See Richard, Jean, *St. Louis*.

8 Richard, *The Crusades*, p.338.

9 See de Joinville, p.141.

269

Chapter 2: The Crusade in the Thirteenth Century

1 In this respect at least, the Crusade differed from Louis's expedition where the King would be the undisputed leader of the force.

2 Some of the Egyptians were Christian Copts who were not unfriendly towards the Crusaders and would have offered advice if any had cultivated good relations with them. Sadly, few did.

3 See Purcell, *Papal Crusading Policy 1244–1291*, pp.74–76.

4 See Barber, *The Knight and Chivalry*, p.185.

5 See Barber, p.225. It should be pointed out that Barber specifically excludes King Louis's later Crusade to Tunis in 1270 from this observation.

Chapter 3: Preparations for Crusade

1 Letter from Robert, Patriarch of Jerusalem, quoted by the contemporary chronicler Matthew of Paris.

2 *Ibid.*

3 The substantial walls that can still be seen are the product of Louis's son, Philip III: a large proportion of Louis's construction was made of timber.

4 See Richard, *Saint Louis*, p.108.

5 See Riley-Smith, J., *The Crusades*, p.159.

6 From the *Registre* of Innocent IV, quoted in Marshall, p.74.

7 See Tyerman, p.109.

8 Louis held high hopes that King Haakon of Norway in particular would commit a number of men to the Crusade, as his fleet would be very useful. Haakon refused, citing amongst other reasons the fact that men of different races would find it difficult to function effectively together in an alien environment. See Richard, *The Crusades*, p.340.

9 See Richard, *Saint Louis*, p.111.

10 Lloyd in *Oxford Illustrated History of the Crusades*, p.54.

11 De Joinville, p.164.

12 Statistics concerning the financing of the Crusade are taken from Riley-Smith, J., *The Crusades*, pp.159–160.

13 Louis was every bit a man of his times in this respect, as evidenced by his purchasing of the Crown of Thorns for his collection in 1239. This relic is still used in ceremonies held every Easter in Paris, though it now resides when not in use in the Treasury of Notre Dame rather than in its original home in Sainte-Chappelle.

14 De Joinville, p.166.

Chapter 4: Rendezvous

1 De Joinville, p.165.

2 Despite his name, Matthew was very much an English chronicler who had no connection with France whatsoever. As such, he sometimes appears to be hostile towards Louis. However, his story does, in this case, ring true. The allusion to poisoners referred to the belief that Louis's father had been poisoned in the city.

3 Some of the medieval Kings of England paid an allowance to certain of their barons close to the Channel Ports, in return for which the barons must accompany the King when he

crossed over to France and hold his head whilst he was sick.

4 Perhaps worst of all for this pious King, the Church placed strict limitations on what could be transported by ship for the purposes of Communion, as a result of which Louis would be unable to properly participate in the ceremony until he reached land.

5 Overall command was given to two Genoese admirals, Ugo Lercaro and Jacopo de Levante, reflecting the large number of ships that Louis had hired from the city.

6 De Joinville, p.167.

7 De Joinville remarked that this was particularly helpful as, when the expedition eventually arrived in Egypt and cut away this sprouting top cover, they found that the grain underneath was perfectly fresh.

8 Matthew of Paris, p.102.

9 The writer Jeremiah Curtin, writing admittedly before the dreadful excesses of the twentieth century in 1908, wrote of the great Genghis that 'he stands forth as the greatest manslayer the world has ever known', estimating that 18.5 million people lost their lives as a result of his actions. See Curtin, *The Mongols – a history*.

Chapter 5: Into Battle

1 De Joinville, p.173.

2 Quotes from Gabrieli, pp.300–1.

3 The humble carrier pigeon played an invaluable role in the Muslim East's communications network, so much so that Christian archers would often try to shoot down the birds or capture them and replace the genuine messages with false information.

4 Gabrieli, pp.284–6.

Chapter 6: The Serpent's Head

1 De Joinville, p.177.

2 De Joinville, p.177.

3 Matthew Paris, p.144.

4 The Egyptians did not have an immensely powerful ocean-going fleet but, as one would expect for a nation with a long coastline and several important ports, they did have a coastal defence force, which was capable of threatening the seaborne lines of communication of the Crusade.

5 See Matthew Paris, p.154.

6 De Joinville, p.181.

7 For further details on arms and armour during the period, see Marshall, pp.86–92.

8 De Joinville, p.181.

Chapter 7: Massacre at Mansourah

1 Gabrieli, 287.

2 Matthew Paris, p.136.

3 See Bradbury, *The Medieval Siege*, pp.270–3.

4 Catapults that hurled rocks at the Crusader forces. For the various categories of artillery in use during the period see e.g. Bradbury, *The Medieval Siege*, Chapter 9.

5 Various references to Greek fire may be found in 'The Medieval Siege' by Bradbury, but

especially pp.277–8.

6 Matthew Paris, pp.166–170.

7 Gabrieli, p.290.

8 Ibn Wasil in Gabrieli, p.290.

9 An impressive memorial to him may be seen in Salisbury Cathedral, though he was in fact interred in Acre.

10 De Joinville, p.223.

11 De Joinville, p.221.

12 See De Joinville, p.197.

13 Ibn Wasil in Gabrieli, pp.291–2.

14 De Joinville, p.196.

Chapter 8: Low-Water Mark

1 The Ibelins were one of the great families of thirteenth-century Outremer, and played a prominent role in many of the great events of that period in the East. They were particularly noted for standing up against the bullying tactics of the Emperor Frederick when he had been in the Outremer.

2 De Joinville, p.204.

3 See Richard, *Saint Louis*, p.125.

4 For a brief assessment of the impact of naval warfare on the Egyptians at this time see Hillenbrand, p.571.

5 De Joinville, p.209.

6 Ibn Wasil in Gabrieli, p.294.

7 Maqrizi in Gabrieli, p.302.

Chapter 9: Prisoners of War

1 De Joinville, 213.

2 In the account of Matthew Paris, the sight of the massacred prisoners is a particularly gruesome one. According to him, the Sultan had offered a bounty to anyone who presented him with the head or feet of a dead Christian, and many of the Saracens had decapitated or amputated the feet from the corpses so that they could claim the money.

3 She had died very young, after giving birth to Conrad whilst still in her teens, after a dreadful marriage to Frederick who had treated her shamefully.

4 Gabrieli, pp.294–5.

5 De Joinville, p.222.

6 Ibn Wasil in Gabrieli, p.296.

Chapter 10: The End of the Beginning

1 Matthew Paris, p.177.

2 De Joinville, p.288.

3 De Joinville, p.218.

4 Matthew Paris, p.178.

5 Ibn Wasil in Gabrieli, p.300.

Chapter 11: Louis in Outremer

1 De Joinville, p.239.
2 The success of the Fourth Crusade led to a Latin empire being set up in what was traditionally Byzantine territory. The Empire was to be short lived – it was surrounded by natural enemies from the start – but was at this time still more or less intact though under increasing pressure. However, its rulers had enough problems of their own to preclude anything but a token force being sent to support Louis.
3 De Joinville, p.242.
4 De Joinville, p.243.

Chapter 12: Louis the Diplomat

1 For further analysis of the Assassins see Bartlett, *The Assassins*.
2 De Joinville, p.251.
3 Fermented mare's milk, *airag*, is still the traditional drink of Mongolia today.
4 De Joinville describes how a Khwarismian gaoler, who was guarding the Franks whilst they were captive in Egypt, opened his pouch of food prepared in such a way.
5 De Joinville, p.258.
6 The Cumans were primarily to be found in Hungary. Given their situation, in between Europe and the nomadic tribesmen who populated Asia, their culture – particularly their armament – had by this time started to become a strange hybrid of East and West.

Chapter 13: Consolidation and Disappointment

1 De Joinville, p.261.
2 The wine of the time was very strong, and should be watered down before consumption. De Joinville had been led to believe when he was young that his constitution meant that he did not need to adopt such measures, but a doctor later convinced him that he had been misled and he therefore took to mixing water and wine along with everyone else.
3 The city of Antioch was one of the first major prizes of the First Crusade. It was taken, after the bloodiest struggle of the entire campaign, in 1098.
4 As princes of Antioch almost invariably were. This Bohemond was the sixth prince to hold that name, which they took from the first prince of Antioch, Bohemond of Taranto, who was an unscrupulous but colourful Norman adventurer.
5 Even when the city was in Muslim hands, Christian pilgrims still regularly had open access to it as pilgrims.

Chapter 14: The End of the Dream

1 De Joinville refers to it as 'Sayette'.
2 De Joinville relates how even then, decades after Richard had returned to the West, the mere mention of his name was enough to frighten Muslim children whose mothers told them terrible tales of the great King's prowess.
3 Called Assur by de Joinville.
4 Called Belinas by de Joinville.
5 De Joinville, p.284.

6 Here, they were remote from the rest of the Byzantine Empire, which was still partly held by the Latins, and they were independently ruled with no allegiance to the larger part of the Greek Empire based around mainland Greece and Nicaea. The very remoteness of the city of Trebizond was for a time its salvation: it was the very last part of Byzantium to fall to the Turks two centuries later, outliving even Constantinople.

7 De Joinville, p.285.

8 Matthew Paris, p.198.

Chapter 15: Homeward Bound

1 See Richard, p.146.

2 The war was about to come to a head. In 1254, Pope Innocent conferred Sicily – the major bone of contention between the Papacy and the German emperor – on Frederick's bastard son, Manfred. He hoped to win the allegiance of Manfred by so doing but the ungrateful ruler switched allegiances and sent an army against the Pope. He defeated the Pope's army at Foggia on 2 December. The news of this was so disturbing to Innocent that he promptly died within a few days.

3 De Joinville, p.289.

4 As one comparison, Louis had contracted thirty-six ships from Genoa and Marseilles in 1246, which would have covered just a small part of those required for his outward journey to the East.

5 For fuller details of the regiment, see Marshall, pp.77–83.

6 It is difficult not to agree with Marzials who felt that Louis would have done much better in summoning his wife and children to supervise their rescue rather than his passive acceptance of fate.

7 Such ships were common votive offerings in the Middle Ages. 150 such vessels were to be found at the shrine of St Thomas Canteloupe at Hereford Cathedral in England.

8 De Joinville, p.301.

Chapter 16: The Last Crusade

1 See Riley-Smith, J., *The Crusades*, p.173.

2 A sleeveless garment that is worn by the celebrant during Mass.

3 De Joinville, p.320.

4 Details from Riley-Smith, J., *The Crusades*, p.174.

5 See Lloyd, *Oxford Illustrated History of the Crusades*, p.63.

6 See Richard, p.314.

7 Variously estimated from 10,000–15,000 strong.

8 See Keen, p.129.

List of Illustrations

1 The Omayyad mosque in Damascus, one of Islam's sacred places. Garry and Julie Lawrence.

2 The walls of Jerusalem, Louis IX's ultimate objective during his great Crusade. Israeli Government Tourist Office.

3 Richard I, still an inspiration to the Sixth Crusade. Author's collection.

4 A clash of religions: a Muslim pulpit in the Crusader castle of Krak des Chevaliers. Garry and Julie Lawrence.

5 The Palestinian landscape: the view from the castle of Krak des Chevaliers. Garry and Julie Lawrence.

6 The effigy of the Crusader William Longspee in Salisbury Cathedral. He was killed in the streets of Mansourah. Author's collection.

7 A Templar chapel from Laon, France; French and Templar fortunes were intertwined during the Crusade. Author's collection.

8 Three medieval monarchs look on from the façade of Notre Dame where Louis IX took his leave of his capital. Author's collection.

9 The struggle of good and evil would have been a symbol for many Crusaders' views of the Crusade: a contemporary piece of architecture from Notre Dame. Author's collection.

10 A riot of colour from the windows of Sainte-Chapelle. Author's collection.

11 Soldiers on the move: from Sainte-Chapelle. Author's collection.

12 Christ in glory, from the façade of Sainte-Chapelle. Author's collection.

13 A statue of Louis IX from his creation at Sainte-Chapelle. Author's collection.

14 Prisoners being dragged into hell by demons: an appropriate analogy for the Crusade in Egypt. Author's collection.

15 A martyr being slain: Louis might well have envisaged such an end at times. Author's collection.

16 A Crucifixion scene from a French medieval manuscript: the association of Jerusalem with such scenes was an important facet of Crusade inspiration. Author's collection.

17 Medieval builders at work: the legacy of the Crusade was as much in the infrastructure of

Outremer as it was on the battlefield. Author's collection.

18 A biblical scene shows contemporary armour. Author's collection.

19 Another biblical scene shows a King in medieval dress addressing knights. Author's collection.

20 Camels, from a medieval manuscript. Author's collection.

21 A knight bids his family farewell, from the Luttrell Psalter. Author's collection.

22 A Crusader in battle with a Muslim warrior. Author's collection.

23 A medieval siege. The scene may depict an allegorical battle for love (the defenders of the castle are women!) but the weapons shown are representative enough of the kind of warfare of the period. Author's collection.

24 A man of war: Western sea power was an important factor of the Crusaders' ability to invade Egypt. Author's collection.

25 A feast scene: such domestic moments form as much a part of de Joinville's chronicle as war scenes do. Author's collection.

26 The calling of the First Crusade at Clermont, from a nineteenth-century French illustration. Author's collection.

27 Crusaders on the march. Author's collection.

28 Christian prisoners paraded in front of the great Muslim leader Saladin. Author's collection.

29 The death of Louis IX. Author's collection.

30 A statue of de Joinville. Author's collection.

31 The horrors of medieval siege warfare. A scene from the crusade against the Cathars. Author's collection.

Acknowledgments

I would like to thank those who have supported me in the writing of this book. Writing a book and working at the same time can be a demanding process as far as an author's time is concerned and it doesn't leave much of it spare for other activities, so thanks to all those who have helped me in this respect.

This is my first book with Tempus and I would like to thank everyone there for their hard work in support of this publication. *The Last Crusade* has been an old friend, in progress for several years, and it is very satisfying to see it in print. I would like to especially thank Jonathan Reeve for his helpful advice and commissioning of the book and look forward to future collaborations together. Last but not least, I would like to acknowledge the support of Pascal Barry in finalising the book. Thanks to you all.

Index

Acre 78, 148, 173, 181, 190,
    194, 195, 220, 234, 235,
    253,
    final fall of 237, 262, 263
    Frederick II in 40
    French regiment in 251
    in Third Crusade 34, 91,
    147
    Louis IX in 156, 167,
    169, 174, 175, 176, 177,
    189, 223, 236
    threatened by Muslim
    army 218, 219, 250
    wealth of 8
    William Longspee
    and 97, 113
Aibek, Sultan of Egypt 203
Aigues Mortes 61, 231, 245
    Crusade assembles at 56,
    65, 67, 68
    construction of port
    at 59
Ain Jalud, Battle of 250
Aix 247

Albigensian Crusade see
    Cathar Crusade
Alenard of Senaingan,
    Norwegian knight 198,
    199
Alexandria 96, 108,
    attack on in 1365 11
    7th Crusade considers
    attack on 79, 100
    Muslims launch
    counter-attacks from 95,
    138
al-Kamil, Sultan of
    Egypt 37, 38, 39
Alphonse of Poitiers, Prince
    of France 55, 95, 99, 177,
    204, 257
    arrives in Damietta 100
    at Mansourah 129, 130.
    in captivity 166, 167,
    168
    in crusade to Tunis 252
    journeys to Egypt 89
    leaves Outremer 188

released 169
Anjou 20
an-Nasir Yusuf, Sultan of
    Damascus 221,
    fights against
    Egyptians 214
    fights against
    Crusaders 217
    fights against
    Mongols 249
    proposed Crusader
    alliance with 189, 203
    proposed Crusader
    alliance against 195, 212
Antioch 31, 173, 196,
    falls to Baibars 250, 251, 253
Aragon 252
Armenians 213, 223
armour 101
Ashmun Tannah 108
Assassins 190, 228
    attempted assasination of
    Prince Edward by 257
    delegation to Louis

IX 193
Louis IX and 10
Ayub, Sultan of Egypt 80,
86,
death of 108, 130, 131
illness of 85

Bab an-Nasr 121
Baghdad 249
Bahr al-Mahalla 133
Bahrites, Mameluke
regiment 116, 139
Baibars, Rukn ad-Din,
Sultan 12, 148, 263
and Battle of Ain Jalud
172, 250
and Prince Edward's
Crusade 257
at Battle of La
Forbie 50, 52
at Mansourah 116, 131
Baldwin II, Emperor of
Byzantium 76
Baldwin of Ibelin, baron of
Outremer 129, 150, 152
Baltic 11, 12, 42, 261
Barbarossa, Frederick,
German Emperor 33, 34
Barcelona 252
Beaucaire 247
bedouins 190, 217
at Damietta 80, 86
at Mansourah 107, 111,
112, 120
in Outremer 217
Bernard of Clairvaux 50
Blanche of Castille, Regent
of France 20, 229,
becomes Regent 19
bids farewell to Louis
IX 63
Crusading antecedents
of 26
death of 230, 232, 233,
234, 239
fear of Mongol
threat 54
receives 'Shepherd's

Crusade' 159
regency of 178, 179, 185
relationship with Louis
IX 17, 25, 55
relationship with Queen
Margaret 161
Bohemond V, Prince of
Antioch 54
Bohemond VI, Prince of
Antioch 213
Boniface VIII, Pope 258
Boulogne, Count of 20
Bourges 57
Brittany 19
Bulgaria 264

Caesarea 195, 198, 207
Caesarea Phillipi 223, 224,
225
Cagliari 254
Cairo 79, 85, 86, 101, 105,
107, 121, 131, 132, 156,
195, 203, 212, 262
Crusader prisoners
in 166
potential assault on by
Crusaders 87, 102, 134,
137
Carthage 254
Castille 20
Cathar Crusade 11, 19, 66,
109
Cathars 13, 35, 42
Cathedral of Our Lady,
Damietta 92, 100
Champagne 21, 194
Charente, River 24
Charles of Anjou, Prince of
France 55, 245, 257, 258
at Mansourah 128, 136
in crusade to Tunis 253,
256
leaves Egypt 166
leaves Outremer 188,
204
relationships with Louis
IX 169
Chateaudun 58

Cheminon 63
Cistercians 63
Conrad, Emperor of
Germany 32, 98
Conrad, King of
Jerusalem 40, 149, 174,
231, 234
Constantinople 76, 199,
200, 229
relics from 61
taken by Fourth
Crusade 35, 75
Corbeil 20, 63
Cross, relic of 8
Crown of Thorns 8
Cumans 200, 201
Cyprus 71, 81, 82,
Louis IX leaves 78
Louis IX on 70, 72, 75,
76, 196
Louis IX returns to on
way back to France 237,
239, 240, 241
supply line to Egypt
from 87, 138

Damascus 47, 52, 80, 141,
189, 203, 210, 212, 214,
217, 220,
al-Kamil plots to
capture 38, 39
and Khwarismians 48
during Second
Crusade 32
taken by Mongols 249
Damietta 97, 100, 101, 103,
107, 131, 138, 154, 156,
168, 254
attempted retreat to 139,
140, 143, 144
attempted ruse by
Egyptians to capture
148, 149
captured by Louis
IX 85–88, 89, 92, 108
Crusade lands at 80
Crusade leaves for Cairo
from 102

Crusader captives return
to 152, 153, 159
Crusader garrison at 94,
151, 160
division of spoils in 90,
98
during Fifth Crusade 35,
36
Louis IX leaves 165, 166
planned assault on by
Louis IX 78
proposed return to
Egyptians 136, 137
Queen Margaret in 162
return of to
Egyptians 157, 163, 164,
167
strengthened defences
of 79
supplies for Crusaders
from 133, 134
traders in 91
Damietta, Great Mosque
of 92
Dean of Marupt 69

Edessa 31, 32
Edward, Prince of England
(later Edward I) 11, 252,
257, 261
Egypt 37, 47, 76, 79, 81, 87,
88, 101, 108, 115, 125,
130, 153, 155, 156, 157,
170, 171, 188, 192, 193,
202, 214, 217, 231, 236,
248, 250
invaded by Seventh
Crusade 9, 78, 80, 102,
172, 196
Louis IX leaves 166
perceived weakness
of 32, 86
strategic designs on 35,
38
Ela, Countess of
Salisbury 117
elephant, gift of to
Louis IX 213

England, English 55,
forces in Seventh
Crusade 58, 95, 96, 98,
117, 122
provision of ships by for
Seventh Crusade 56
relationships with
France 23, 264
Epirus 200
Erard de Sibery, knight 120
Eudes of Chateauroux,
Papal Legate
at Damietta 90, 95, 100,
151
in Outremer 180, 182,
233, 234, 235
involvement in
canonisation of Louis
IX 259
preaches Seventh
Crusade 53, 57, 58, 62
Everard of Brienne 81

Fakhr ad-Din, vizier of
Egypt 80, 114, 116, 131
Farris-Eddin Octay 154
Ferdinand Sanchez, Prince
of Aragon 253
Fifth Crusade 35, 43
financing of the
Crusades 46, 59, 60, 61
First Crusade 30, 32, 34, 42,
44, 77, 171, 172
Fourth Crusade 34, 56, 75
France 19, 28, 33, 61, 63,
66, 68, 69, 92, 140, 159,
160, 166, 167, 170, 180,
181, 183, 185, 187, 231,
235, 236, 239, 240, 244,
245, 258
chivalric code in 44
relations with
Latin empire in
Constantinople 75
relations with
England 23, 24, 55, 179,
264
Franciscans 252

Frederic of Loupey,
knight 120
Frederick II, Emperor of
Germany 145, 146, 149,
174,
and Sixth Crusade 10
and Outremer 41
character of 37
confrontation with
Papacy 12, 43, 55, 234
death of 231
gains control of
Jerusalem 17, 39, 40
links with Teutonic
knights 51
relationships with France
and Louis IX 18, 46, 71,
189
relationships with
Islamic East 38, 80, 191

Gascony 24
Gaucher of Chatillon,
knight 126
Gaza 52, 217
Egyptians and Syrians
battle at 214
plans for negotiations
at 212, 213
Genghis Khan 47, 73
Genoa, Genoese 87, 165,
257
at fall of Acre 262
in Acre 173
in Damietta 162
provision of ships
toThird Crusade 56
provision of ships to
Seventh Crusade 46,76
provision of ships for
Crusade to Tunis 252
ships bring supplies to
Crusade 95
Geoffrey of Sargines, French
knight
in attack on Caeserea
Phillipi 224
in retreat from

Mansourah 139
leads Franch regiment in
Outremer 222, 236
returns to Damietta 163
Germans 58
Giles le Brun, Constable of
France 224, 239, 240
Giles of Saumur, Archbishop
of Damietta 92
Greek fire 109, 110, 119,
128, 129, 143, 144, 154
Gregory IX, Pope 12, 38, 40
Gregory X, Pope 78, 258
Guillemin, servant of de
Joinville 175, 177
Guy of Ibelin, baron of
Outremer 129, 150, 152
Guy of Flanders 252
Guy of Mauvoisin, French
knight 129, 181
Guyuk, Mongol khan 73,
74

Harbiyah, Battle of see La
Forbie
Hattin, Battle of 33, 51,
52, 251
Henri de Ronnay, Provost
of the Hospitaller
order 123
Henry III, King of
England 25, 40, 46, 55,
58, 67, 96, 98, 178, 231,
246, 264
and wars with
France 24,
attitudes to
tournaments 43
Henry of Champagne 21,
22
Holy Sepulchre, Church of
the 49, 78
Homs 80
Hospitallers, Military
order 48, 172, 210, 222,
257
at Battle of La
Forbie 51, 53

at fall of Acre 262
at Mansourah 117
dispute with de
Joinville 208
in battle at Ramleh 215
in battle at Caeserea
Phillipi 224
position of in
Outremer 50, 149
Hugh of Juoy, Templar
knight 210
Hulagu, Mongol khan 249
Hundred Years War 264
Hungary, Hungarians 47,
54, 73, 191, 198
hunting 199, 208
Hyeres 245, 246

Ibn Abd al-Zahir, Muslim
chronicler 134
Ibn Wasil, Muslim historian
86, 114, 150
Imbert of Beaujeu 92, 111
Innocent IV, Pope 58, 178,
263
calls for Crusade 12, 53,
57
confrontation with
Frederick II 40, 41, 55
offers of Indulgences
by 42, 56
relationships with Louis
IX 54, 67, 71
sends embassy to the
Mongols 73, 74
Inverness 56
Ireland 198
Isabella, Princess of
France 18
Isabelle of Angouleme,
Queen of England 24
Italians 58, 262

Jaffa 213, 218, 220, 221
attacked by Muslims 236
Louis IX strengthens
defences of 212, 222,
234, 235

Jamal al-Din, governor of
Damascus 141, 151
Jamdarites, Mameluke
regiment 116
James I, King of
Aragon 252, 253
Jerusalem 8, 46, 72, 77, 138,
171, 173, 189, 195, 196,
213, 214, 221, 223, 229,
255,
alledgedly offered by
Ayub to Louis IX 108
and Third Crusade 34
captured by First
Crusade 30, 31
captured in First World
War 264
gained by Frederick
II 37, 39, 40
importance of to
Christendom 13, 35
Louis IX negotiates for
136
sacked by
Khwarismians 16, 48, 49
taken by Saladin 17, 33,
51, 250
Jews 61
John, Count of Jaffa 83, 84,
181, 182
John de Voisey, priest 126,
146
John le Grand, Genoese
knight 219, 220
John of Beaumont 92, 183
John of Brienne, King of
Jerusalem 35, 36, 90
John of Bussey, knight 226
John of Valenciennes 194,
195, 226
John of Valery 90, 150
John Vatatzes, Greek
Emperor 200
John Tristan, Prince of
France 254
John, King of England 24,
34
Joinville 245

Joinville, Jean de, chronicler
and Crusader 9, 10, 19,
65, 78, 155, 196, 251,
252, 259
and Mongol
embassy 198
arrangement with Louis
IX 187, 188, 194, 195,
208
at Acre 174, 175, 176,
177
at Mansourah 118, 119,
120, 123, 133, 137
capture of 143–147
decides to return to
France 233, 234, 235
decision to stay in
Outremer 180, 182–184
dispute with
Hospitallers 208–209
during the march to
Mansourah 104
illness of 136
in battle at Caeserea
Phillipi 224–227
in battle at Ramleh 215
in battle with An-Nasir
Yusuf 217, 218
in conversation with
Armenian pilgrims 223
in flight from
Mansourah 140
involvement in
canonisation of Louis
IX 258
journeys to Aigues
Mortes 67
in Muslim
counter-attack at
Mansourah 125, 126,
128, 129
involvement in the
attack on Damietta 81,
82, 83, 84
leaves on Crusade 60
life in Outremer 204,
205, 206, 228, 229, 230
on Blanche of

Castille 161
on internal conflicts in
France 22, 25
on murder of
Turanshah 152–154
on Robert of Artois 99
on sea crossings 69, 70
on the death of Louis
IX 256
on the piety of Louis
IX 26
on the storm at
Damietta 100
on the Third
Crusade 34
return journey to
France 237, 238, 240,
244, 245, 247, 248
returns to Damietta 163,
165, 168
stay at Damietta 91, 92,
94
stay in Cyprus 71, 72
Joinville, Simon lord of 21
Jordan, River 223
Joscelin of Brancion, knight
130

Khwarismians 16, 47, 49,
50, 52, 53
Krak des Chevaliers 173

La Forbie, Battle of 52, 53,
102, 113, 116, 117, 171,
172, 174
Languedoc 66
Limassol 70, 80
Louis VII, King of
France 26, 32, 98
Louis VIII, King of France
18, 19
Louis IX, King of France 7,
8, 9, 10, 11, 13, 14, 29, 44,
53, 66, 67, 102, 103, 146,
149, 156, 157, 160, 189,
202, 213, 216, 217, 218,
220, 222, 223, 232, 261,
262, 264

and building of Aigues
Mortes 57
and ceremonial
departure from Paris 62
and contacts with the
Mongols 72–74, 196,
198, 249
and Crusade to
Tunis 250–253
arrangement with de
Joinville 187–188, 204,
205
at Mansourah 107, 108,
110–112, 114, 118, 120,
121, 123
at Sidon 227–228
and Philip of
Toucy 200–201
attraction of Indulgences
to 42
becomes king 19
canonisation of 258, 259
character of 26–28
confrontations with
French barons 20–23
considers return to
France 178–185
death of 255–256
decides to march on
Cairo 101
decides to return to
France 233–236
departure from France
of 65,68
early life 18
falls out with the
English contingent 96–
97
in Acre 174–175
in captivity 143,
150–152, 159
in Muslim
counter-attack at
Mansourah 127–128
judgement of 207
lands in Egypt 80–81,
84, 85
leaves Egypt 167–170

meets Assassin
envoy 190–192
negotiations with
Muslim powers 194,
195, 203, 214
organisation of Crusade
by 45, 46, 56, 59, 61
prevaricates after capture
of Damietta 89
reaction to death of his
mother 230
relationship with
Frederick II 40, 41
relationship with
Latin empire in
Constantinople 75, 229
relationship with Pope
Innocent IV 54, 55
relationship with
Templars 209–211
retreat to Damietta 136–
141
return to Damietta 165,
166
return journey to
France 238–246,
247–248
takes Damietta 88,
90–92, 94, 99, 100
time on Cyprus of 70–
71, 76
vows to go on
Crusade 15, 17
wars with the
English 24, 25
Low Countries 252
Lucienne, Regent of
Antioch 213
Lyon 40, 55

Malta 11
Mamelukes 50, 52, 53, 116,
131, 139
Mansourah 108, 131, 134,
136, 137, 146, 161
aftermath of battle
at 132
attacked by

Crusaders 102, 107, 111,
114–117, 121–123, 125
constructed to defend
Cairo 79, 105
Crusader captives taken
to 147
Maqrizi, Muslim
chronicler 79
Marcel, French soldier 140
Marche, Count of la 24, 25
Margaret, Queen of
France 55,
arrives at Sidon 229
at Damietta 95, 151, 161,
162
return journey to
France 240, 243, 244
Marseilles 46, 56, 252
Mary, Empress of
Byzantium 75, 76
Mary Magdalene 247
Master of Hungary 159
Matthew Paris,
chronicler 10,
criticism of Innocent IV
by 42
on disputes between
English and French 96,
97
on Muslim attempts on
Damietta 148, 161
on revenues of Acre 173
on Robert of Artois 99,
113, 115, 117
on Sultan Ayub 108
on the capture of Louis
IX 150
on the Crusade at
Damietta 94, 95, 163
on the debacle to
Mansourah 118
on the progress of
Crusade through
France 66
Mayyafaraqin 249
Mongolia 47
Mongols 10, 45, 48, 263
attacks on Europe by 54

attacks on Middle East
by 72, 172, 248, 249, 250
calls for Crusade
against 11
Christian embassy to 74,
196, 197, 198
violence of 47, 73
Montjoie, ship 77
Montlheri 20
Moors 26, 42, 261

Narbonne 26
Nestorian Christians 74
Nicaea 200
Nicopolis, Battle of 264
Nile, River 35
Normandy 24
Norway 198, 199
Nosairi Mountains 190
Notre Dame Cathedral 61,
62
Nur-ed-Din, Muslim
leader 32, 33

'Old Man of the
Mountains' 190, 191,
192, 193
Oliver of Termes,
mercenary 151, 226, 240
Outremer 9, 10, 32, 46, 47,
80, 138, 171, 176, 180,
181, 182, 195, 202, 203,
204, 207, 211, 222, 230,
231, 235, 237, 238, 248,
253, 263
attacked by
Khwarismians 16, 49, 50
alliance with
Damascus 48
castles in 149
eventual loss of 262
Frederick II in 38, 39,
40, 41, 189
importance of military
orders to 117, 209, 212
in Third Crusade 34
thirteenth-century life
in 205

Louis IX's arrival in 160, 174
Louis IX leaves 236, potential effect of Louis' departure on 179, 185
Prince Edward's Crusade in 257, 261
relevant insignificance to Islam of 172
Sultan Baibars and 250
territories of 31, 173
vulnerability of 206

Palermo 257
Palestine 30, 33, 199
Papal Indulgences 30, 41, 42, 56, 60, 261
Paphos 75
Paris 7, 20, 27, 65, 67, 141, 242, 247, 263
body of Louis IX returns to 258
French nobles take the cross in 57
Louis IX leaves 63
Louis IX discusses Tunis Crusade in 251
'Shepherd's Crusade' reaches 159
Pelagius, Cardinal 35, 36
Perche 20
Persia 47
Peter of Avalon, Crusader 109
Peter of Bourbonne, knight 175
Peter of Neuville, Crusader knight 119
Peter, Count of Brittany at Mansourah 112, 119, 128
death of 167
in captivity 149, 150, 152
involved in rebellion in France 20, 21
Peter Fernandez, Prince of Aragon 253
Philip Augustus. King of

France 221
and Cathar Crusade 19
and relationships with England 179
and Third Crusade 17, 33, 34, 98, 221
Philip, Count of Artois 264
Philip of Montfort, knight 140, 150
Philip of Nemours 184
Philip of Toucy, Cousin of King Louis 199, 200, 201
Philip, Prince (later king) of France 18, 254, 256
Philip the Fair, King of France 263
Pisa, Pisans 87
at Damietta 162
provide shipping to Seventh Crusade 56
rivalry with Genoese 76
trading relationships with Outremer 173
Plonquet, knight 82
Poland, Poles 47, 54, 73
prostitution 207
Provence 247

Qutuz, Sultan of Egypt 250

Ramleh 214, 215
Raoul of Albano, Bishop of Albano 252
Raymond, Templar brother 237
Raymond VII, Count of Toulouse 67
Renaud de Vichiers, Marshal of the Temple 104, 176, 211
Rheims 18, 55, 57
Rhone, River 66
Richard de Bures, Master of the Templars 113
Richard, Jean, historian 253
Richard of Cornwall, English noble 173

Richard I, King of England 24, and fund raising for Crusade 60
and Third Crusade 17, 33, 34, 91, 98, 147, 201, 221
and wars with France 23, 179
conquers Cyprus 70
Robert de Vere, English knight 117
Robert of Artois, Prince of France 55, 123, 264
argues for advance on Cairo 101
death of 117
in attack on Mansourah 112, 113, 115
in dispute with English contingent 97, 99
intransigence of 108
Robert the Monk 77
Robert, Patriarch of Jerusalem 49
Roche-de-Glun 66
Roger of Clerieu 66
Rome 234
Royaumont 27

Safed 173
Saint Antione, Abbey of 62
Sainte-Chapelle 7, 8, 61, 62, 141, 157
Saint-Denis Cathedral 62, 258
Saint Genevieve 255
Saint James 255
Saint Nicholas 241
Saladin 50, 221
death of 34, 38, 47
in invasion of Egypt 33
takes Jerusalem 17, 51
Samaria 222
Sardinia 254
Scotland, Scots 58, 252
Second Crusade 32, 34, 98
Setton, Kenneth,

historian 13
Shajar ad-Durr, wife of
    Turanshah 155
Shepherds Crusade 159
Shirkuh, Muslim warrior 33
Sicily 254, 257
Sidon 222, 230,
    Louis IX rebuilds 223,
    227–228, 233, 234, 235
    sacked by Muslim
    army 220
Simon de Montfort 109
Simon of Brie 252, 258
Simon of Montbeliard,
    commander at
    Sidon 220
Soissons 19
Stephen of Otricourt,
    Commander of the
    Temple 168
Straits of Gibraltar 199
Subeibe 225
Sur 235, 236
Syria 30, 48, 70, 76, 248,
    249

Taillebourg 24
Templars, Military
    order 125, 222, 257,
    and advance on
    Mansourah 103, 104,
    105, 109
    and battle at Caeserea
    Phillipi 224
    and Battle of La
    Forbie 51, 53
    and defence of
    Outremer 48, 149, 172
    at fall of Acre 262
    at Mansourah 112, 113,
    114, 117, 122
    at Ramleh 215
    dispute with Louis IX
    over relations with
    Damascus 209–212
    eventual destruction
    of 263
    financial disputes

with 168, 175
    in aftermath of
    Mansourah battle 129
    purpose of 50
Temple Church,
    London 264
Teutonic Knights 39, 50,
    52, 118
Thibaud of Navarre 258
Third Crusade 33, 91, 147,
    179, 201, 221
    Cyprus falls during the
    lead-up to 70
    outcome of 34
    provision of spoils in 98
Tibald II, Count of
    Bar 71
Tibald IV, Count of
    Champagne 20, 21
Tiberias 33
Tortosa 229
tournaments 43
Trebizond 229
Tripoli 31
Troyes 21
Tunis 253, 254, 257
Turanshah, Sultan of
    Egypt 141, 156,
    becomes Sultan 130
    murder of 153, 154, 155,
    189
Turks 32, 45, 54, 264
Tyre 33, 222

Urban II, Pope 29, 31, 41

Varangeville 241
Veni creator spiritus,
    Crusader hymn 69
Venice, Venetians 87,
    at fall of Acre 262
    provision of ships by for
    Fourth Crusade 56
    relationships with
    Egyptians 35, 38, 80
    relationships with
    Outremer 173, 257
    supply of transport to

Louis' Crusade by 71

Walter of Autreche,
    knight 93, 94
Walter of Brienne,
    knight 194
Walter of Chatillon,
    knight 135
William Longspee, English
    knight 98
    at battle for
    Mansourah 113
    death of 117
    launches raid in
    Egypt 96
    leads English contingent
    in Crusade 58, 95
    leaves Egypt 97
William of Beaumont,
    Marshal of France 182
William of Boon,
    knight 119
William of Sonnac, Master
    of the Templars
    at battle for
    Mansourah 113, 114, 117
    death of 129
    wounded at
    Mansourah 122
William, Count of
    Flanders 129, 133, 167,
    181

Yolande, Queen of
    Jerusalem 40, 149
Yves le Breton, priest 189,
    193

Zengi, Emir of Mosul 31,
    32

Also by W.B. Bartlett

ASSASSINS
THE STORY OF MEDIEVAL ISLAM'S SECRET SECT

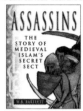

£8.99 paperback   ISBN 978 07504 4609 4

ROAD TO ARMAGEDDON
THE LAST YEARS OF THE CRUSADER KINGDOM OF JERUSALEM

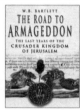

£20 hardback   ISBN 978 07509 4578 3

AN UNGODLY WAR
THE SACK OF CONSTANTINOPLE & THE FOUTH CRUSADE

£20 hardback   ISBN 07509 2378 4

THE CRUSADES
AN ILLUSTRATED HISTORY

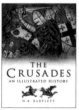

£14.99 paperback   ISBN 978 07509 3919 5

If you are interested in purchasing these books published by Sutton, pleasse contact our
Sales Department on 01453 883300

TEMPUS – REVEALING HISTORY

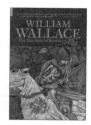

William II Rufus, the Red King
EMMA MASON

'A thoroughly new reappraisal of a much maligned king. The dramatic story of his life is told with great pace and insight'
John Gillingham

£25

0 7524 3528 0

William Wallace The True Story of Braveheart
CHRIS BROWN

'A formidable new biography... sieves through masses of medieval records to distinguish the man from the myth' **Magnus Magnusson**

£17.99

0 7524 3432 2

Elizabeth Wydeville: The Slandered Queen
ARLENE OKERLUND

'A penetrating, thorough and wholly convincing vindication of this unlucky queen'
Sarah Gristwood

'A gripping tale of lust, loss and tragedy'
Alison Weir

A **BBC History Magazine** Book of the Year 2005

£9.99   978 07524 3807 8

The Battle of Hastings 1066
M.K. LAWSON

'Blows away many fundamental assumptions about the battle of Hastings... an exciting and indispensable read' **David Bates**

A **BBC History Magazine** Book of the Year 2003

£12.99   978 07524 4177 1

The Welsh Wars of Independence
DAVID MOORE

'Beautifully written, subtle and remarkably perceptive' **John Davies**

£12.99

978 07524 4128 3

Medieval England
From Hastings to Bosworth
EDMUND KING

'The best illustrated history of medieval England' **John Gillingham**

£12.99

0 7524 2827 5

A Companion to Medieval England
NIGEL SAUL

'Wonderful... everything you could wish to know about life in medieval England'
Heritage Today

£19.99

0 7524 2969 8

The Prince In The Tower
MICHAEL HICKS

'The first time in ages that a publisher has sent me a book I actually want to read' **David Starkey**

£9.99

978 07524 4386 7

If you are interested in purchasing other books published by Tempus, or in case you have difficulty finding any Tempus books in your local bookshop, you can also place orders directly through our website:
www.tempus-publishing.com

TEMPUS – REVEALING HISTORY

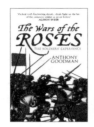 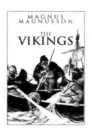

The Wars of the Roses
The Soldiers' Experience
ANTHONY GOODMAN
'A fascinating book' *TLS*
£12.99
0 7524 3731 3

The Vikings
MAGNUS MAGUNSSON
'Serious, engaging history'
BBC History Magazine
£9.99
0 7524 2699 0

 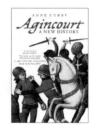

William the Conqueror
DAVID BATES
'As expertly woven as the Bayeux Tapestry'
BBC History Magazine
£12.99
0 7524 2960 4

Agincourt: A New History
ANNE CURRY
'A tour de force' *Alison Weir*
'*The* book on the battle' *Richard Holmes*
A *BBC History Magazine* book of the year 2005
£12.99
0 7524 2828 4

Hereward The Last Englishman
PETER REX
'An enthralling work of historical detection'
Robert Lacey
£17.99
0 7524 3318 0

The English Resistance
The Underground War Against the Normans
PETER REX
'An invaluable rehabilitation of an ignored
resistance movement' *The Sunday Times*
£12.99
0 7524 3733 X

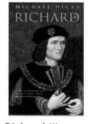 

Richard III
MICHAEL HICKS
'A most important book by the greatest living
expert on Richard' *Desmond Seward*
£9.99
0 7524 2589 7

The Peasants' Revolt
England's Failed Revolution of 1381
ALASTAIR DUNN
'A stunningly good book... totally absorbing'
Melvyn Bragg
£9.99
0 7524 2965 5

If you are interested in purchasing other books published by Tempus, or in case you have difficulty finding
any Tempus books in your local bookshop, you can also place orders directly through our website:
www.tempus-publishing.com